The Labor of Care

THE ASIAN AMERICAN EXPERIENCE

Series Editors
Eiichiro Azuma
Jigna Desai
Martin F. Manalansan IV
Lisa Sun-Hee Park
David K. Yoo

Roger Daniels, Founding Series Editor

A list of books in the series appears at the end of this book.

The Labor of Care

Filipina Migrants
and Transnational Families
in the Digital Age

VALERIE FRANCISCO-MENCHAVEZ

UNIVERSITY OF
ILLINOIS PRESS
Urbana, Chicago, and Springfield

Library of Congress Cataloging-in-Publication Data
Names: Francisco-Menchavez, Valerie, 1983- author.
Title: The Labor of Care: Filipina Migrants and Transnational
    Families in the Digital Age / Valerie Francisco-Menchavez.
Description: Urbana : University of Illinois Press, [2018] | Series:
    Asian American experience | Includes bibliographical
    references and index.
Identifiers: LCCN 2017048961| ISBN 9780252041723 (hardback) |
    ISBN 9780252083341 (paper)
Subjects: LCSH: Transborder ethnic groups—Philippines. |
    Women immigrants—Philippines. | Mothers—Philippines.
    | Digital communications—Philippines. | Internet—Social
    aspects—Philippines. | Transnationalism. | BISAC: SOCIAL
    SCIENCE / Ethnic Studies / Asian American Studies. |
    SOCIAL SCIENCE / Women's Studies. | SOCIAL SCIENCE /
    Emigration & Immigration.
Classification: LCC HM1271 .F725 2018 | DDC 305.8009599—dc23
    LC record available at https://lccn.loc.gov/2017048961
Ebook ISBN 978-0-252-05039-8

For my parents Irma and Vernon
For my children Aya Gabriela and Cy Andres
For my family's sweet baby angel Melana Reme

Contents

Acknowledgments

Kahit magkalayo kami, hindi kami magkahiwalay.
Even if we are separated, we are never apart.
—Unknown

Separated but never apart. An encompassing description of what this book is about: the experiences of transnational families and my experience of researching and writing about them. In Tagalog, this quote can be interpreted as separation by physical distance and as separation in the abstract, a distance felt in the heart. I begin with it because it sums up the long and arduous process of completing this book, and more importantly, all the people that helped me do it. The next few pages are an ode to everyone who has held me up and through the process of writing this book to let them know that each person who has touched this project made it that much better. Even if I am far in physical distance from many of the people acknowledged below, we are never really apart in our hearts through the pages of this book. The completion of this work allows me to thank and acknowledge the people spanning the Filipino diaspora—from New York City, to San Francisco, to Portland, to Manila—who inspired, supported, and believed in me to fulfill the larger objective of this work: to bring to light the struggle and resilience of Filipino migrants in the diaspora and their families.

The first people to thank are the brave women and men in the Kabalikat Domestic Workers Support Network in New York City and their families in the Philippines. In New York City, a mostly Filipina group of undocumented immigrants did not have to share their life stories of pain and joy with me. They did not have to invite me to their group gatherings to meet their friends' friends' friends. They did not have to let me into their homes to record their lives on a digital recorder. They did not have to introduce me to their families in the Philippines through Skype or Facebook. They most definitely did not have to give their addresses in Manila to me and let me meet their loved ones. But they did. They not only told me their life stories; they also let me in, all the way in. During their moments of utter sadness about being away from home for so long and the times of relief when their sons and daughters graduated college or celebrated birthdays, I was allowed in to hold their hands and cry with them. They invited me to sing karaoke and eat *lumpia* and *pancit* and laugh at Tagalog movies with them. They linked arm in arm with me during mobilizations for domestic worker rights and Filipino independence day parades. They let me into their homes, in both Queens and Manila, and trusted that I would care for their stories so that I could tell the whole world a story of migrants and their families that can resonate with us all. To the main core of Filipina heroes whose stories and personalities anchored this book, thank you: Lorena, Tuts, Nanay Emy, Tita Olet, Ate Edna, Tatu, Ate Nitz, both Tita Lucys, Ate Maribel, Ate Thea, Ate Anabel, Tita Hermie, Jessica, Ate Ana G, Tita Pinky, Tita Susan and Tito Toti, and Nanay Frances. These women would eventually introduce me to so many more Filipina domestic workers in Queens. I'm equally grateful to those who remain unnamed but forever close in my heart. To the families in the Philippines: from Tondo, to Novaliches, Laguna and Marikina, Quezon City, and Sucat, thank you for trusting a stranger from New York to come into your homes and ask intimate questions about probably the hardest events in your lives—separation and migration. These families not only shared their experiences with me; they cooked amazing meals, picked me up from bus stations, and reserved whole afternoons to walk and talk at the mall with me. Their kindnesses went beyond participating in a research study. They offered me friendship, and they continue to do so to this day. So to this powerful group of people who continue to conquer the distance in between, thank you. Your *Labor of Care* is what this book is about. Your stories are what I hope to bring to life so that people understand that all of you are working so hard to stay together, even though you're apart.

When I chose to pursue a PhD in sociology, I already knew that I wanted to work on a project that could facilitate the development of leaders in the Filipino community wherever I landed. I wanted to do something meaningful to help build mass organizations that could advance the struggle against the exploitation of my people. Community organizers and activists in progressive Filipino organizations in the United States and the Philippines, as well as in places like Hong Kong and the Netherlands, sharpened my ideal and helped me put my ideas into practice. Organizations and activists that support Kabalikat are in need of countless thank yous for their relentless faith that this project would help create leaders and build solidarity among our Filipino immigrant and Filipino American community to advocate for the rights and welfare of Filipino migrants: the Philippine Forum, the Bayanihan Community Center in Queens, Migrante New York, GABRIELA New York City, Anakbayan New York and New Jersey, the New York Committee for Human Rights in the Philippines, the National Alliance for Filipino Concerns (NAFCON), GABRIELA USA, and BAYAN USA. In the years of researching, writing, and editing this book, it was my comrades, or in Tagalog *mga kasama*, who helped me keep the big picture in mind. First, that research and scholarship should rightfully serve the people. And second, that the theory and insight gleaned from the stories of Filipino migrants must critique the systems of power that seek to exploit them. To this end, these activists and organizers, both Filipino American and Filipino immigrants, are the beacons of light that guided me through what would have been a solely academic project. Thank you, *mga kasama*, Elaine Villasper-Dizon, Sandra Panopio, Donna Denina, Terrie Cervas, Tina and Irma Shauf-Bajar, Melanie Dulfo, Jackie Mariano, Christina Hilo, Candice Sering, Jennine Ventura, Jonna Baldres, Julie Jamora, Tina Cocadiz, Maria Marasigan, Mona Flaugher, Vanessa Banta, Bernadette Ellorin, Gary Labao, Michelle Saulon, Lorena Sanchez-McRae, Hanalei Ramos, Raquel Redondiez, Joy Sison, Arlene Rodrigo, Rossella De Leon, Angelica Lim, Kenneth Crebillo, Justin Katigbak, Nikki De Leon, Julian Jaravata, Michael Tayag, and Peter Chua. I have deep love for *kasama* families who applauded my efforts on writing this book, continuing on with my movement work and growing a little family. Thank you to Mario, Josie and Kamilo De Mira, Joal, Amy and Kailea Truong-Vargas, Alexis, Jason, Emory and Marcello David-Ortega, and Melissa Reyes and Solisia Ixchel Almuina. Thank you for being patient as I worked out the kinks and for helping me figure out how academic research can be of service to political struggle. Thanks for always holding the big picture over my head to help me understand that this research is a small piece of a much bigger movement.

The aforementioned activists and organizations in the United States are integral to the national democratic movement in the Philippines and therefore, I'd like to thank organizations and activists in the Philippines who supported me as I collected my research in the Philippines: GABRIELA Philippines, Bayan Philippines, Center for Women's Resources, Joan Salvador, Joms Salvador, Emily Cahilog, Liza Maza, Gert Libang, Rita Baua, Renato Reyes, Marie Boti, Coni Ledesma, Sarah Raymundo, Judy Taguiwalo, Lana Linaban, and Jojo Guan. My *kasamas* number in the thousands. Please know I carry you in my heart and, hopefully, this book contributes to our ultimate goal.

I want to acknowledge the many circles of support from brilliant scholars and academics who have supported this project from its nascent stages. First, my mentors at the City University of New York, The Graduate Center (GC), have read countless drafts and provided line-by-line comments to earlier drafts of this book. Michelle Fine and Hester Eisenstein emerged as stalwart partners in developing theories in this work that intersected with progressive politics. I thank them for being brave in that intersection and allowing me to find my way in. Carolina Bank-Munoz valiantly took me on as her first doctoral student and I am thankful for her solid politics and her willingness to share her rich experiences in the academy with me. Thank you, Carolina, for reading every line, asking hard questions, asking the right questions, and forcing me to sharpen, always sharpen, my argument. I thank GC sociology faculty members Robert Smith, Margaret Chin, and Vilna Bashi for their feedback on my research.

I was able to begin transnational ethnography from New York City to Manila through the generous support of institutional supports and fellowships. I was a research associate at the University of the Philippines (UP), Diliman, Women and Development Studies, in the summer of 2009 where my mentor Judy Taguiwalo guided me through the ethics of collecting research with families in the Philippines. I am thankful to sociologist Sarah Raymundo for allowing me to sit in her classes and talking with me about the emergent themes in my research. I met Dennis Raymundo in my time at UP Diliman and he became the chief transcriber for many of my interviews held in Tagalog. I'm also thankful to Joi Barrios, who was in the past affiliated with UP but is now at UC Berkeley and who helped me develop one of the key concepts in this book, *sukli*. These Philippine scholar-activists braid revolutionary politics, brilliant intellectualism, and humor so easily. I also thank my Pasig-based familiy, Agnes and Bebs Manlangit, who housed and fed me during these stints of research in the Philippines.

I benefited greatly from the weekly conversations as a graduate fellow at the Center for Place, Culture and Politics with David Harvey in 2010–2011 where I was in conversation with brilliant scholars that made room for my thinking and also challenged it: Ruthie Wilson Gilmore, Premilla Nadasen, Manny Ness, Setha Low, and Diana Polson. I am thankful for Maria Torre and Michelle Fine at the Public Science Project (PSP) at the GC, who gave me a postdoctoral fellowship while I was developing my second project on Filipino caregivers in San Francisco. My amazing colleagues at the GC have listened to my academic woes and my practice presentations; they also have reminded me to eat, laugh, and dance. To C. Ray Borck, Allison Padilla-

Goodman, Tsedale Melaku, Alyson Spurgas, John Boy, and Colin Ashley, my cohort homies, thank you for the countless meal breaks that you gave me to rant about the current burning academic issue. Thanks for reading drafts and giving me feedback on bibliographies. Through the years, you have all supported this book and my development as a human being; thanks for being awesome friends. To Patricia Krueger-Henney, thank you for understanding that my academic project was always tied to my community; our unsaid unity helped me ask questions beyond the academe and toward movement building. I am thankful for the 2011–2012 Ethnic Minority Writing Fellowship Program at the University of San Francisco for bringing me home to the Bay Area. I needed to finish my data analysis and commit to writing and luckily, I found myself with Dawn Lee Tu, Evelyn Rodriguez, Evelyn Ho, Hwaji Shin, and Stephanie Sears, who offered me not only intellectual enthusiasm but also exciting collegial relationships.

This book has had many homes. My first job was at the University of Portland (UoP) and there I found support for my transnational research through the Butine Grant for Faculty Development, which funded my last data collection trip to the Philippines and New York City in 2014. I also enjoyed the affirmation of colleagues Christi Hancock, Alice Gates, and Alexa Dare, who committed to weekly writing groups. These colleagues not only gave me courage to write but also helped me learn my politics around race and gender in an institution where we shared the margins. I was also lucky enough to be able to work with sharp and dedicated Filipina students who are also my *kasamas*. Angelica Lim and Geleen Abenoja became my research assistants and co-authors. I want to thank them for looking at the stories in this book in a different way. During my time at UoP, I was able to participate in a workshop at York University organized by Kabita Chakraborty about emotions and migrations. The opportunity to expand my thinking around emotionality gave this book a deeper dimension. In the Portland academic community, senior scholars Patti Duncan from Oregon State University and Johanna Brenner from Portland State University read early drafts of this manuscript. I'd like to thank Patti for reading my drafts and providing avenues for publication and presentation of the theories in this book. She also reminded me as my oldest child was just turning a few months old that scholars could aspire to getting back "home" to where their family was—mine, the Bay Area—because my scholarship was valuable. Oh, how I needed to hear that at that moment with a little babe in my arms, wanting to close the distance between me and my family.

Patti was right. I landed my second job at San Jose State University (SJSU) and I set out to finish a draft of this book to send out to reviewers. I'm grateful to the Research, Scholarly and Creative Activity Course Release, 2015, in the Department of Sociology and Interdisciplinary Social Sciences. But more importantly, I am so grateful to my weekly writing group, Maggie Barrera, Faustina DuCros, and Amy Leisenring, who gave me consistency and structure to finish the draft. The cocktails and laughter were a plus. I'd also like to acknowledge other colleagues at SJSU who supported my research and teaching: Susan Murray, Tanya Bakhru, Maria Alaniz, Walt Jacobs, and Peter Chua. After one short year at SJSU, I received an offer for my dream job at my alma mater San Francisco State University (SFSU).

At SFSU, I have deep appreciation for my colleagues in the Department of Sociology and Sexuality Studies—those who were my undergraduate teachers became mentors and now colleagues. I want to thank my undergraduate mentor Jessica Fields, who put into place a rigorous diet of planning, deadlines, and discipline when I was an undergraduate and aspiring scholar. I'm grateful for Jessica's commitment to transform our mentor-mentee relationship into collegial respect and a wonderful friendship. Special thanks to Marla Ramirez, Alexis Martinez, Andreana Clay, Christopher Carrington, Karen Hossfeld, Clare Sears, Allen LeBlanc, and Chris Bettinger for believing in me and my work. They encouraged me to close my office door and applauded the booming music in the background of my writing sessions. I have a set of colleagues in the university who have been caring and supportive of this book through our writing groups, over lunches, and checking in with me in hallways. Thank you to Dawn Bohulano Mabalon, Ron Hayduk, Susanna Jones, Autumn Thoyre, Dilara Yarbrough, Oscar Stewart, Ché Rodriguez, and Melissa Guzman. Lastly, although I am technically in the sociology department, I also have a home in the Department of Asian American Studies in the College of Ethnic Studies and I'm grateful for the support of Grace Yoo, Allyson Tintiangco-Cubales, and Anantha Sudhakar. At SFSU, I've also had the great privilege of working with amazing students who have challenged and supported this book as research assistants. I'd like to recognize Katrina Liwanag, Christopher Dokko, Sophia Mortera, Colleen McCullough, Knoble Tankiamco, and Tiffany Mendoza for helping me with logistics but also reading my almost-final chapters and challenging me to think through the concepts I'm proposing here. I'm lucky to be working with brilliant students who become my teachers.

I am indebted to my editor Dawn Durante at the University of Illinois Press, who ushered me through the process of completing this book. At the publication of *The Labor of Care*, Dawn will have seen me through three institutional moves and two births. She has been patient and unwavering in her commitment to this book, and more importantly, she has shared my joys and losses both in this book and in life. I am also thankful to the editors Adi Hovav, Laura Helper-Farris, and Maria denBoer, who treated my pages as carefully as I would and I'm thankful for their care.

A special group of people who have supported me through this work are those who share my passion for critical scholarship and research, teaching, activism, and family. I'm indebted to them for seeing me holistically and supporting my writing by supporting my heart, appetite, and children. Thank you to Suzanne Schmidt and Michael Viola for providing writing retreats and childcare as I did the important work of editing and clarifying my writing. Thank you to Faith Kares and Jan Padios, sisters whom I met in this academic journey just at the right time when we were growing our projects and learning how to let them fly. Lastly, I'd like to acknowledge the brilliant kasama, editor, indexer, friend, and supporter, Rossella De Leon for her work on this book. Her invaluable eye to detail and commitment to success of this project pushed me through the last stages.

All throughout this journey, Robyn Magalit Rodriguez has consistently taken on the task of guiding me through the academy, our shared political commitments, and personal growth. I thank her for taking nuggets of coherence in my work and showing them to me so I could actually turn them into fully formed ideas. Robyn, thanks for seeing potential in me and then committing to a lifetime partnership of growth as scholars, *kasamas*, and sisters.

I would not have been able to complete this book without the scholars I met in professional organizations, groups, and spaces. In discussion with the famous and going-to-be-famous thinkers, activists, and writers in these spaces, I have been able to situate myself as a scholar, activist, and scholar-activist. I want to acknowledge the Association for Asian American Studies, the National Women's Studies Association, the Labor/Labor Movements, and the Asia/Asian America sections at the American Sociological Association, which have been reliable sources of inspiration and refuge for a scholar with commitments to social justice. I want to acknowledge these critical Filipino scholars for supporting and affirming my work: Martin Manalansan, Rick Bonus, Allan Isaac, Anna Romina Guevarra, Amanda Solomon Amorao, Mark Villegas, Tracy Buenavista, Neferti Tadiar, Catherine Choy, Kevin Nadal, Matt Andrews, James Zarsadiaz, Anthony Ocampo, Celine Shimizu Parreñas, Johanna Almiron, Ethel Tungohan, Robert Diaz, Melissa Nievera-Lozano, Sherwin Mendoza, Faye Caronan, Josen Diaz, Joyce Mariano, Linda Maram, Armand Gutierrez, and Joy Sales. Your presence in the academy as Filipino

American scholars helps me feel like we are experiencing a renaissance in the field of Filipino Studies.

When I finished grad school, my sister said to me, "Where we come from, not a lot of people get college degrees. Much less PhDs." My sister Alexie Rae, my brother Arve, and I grew up not knowing what we would do after high school. They have always reminded me to look back and see the long distance we have come. They remind me that I represent the people from whom we come, from Manila, Philippines, by way of Concord, California. I thank them and their families for not always understanding what I do but for always having confidence in me. In 2016, my sister Alexie, my brother-in-law Bill, and their son Kanoah went through an unimaginable loss, as their sweet 3-month-old Melana Reme transitioned to be with our ancestors. In the thick of their grief and mourning, these three people showed me true strength of the spirit, the true definition of being separate but never really being apart, at least in their hearts. I thank Alexie, Bill, and Kanoah for their smiles, love, and giving me the honor of knowing Melana Reme, our beautiful angel.

I want to thank my parents Irma and Vernon, the first transnational family in my life. These two people endured unimaginable sacrifices to bring my siblings and me to the United States and then they faced more sacrifices when they got here. Their hope for me was always to be a doctor. I think they thought that I'd be the kind of doctor that could write prescriptions. But now, I don't think they mind. Even though they had no idea what a PhD was or how I was going to get a job with it, they still cheered me on. They always saw the long road ahead of me, knowing that that road is filled with possibility. I want to thank my grandmother Remedios and the grandmother she left me with, Priscilla. They both believed that I could do whatever I put my mind to, and so I did. I want to acknowledge my friends whom I'm lucky to call my extended family: Thieny Hoang, Lina Nguyen, Hamida Yusufzai, Socorro Dalton, Connie Huang, Kerry and James Flores, Kraig Hengst and Vanna Beepat. My family helped me plant my feet with strong roots down to the humble earth so I could reach for the stars. For this, I'm forever grateful.

I want to thank two people who weren't around when I started this project, my daughter Aya Gabriela and son Cy Andres. When I began to do the research for this book, I would cry alongside mothers who missed their children's birthdays and graduations because I felt their sadness. When I birthed my two children, they taught me how to be a mother (they continue to do so) and in that process I came to understand a different dimension of migrant mothers' sacrifice when they leave the Philippines and the pain they feel when they can't hug their children. I am privileged enough to be able to raise my children in the same house, same city, and same nation, so because of Aya and Cy I understand so intimately what is at stake. Aya and Cy came into my life as I was finalizing these pages, changing me and the analysis in this book as well. I want to thank them for their life-changing presence: teaching me patience, granting me perspective, and giving me so much joy.

Lastly, I want to thank my love Raul Francisco-Menchavez for believing in me at the moments when I didn't believe in myself. Raul, thank you for always seeing me for who I am and reminding me when I get lost, then helping me see who I can become. Thank you for moving so many times across the country and up and down the West Coast. Thank you for your patience and relentless confidence in me. Thank you for giving my life color. We have so many more places to go and so many more dreams to catch. Thank you for finding me in this lifetime and riding shotgun with me through it.

Introduction

Filipino Transnational Families
and New Caring Strategies

Mother's Day is a big event at the Filipino community center in Queens, New York. Today, everything in Kalayaan (Freedom) multipurpose hall is decorated in a Mother's Day color, purple—from the flowers to the tablecloths to the fanciest disposable wares the organizers could find at the dollar stores on Sixty-ninth Street in the Roosevelt neighborhood. Young Filipino and Filipino American men and women volunteers usher fifty Filipina migrant women to their seats around decorated banquet-style tables. Many of the women belong to the Kabalikat Domestic Workers Support Network, a program of the Filipino community center dedicated to leadership development, rights, and welfare. The annual Mother's Day event is part of Kabalikat's effort to provide a space for celebration for mothers and women who are away from their own mothers and children on this emotional occasion. After an elaborate Filipino-style lunch, Filipino American volunteers begin the formal program. Volunteers have spent weeks working with Kabalikat members' families in the Philippines through Facebook posts, emails, and Skype calls, gathering moving missives and other forms of greetings. First, volunteers read aloud letters of dedication from the women's children; then, as the lights in the room dim, one of the Kabalikat coordinators, Andrea, turns on a projector. The second part of the program consists of video greetings from family members in the Philippines.

The first video greeting features Joan's children. Joan is a migrant mother working as a domestic worker in New York City who has been separated from her family for about five years at the time of this celebration; as the face of Melann, Joan's only daughter, is projected onto the wall, Joan sighs aloud in awe. The audience hears music in the background as Melann greets her mother: "Happy Mother's Day, Mama!" Melann then turns the camera over to Christopher, Joan's youngest son. He says, "Happy Mother's Day, Mama! Here it is!" He is smiling with pride as he holds up his high school diploma. As he zooms the diploma in and out of his computer camera, a teary Joan exclaims aloud, "I'm so proud of you, Chris! Tapos na ang aking trabaho! My work is done! Tapos na ako sa paglilinis ng arinola! I'm done with cleaning toilets!" As the video comes to an end, Chris addresses the rest of the Kabalikat women in the audience, reassuring them that their children are celebrating on Mother's Day as well. He says, "Huwag kayong mag-alala, pinagbubutihan namin ang aming pag-aaral dito, mga titas. Don't worry—we're all doing our best in our studies here, aunties."

Several women turn to Joan to offer their congratulations. Lily, another migrant mother, turns to Joan and says, "See, after all of that, ang galing pala ni Chris! Chris is so good after all! Didn't I tell you that you just have to always remind him about going to school? Didn't I tell you that you should ask him to tell you about the different classes he is taking?" Joan, teary-eyed, says, "Yes, I remember. And now, he's graduated. What a relief." Lily and Joan embrace. Their friendship has seen both of them through so many trials—from issues with their families in the Philippines to their everyday struggles in New York City. But today, on Mother's Day, they revel together in this victory.

*   *   *

Christopher's display of his diploma was his acknowledgment of his mother's work and his gratitude for all that she does all the way across the world. In that moment, Joan saw her years of separation and work abroad repaid through her son's accomplishment. As Christopher addressed the audience, he spoke for all children who could not be with their mothers on Mother's Day in New York City. His diploma exemplified one of the ways that families in the Philippines honor their migrant family members abroad. Although he only knew a few of the Kabalikat women through his mother introducing them on Skype, Christopher's act of offering his high school diploma to his mother and then to all of his *titas* (aunts) is symbolic of how families in the Philippines are repaying the sacrifices of the migrant women in their families.

Even if Joan could not make it to Christopher's graduation, watching him show off his diploma through a video greeting in front of all of the Kabalikat women on Mother's Day was memorable. It allowed her to share Christopher's accomplishment with the women at the center, many of whom she considers as close as sisters and family members. The Kabalikat women have worked housecleaning jobs with Joan, accompanied her to doctor visits, and talked her through financial problems in the Philippines. Many of them have school-age children of their own back in the Philippines, looking to Joan and Christopher as exemplars. As the Kabalikat women showered Joan with congratulations, they took that moment to share in the hope that the sacrifices they were making for their families back home would be rewarded with equally positive outcomes. This opening vignette represents the rich and dynamic textures of the many people involved in transnational family arrangements (family members in the Philippines, migrant mothers, migrant communities) and the types of care work present in these contexts. The Mother's Day celebration invites us to think about how longing, pride, and resilience encapsulate the experiences of those who are trying to make meaning of their families from a distance and just how much work it takes to keep families together while apart.

This book is about the intimate relations of transnational families exemplified through the lives and experiences of Filipina migrants living in New York City and the families they left behind in the Philippines. Filipino families have a long history of institutionalized migration, separation, and transnational experiences.[1] The need to examine macrostructural forces and how they shape the microinteractions of separated family members (Laslett and Brenner 1989) is more pressing than ever as Filipina women are migrating at an increasing rate given the global demand for domestics and the lack of opportunities for work in the Philippines. Through the lives of Filipino transnational families, I examine the care work, both paid and unpaid, which sustains families shaped by neoliberal conditions. Indeed, this book balances the seemingly abundant advances of our increasingly globalized world (such as mobility, transport, technology, etc.) with the testimony of the people who contend with and attempt to survive the consequences of globalization's discontents (migration, separation) on a daily basis.

The work of transnational families is filled with numerous actors, forms, and definitions of care simultaneously keeping these families' expectations and practical functions afloat. Anchored in the lives and experiences of Filipina migrants in New York City and their families in the Philippines, the purpose of this book is to draw out the myriad of innovative engagements in care work by both migrant and nonmigrant members of transnational families, to recognize their reconfigured practices of care as labor and active agency. Families, both biological and fictive, in the homeland and the hostland, are putting in tremendous amounts of work to keep the transnational family arrangement a viable one. Migrant and nonmigrant family members are tailoring their definitions of the family form based on the conditions of their lives while global processes are restructuring intimate family dynamics. Insomuch as this book is about the affliction of migration and globalization, it is also about the courage and durability of families. Therefore, my central research questions are: How are members of transnational families transforming and negotiating care work under the development of neoliberal conditions that present migration as the only form of livelihood and technology as a form of connectivity? How does this historically specific neoliberal moment impel migrants and their families to develop care strategies that accommodate long-term separation over long distances? What are those strategies and how are migrants using these social processes to create new types of familial adaptation and resilience?

Broadly, my inquiry is focused on how neoliberal structural shifts in induced and sustained migration shape and ultimately change the intimate relations and definitions of care in Filipino families. I am critical of the social, political, and economic conditions under which families are forcibly separated. By framing the laboring lives of Filipina migrants and their transnational families through the theory of social reproduction,[2] I critically examine the export of Filipino labor and reliance on the contemporary transnational Filipino family for profit in a neoliberal era through the Philippine "labor brokerage state" (R. M. Rodriguez 2010; Guevarra 2009).[3] While I hold in tension the inventive practices of care in transnational families, I assert that they necessarily reconfigure the functions, operations, and definitions of family as a result of forced separation due to various dimensions of neoliberal globalization, specifically migration and technology (Harvey 2007). I maintain that the family is often deployed as an auxiliary mechanism to the neoliberal strategy of managed and regulated labor migration of Filipinos. Filipino migrant citizens are deemed as labor to the world with huge returns for the Philippine national economy. And therefore, the transnational family is folded into the capitalist enterprise as a site of (re)production and accumulation (Katz 2004; Ninh 2011). However, I also assert that the social reproductive labor of transnational family members can be a site for hopeful potential in challenging gender roles, pushing back against which currencies of care work count in the family, and even creating new types of solidarity in diasporic sites that center fictive kinship as a form of transnational family operations. My focus in highlighting the circulation of care work transnationally in its many forms relies on the feminist sensibility of visibilizing the work in "doing family" and in investigating these questions, new roles, alternative care providers, and shifting gendered ideas that surface in the unseen work of reproducing the family, specifically in a transnational arrangement.

I use the term "transnational family" to describe the organization, operations, and production of a family with members who reside in two or more nation-states. I operationalize this term to go beyond the Western idea of the nuclear family to account for both biological and fictive kin, which includes but is not limited to grandparents, aunts, uncles, cousins, siblings, nephews and nieces, and those who are treated and labeled as such. I start from an expansive understanding of the membership and definition of a transnational family as the form is changing relative to the conditions and the extended periods of separation over long distances (Bryceson and Vuorela 2002). As a result, families, communities, and people left behind are actively negotiating, rethinking, and reassigning who provides care, what types of care are necessary, and who receives that care. In this work, I prioritize the extended family formation and fictive kin as the *primary* form for Filipino families, shifting the focus away from the bourgeois family ideal of the Western nuclear family form (Alipio, Lu, and Yeoh 2015).[4] The Philippine family rarely follows the nuclear form; for Filipinos, family is upheld by *pakikisama*, literally translated as "being with," thus placing importance on interpersonal relationships that then bolster a feeling of being in the family (Agoncillo and Guerrero 1974). Membership in Filipino families is extensive, with Filipinos tracing lineage through both mother and father and considering relatives regardless of how distant or close as "family" (Asis 2006). By considering a wider set of people as contributors to a transnational family, I give research participants the authority to define for themselves whom they deem as members in maintaining their families.[5]

Throughout this book, gender is integrated in my study of the development of multiple directions, providers, and interpretations of care work in the transnational family. Gender roles for migrant mothers shift as they become breadwinners and decision makers in their households in ways that they have not before (Curran et al. 2006; Alicea 1997). Although historically men have migrated more frequently, the concern about the disintegration of family was less connected to men's migration and more intense for women's migration.[6] Still Alicia Pingol argues, "When economic realities limit men's capacity to provide for their families but open opportunities for women to assume this function, the dynamics of the family changes. Men as well as women are confronted with the task of redefining their own notions of the masculine and feminine" (Pingol 2001, 6). I take this on by accepting that gendered construction of family occurs for all members of the family producing a range of masculinities and femininities.[7] Therefore, I examine how gender identity and performance are affected by the shifts in productive and social reproductive labor in transnational families (Connell 2005; Pingol 2001). Instead of a silo discussion of gender, I integrate a gendered analysis of ascribed care work, attending to the ways in which gender and sexuality organize processes of migration and dialectically how migration experiences impact the way in which gendered and sexualized identities and performances are formed in the transnational family.

This book's aim is to illuminate the work, in both sending and receiving contexts, in the reconfiguration of domestic and social reproductive relations for transnational families. Scholars have established that specifically for women and girls, global and feminized migration rearticulates traditional conceptions and strategies of motherhood for migrants (Hondagneu-Sotelo and Avila 1997; Parreñas 2001b; Dreby 2010). These new definitions compel migrant mothers to redefine their work and participation in family life through remittances (Hoang and Yeoh 2015b) and technology. Still, as migration becomes institutionalized, especially in developing countries like the Philippines, these new definitions of family also affect the strategies that *all* family members left behind deploy in terms of who takes up social reproductive labor, its forms, and its meanings. I pay attention to the particularly understudied work of children and young people in transnational families and how they are continuously engaged in the work of the family (Ní Laoire et al. 2010; White et al. 2011; J. L. Waters 2015; Hoang et al. 2015). Additionally, migrants in their host cities are often changing their social relations and producing new types of care for one another as they find themselves without the family networks they had previously relied on. Throughout this work, I highlight care work through the vantage points and sites that are often conceptualized as passive or vacant of work: nonmigrant family members in the place left behind, specifically children, husbands, and extended kin, and also among migrants in their diasporic place of residence. In the opening vignette of Kabalikat's community celebration, I locate the different actors and processes involved in the transnational lives of migrant women but I seek to widen that perspective by not only focusing on the migrant's absence, but also on the presence of other types of care work emergent because of the neoliberal conditions under which migrants and their families live. This book prioritizes an optic of transnationalism in a critical discussion of the family, gender, and migration that insists that the transnational family is a generative site to study labor and political economy. The transnational family, in fact, can be an important nexus to uncover the links between the global and the intimate, and perhaps a generative empirical field to consider and create critical hope in times of seemingly overdetermining forces of neoliberal globalization.

Multidirectional Care in Transnational Families

The overall argument in this book is that multiple sets of people from multiple locations do work to maintain the transnational family as a functioning and viable family form. Chris's graduation was his way of holding up his end of the deal that his mother entered into when she migrated to the United States. Melann and Chris, two of Joan's three children, were supporters of each other's success in college after their mother left. And for the most part, this partnership contributed to a sense of relief for Joan, working as a nanny thousands of miles away. Joan funded Chris's and Melann's college education, but the siblings worked hard together to support their education journeys, which in turn reassured their mother that her decision to migrate was not in vain. Transnational family members from different places in the diaspora exchange care work in many different forms. Although the care work from transnational families is not similar in form (monetary remittances versus high school graduation), they generate labor nonetheless. The incommensurability of the currencies and capital of care work in transnational families is the focus of this work because these labors are often circulating in various political, financial, and affective economies, yet some of them are valued less, or worse, invisible. Therefore, it is my aim to identify these currencies and to analyze the consequences and reception of the incommensurability of care work between transnational family members. To this end, I introduce a concept called "multidirectional care" to describe the ways in which transnational family members activate multiple resources, people, and networks to redefine care work in the family (Baldassar and Merla 2013).[8]

It is increasingly apparent that the character of the contemporary family in an era of globalization continues to move toward transnationality. The idea of a nuclear family that is reified in much of Western sociology of the family scholarship is constructed in and through an assumption of economic stability that accepts that family members live under the same roof and even in the same nation. This is no longer the form of the contemporary family. Migration characterizes the childhood experience in Asia (Alipio, Lu, and Yeoh 2015), among other regions of the world. As a result of the long-term separation driven by an acceleration of migration under globalization (Castles and Miller 2003), parents are not only physically absent from their children for long periods of time, but the transnational family form is also reorganized into a complex constellation of biological and nonbiological kin. With the transnational family as the unit of analysis, I trace the flows and directions of care work that are circulating in the process of migration and separation. I focus on the transnational family to make visible the labors necessary to challenge the idea that any "good" care work requires proximity (Baldassar and Merla 2013). I join scholars of migration studies in demonstrating that care work and family are adaptive and expansive in the definitions of roles and form, especially under the neoliberal conditions of accelerated migration.

The multidirectional care in the lives of Filipina migrants and their families is at the center of the complex relationship between productive and social reproductive labor, global capital accumulation, and neoliberal states. This transnational process embedded in the tensions of paid and unpaid domestic labor is best situated in the feminist political economy theoretical frame of social reproduction, wherein the term "social reproduction does more than identify the activities involved in the daily and generation reproduction of life. It allows for an explanation of the structures, relationships, and dynamics that produce" (Luxton 2006, 39) the lives of Filipino transnational families. In an effort to expand conceptualizations of care within the transnational family, I adopt an expansive definition of social reproductive labor offered by Barbara Laslett and Johanna Brenner (1989, 382):

> Among other things, social reproduction includes how food, clothing and shelter are made available for immediate consumption, the ways in which the care and socialization of children are provided, the care of the infirm and elderly, and the social organization of sexuality. Social reproduction can thus be seen to include various kinds of work—mental, manual, and emotional— aimed at providing the historically and socially, as well as biologically, defined care necessary to maintain existing life and to reproduce the next generation.

Applied to migrants and their transnational family, this definition captures the daily, local paid work of Filipina migrants in New York City as housekeepers, nannies, and caregivers to the elderly for "immediate consumption" *and* it also describes the work migrants and nonmigrant family members engage in transnationally, often after-hours, invisibly, and automatically. Filipina migrants and their families subsist on the wages earned from paid domestic work in New York City but Filipinas also participate in the unpaid domestic labor for their families in the Philippines from New York City. Likewise, migrants are also dependent on the domestic labor done by their family members left behind.

This integrated and symbiotic process of waged production of domestic services and unwaged production of life are both regulated by a neoliberal capitalist economy that necessitates the migration of low-wage, migrant domestic workers to the Global North and their separation from their families in the Global South (Luxton 2006). These are the systemic political and economic conditions required for the emergence of multidirectional care in transnational families. Social reproduction as an analytical frame that links the state in collusion with neoliberalism has become central to endorsing the ongoing reconfiguration of social reproductive labor within Filipino families as they export Filipina migrants as paid domestic workers globally.

Migration jumpstarts emotional changes in the family (Boccagni and Baldassar 2015). The model of multidirectional care captures the invisible social reproductive labor flowing between and among members of transnational families undergirded with affective and emotional charges, both good and bad. In my application of multidirectional care, I count acts of labor and service even through experiences of emotional strain and conflict between members of transnational families as part of the formula of circulating care. Although emotions may contradict transnational family members' desire to care for one another, they still attend to deeds of service, communication, and labor to sustain their family operations from a distance. Idealized notions of care and love do not always exist in the care work between transnational families (Coe 2008). Yet for transnational family members, unavoidable tasks like remitting money or communicating current developments are tasks that need to be accomplished. Multidirectional care contains these types of labor regardless of its emotional underpinnings. Though emotions are at times overlooked in migration and transnationalism studies (Mai and King 2009), I hold them within the multidirectional care model because while it is an intrapsychic process it is also produced by political, economic, and social processes such as migration. Feelings such as guilt (Baldassar 2015; Baumeister, Stillwell, and Heatherton 1994; Vermot 2015), sacrifice (Park 2005), and even hope (Raffaetà 2015) are shaped by migration and the moral economies of family obligation (Velayutham and Wise 2005) and responsibilities that come with it. Unavoidably, a transnational affect (Wise and Velayutham 2006) that is relational, embodied, and socially structured by the capitalist processes of migration becomes key in understanding the multidirectional labor of care in transnational families. Thus, a turn to emotionality is not merely a descriptive analytic; rather, it is a commitment to understanding the seemingly "natural" or "biological" nature of emotions as politically and socially constructed phenomena (Lutz and Abu-Lughod 1990).

Most importantly, recognizing that care work is multiple in form and direction also draws attention to family members both biological and fictive, in both the place left behind and the diaspora, doing the work of the family. Often exchanges of care work are centered on a linear relationship from migrant family members toward families left behind. This formulation assumes that all the care work that families left behind engage in is only in reaction to the absence of one person; however, families left behind have many more concerns beyond their migrant family members. Their lives continue without that one person who migrated, and production of life in the place left behind is ongoing: Children have to be sent to school, bills need to be paid, and dinners need to be cooked. Thus, multidirectional care considers the transnational practices of care and labor enacted by *all* members involved in transnational arrangements and how they make meaning of those practices.

In conceptualizing these transnational circuits of care, the heavy demands of global capital accumulation are apparent on those who carry the burden of social reproductive labor in the transnational family. Moving beyond a microsociological study of Filipina migrants as paid domestic workers and/or as providers for their transnational families in the Philippines, this book demonstrates that capital's gluttonous need for cheap domestic labor pulls in more than migrant women in the "care chain" (Ehrenreich and Hochschild 2002) or those involved in "global householding" (Douglass 2006). In fact, the political economy of care necessitates all types of social reproductive labor (from the place left behind, within migrant communities, etc.) and requires many more laboring bodies to maintain the transnational family. This argument follows an emergent field of studies on care circulation in transnational families as Loretta Baldassar and Laura Merla (2013) write:

> We think a care circulation lens, with its focus on the practices and processes of the asymmetrically reciprocal exchanges of transnational caregiving, offers a productive way to trace and retrace the links and connections between members across distance and time, which constitute the workings of "global households."

In the context of coerced separation through neoliberal immigration policy, a care circulation framework aptly describes the work of Filipino transnational families. In mapping the forms, providers, and directions of care, Filipino members of transnational families have demonstrated that there are various dimensions of care and a myriad of people making sense of the care they are giving. The circulation of care allows us to see how migrants are not the only people providing care in their transnational arrangement; they are also receiving care from their families at home. Tracing from whom that care comes allows us to break open the nuclear family form and accept the many members who contribute to constellations of care in a transnational family. We are able to then redefine the labor in care work, what constitutes care activities, forms of care, and acts of service if we take on a framework that care is always in motion, albeit asymmetrically (financial versus emotional versus communication, etc.). Remapping care work as multidirectional and in circulation leads us to see the myriad of forms and actors crafting and negotiating with the conditions of absence and separation.

"My Mom is My Facebook Friend!": Technology as Care Work and Globalization

Christopher proclaimed, "*Hindi ako shy, Facebook friends kami ni Nanay!* I'm not embarrassed, my mom is my Facebook friend!" when I asked him if he shared some of his girlfriend's pictures on Facebook. Christopher, who was 13 years old when he claimed proudly that he was friends with his mom Joan on Facebook, did not seem ashamed about sharing the personal and youthful online platform with his mom. He told me that although his mother hangs on to every post and picture he posts on Facebook, he considers it a passive service to her given that he would post those things anyway. And since they are friends she is able to stay updated on his daily musings without Christopher having to "try." In some sense, Christopher's lackadaisical perspective on his friendship with his mother on Facebook is a form of providing care work through communication with her.

The multidirectional care model leads to my second argument: With increased use of technology in a neoliberal context, *who* attends to social reproductive labor and care work can shift from adults to children, from migrants to family members left behind. The advancement of technology through personal computers, video software, and web-based social networks makes possible ever quicker and more intimate interactions between family members who live transnationally (Aguila 2011). As the example of the video played at the Mother's Day celebration demonstrates, technology—especially technology that contains video capabilities—establishes a new kind of intimacy for families separated by migration. Likewise, social media platforms introduce novel means of relating for separated families. Specifically, presence and intimacy are greatly facilitated by these emerging avenues of communication technology. They enable a simultaneity (Levitt and Schiller 2004) that powers the continuum of multidirectional care work as a transnational practice.[9]

Every member in the transnational family who engages in learning, teaching, and participating in technology to communicate with one another becomes part of a circulating "virtual form of care" (Baldassar and Merla 2013, 12). The theory of simultaneity is a heuristic to capture the dynamism of transnational life, changing social relations and experiences in all places all at once. This concept makes it possible to understand that not only the forms of care work can be varied but also the people who take up roles as care providers are often redefined simultaneously in the transnational family.[10] More specifically, it highlights nonmigrant members and nontraditional actors of transnational families taking up new roles as care providers, especially vis-à-vis developments in technology as opportunities to exchange skills as part of the necessary communication entailed in care work for transnational families.[11]

Care circulated through the use of technology and framed in simultaneity adds new dimensions to the direction and providers of care in the transnational family. The use of technology in the transnational family allows for an exchange in skills and knowledge as well as care and communication. Joan's children Chris and Melann have spent countless hours as "tech help" for Joan, teaching her how to turn on a computer or create an account on the instant messaging client and video-conferencing software Yahoo Messenger. After all, Joan, a middle-aged immigrant woman who has worked low-wage jobs in the Philippines, has never had to deal with any type of technology. Chris and Melann have both internalized their roles as care providers to their migrant mother by teaching her this set of critical skills that is a key component to the care work in their transnational family. Scholars have argued that age is an important determinant in how children in transnational families experience separation and migration (Hoang and Yeoh 2015a; Huijsman 2011); I would add that the types of knowledges they possess as youth can also influence how they interpret their roles as care providers in their transnational relationships with parents. The two-way directionality of care happens all at the same time: Joan sending back tuition money, Chris chatting with Joan on Yahoo Messenger about next steps after graduation, Melann showing her how to log on to Facebook. Care circulation and simultaneity capture the reciprocity that includes the different forms of care and roles of care providers that emerge in the changing social relations with the development of technology. Throughout this book, I draw on the care circulation frame and the theory of simultaneity to examine the processes and dimensions of care for Filipino transnational families.

Transnational families' engagement with technology is fixed to the context of neoliberal globalization just as the argument of multidirectional care is produced in and through these political economic conditions. The advancement of information economy and communication technology is a different side of the same capitalist economy that produces the regulated management of Filipino labor migration. Therefore, it is no surprise that all of the family narratives in this book include stories of dispossession as a result of globalization in the Philippines, migration as a direct result, and technology as a way to deal with their circumstances. I hold in tension these dynamics of globalization as the framework that produces the migrant worker industry and the technology that keeps families together from afar. Just as I explore the creative technological strategies of migrants and their families left behind, I remain critical of globalization because it requires separation and migration so that transnational families must use Skype and Facebook as their forms of relationship building.

Chosen Migrant Families, Fictive Kinship, and Communities of Care

Migrants' experience in multidirectional care within their own transnational families becomes the basis for fictive kinship abroad. When Lily embraced Joan at the Mother's Day celebration, she was congratulating her on her son's graduation because she understood deeply what that sacrifice is about. Lily was putting her daughter through college and she shared Joan's hopes that their children could finish with a college degree. For Lily and Joan and other migrant women, acknowledgment from one another was a high compliment, as they all held their transnational families' hopes and dreams in common when they migrated to New York City. They relied on that solidarity to build relationships with each other.

This application of the multidirectional care model demonstrates how Filipina migrants take their intimate knowledge of social reproduction relations, as redefined in their families, and apply it to new relationships with other migrant women in their migrant communities. The care work exchanged between fellow migrants, through fictive kinship and immigrant social networks in their diasporic location of New York City, is an integral part of explaining the circulation of care in the transnational family. I look closely at the women-centered networks that emerged when gendered experiences of being a migrant, a family member and a domestic worker produced points of unity and relationships of solidarity. Migrants use the likely mechanisms of fictive kinship and immigrant social networks in their daily lives for pragmatic reasons[12]; however, the people in this book exhibit an alternative basis of solidarity in the destination context of New York City. Migrants' transnational life and practices provide a deeper basis for the creation and function of immigrant social networks. Relying on black feminist theories (Collins 2002; Stack and Burton 1993) and queer migration studies (Lubheid and Cantu 2005; Manalansan 2006), the discussion on the care circulation of migrant communities considers the structural constraints of gendered migration, transnational family separation, and racialized labor in an urban economy mooring those conditions to the capacities of migrant women to create deeper kinship ties to one another.[13]

In rethinking the basis for immigrant networks, I submit that an integral and often unrecognized type of care in the transnational lives of migrants is in what I call "communities of care." In communities of care, the care work *between* Filipina migrants is the unit of analysis; through their stories of fictive kinship and solidarity with one another the care found abroad among migrants is another redefinition of care arrangements in a transnational context. Care work exchanged among migrants yields a new "sisterhood" with new "daughters" and "mothers" incorporated into what migrants call their "family away from home." Communities of care function like immigrant social networks through mutual assistance in practical issues of migrant life. For example, Filipina migrant workers help one another with job hunting, housing, and various kinds of support (emotional, financial, and practical) related to maintaining families left behind and the transition to a life abroad. However, this definition of care fomented in and through transnational reconfigurations of care must not be viewed simply as exchanges in resources.[14] Rather, the connections and identifications with one another are embedded in identities of migrant, mother, and worker, which are all context dependent.[15] Migrants living in New York City become intelligible to one another on the basis of their experience in transnational families and the particularity of living in a global city as undocumented immigrants in a highly precarious labor industry under the conditions of long-term separation from their families. These are the conditions under which their immigrant social network is activated and transformed into communities of care. Migrants are defining new family relations in New York City; informed by their shared experience with the reorganization of care work in their transnational family arrangements, Filipina migrants are always fostering new fictive and filial relations with one another. Communities of care go beyond the simple activation of contacts in a network to produce job or housing opportunities. They activate identities that are produced through systems of power resulting in fictive kinships, or what scholars of African American families call the motherwork of "othermothers," yet another iteration and reorganization of multidirectional care (Stack 1997; Collins 2002).[16] While the work of othermothers in transnational families is counted as the work of women in the place left behind (Schmalzbauer 2004), I bring that concept into the place of destination in the context of Filipino migrants to highlight how a migrant community is an extension of what becomes part of the transnational family and what labor goes into sustaining that family away from family.

Redefining family more broadly as communities of care in the destination sites of migrants helps us see the creative strategies for survival for migrants who are already dealing with the reconfiguration of care in their families and in their paid work. Many migrants often take from their experiences of worker exploitation, classed racism, and isolation to create transformative bonds through political organizing and community associations.[17] However, the migrants in this book have shown that their transnational lives are equally as important to community building as the experiences they have in their new homes. Migrants may not always make their communities safe or caring, and I do not claim that all migrant communities are communities of care. The broader argument I advance here is that their diasporic and transnational practices are part of how migrants construct and interact within their social network. The communities of care framework allows us to see Filipina migrants as diasporic subjects who construct their own brands of care, and use transnational sensibilities to relate to one another, thus forming both practical and affective bonds of support.

I introduce communities of care as a lens to have a different conversation about immigrant social networks that pulls in a discussion of power and inequality produced by neoliberalism, coerced and gendered Filipina labor migration, and classed racism as the basis for building solidarity. I pay close attention to the meaning-making politics that motivate migrant women to define immigrant social networks as families away from home.[18] I consider communities of care an expression of multidirectional care in the transnational family as the lived experience of Filipina migrants renders women-centered, immigrant networks into a sort of "chosen family" (Weston 1997). Naturalizing heteronormative ideas about Filipina migrant women solely reproducing care as domestic workers who attend to host families and then again to their own transnational families provides an incomplete understanding of the sexualized nature of their occupations and migrations (Manalansan 2003). I argue that queering systems of labor diaspora—incorporating gender and sexuality as axes of analysis—can trouble the normalized conception of migrant Filipino women by reproducing only heteronormative families (in their paid and unpaid work). I offer a new homosocial analysis of the immigrant network that is a reimagining of social reproductive labor distributed horizontally among women because of the political economic context that has radically reconfigured their paid public and unpaid private care work. I continue the work of Filipino migration scholars in critiquing the structural powers that produce such dire conditions for Filipino migrant workers,[19] but I go further to redefine migrant networks as communities of care, thus prioritizing migrant women's gendered intersubjectivity. Through the concept of communities of care, I highlight the significance of the fictive kinship ties between migrant women as they redefine care work between themselves in diasporic locations.

Transforming Labor in the Family in a Neoliberal and Digital Age

The focus of this work is on the negotiations of care work in the transnational family. Given that the transnational family is the unit of analysis, the people's stories that populate the following pages demonstrate that the work of the family is being done beyond normative conceptions as the complex coordinates and flows look like a constellation of multiple directions, providers, forms, and arrangements, and it can even look like care between, across, and among migrant workers. However, even more broadly, I deploy the narratives in this book as a critique of the current political and economic system that relies on separating families as a form of economic development and profit.

Multidirectional care as a pattern of care work for transnational families is always undergirded with an inherent critique of the failing Philippine state and the contradictions of globalization. At the Mother's Day celebration at the community center, after the video messages, photomontages, and emailed poems and letters were presented, the organizers of Kabalikat asked people to come forward and share their proudest moments of being a mother. One after another, each Kabalikat mother went to the front of the room to share her family's most recent achievements: the building of a house, the graduation of a young person, a nice gravestone for a beloved one. Helen, one of Kabalikat's oldest members, remarks, "All of this we've achieved even if we're far. Only if the jobs were closer to home, only if the government would get it right."

By linking the intimate to the global, just as Helen does, we see the complex relationship between the radical reconfiguration of care and the reorganization of the family in the context of migration under neoliberal globalization. The conditions of migration are directly related to the transformation of families, the social costs they take on, and the resilience of migrants and of their families left behind. The movement of care from one place to another demonstrates that some people's (First World) care is privileged over that of others (Third World), that migration is often the only option for Filipinos to imagine a better future for their families. Unfortunately, this option means that a better future can never be in close proximity to their loved ones. These most intimate of decisions and the pulling apart of the most intimate of relationships are always linked to the access to opportunities for livelihood. I insist on contextualizing the family in the labor brokerage state and the neoliberal political economy to establish that the transnational family form is produced through commodification of people through migration. Hence, the forms of care that follow the neoliberal version of labor migration reflect the multiple actors and places that are activated and affected by labor brokerage. Multidirectional care is necessarily established in response to the state's reorganization and recuperation of the family in brokering parents, siblings, and children as migrant exports.

Still, I resist telling the stories of these families as mere victims in the throes of globalization. Within these pages, I hope you find that migrants and their families are often devising inventive strategies for "doing family" despite these consequences. Often, they are engaged in trial-and-error methods and there are many moments of joy and despair. In some ways these families are dealing with issues similar to those families who live under the same roof or even in the same country face. But the key difference about their stories is that they are innovating their labor in the family under extremely different conditions, often using a dimension of the very same globalization that has pulled them apart in the first place, technology. The paradox in the lives of Filipino transnational families is in the way they are revising their family formation and operation because of and in spite of the context of migration and long-term separation. Filipino migrants are ensnared in the decision to leave their families, often reluctantly, but they are also using the advances in information and communication technology to narrow the physical gaps between themselves and their families. My hope is that this book provides a nuanced analysis of the lives and labor of Filipino transnational families from their multiple sites while analyzing the larger context of neoliberal globalization that produces their situations.

Researching Transnational Families' Lives

A few of the fifty Filipina migrants living and working in New York City included in this research study insisted that the narratives of their family members in the Philippines were necessary to understand their transnational experiences. They asserted that the multisited character of transnational families must shape the design of this research. To them, migration was an unfolding process rather than an event of departure or arrival. Similarly, many family members articulated the changes in their family structure and practices over a span of time. The experiences of family members called for sustained and continued examination as roles of care providers or the meanings of migration shifted as migrant women left and stayed abroad for years. Thus, this book's research is a product of that insight, wherein the transnational family, their histories and experiences of migration, is the unit of analysis. Instead of snapshots of just migrant mothers or just families left behind, this book relies on the narratives of whole families separated and living in multiple locations over a period of five years.

The multisited and longitudinal approach to studying transnational families is the methodological innovation that ultimately informed the overall argument of multidirectional care. Travel to multiple sites and maintenance of internet practices for the transnational families in this study allowed for a study of transnationalism "from below," where I was able to study the day-to-day regimen of separated family members. Interviewing both migrants and their family members provided a deeper dimension to transnational life, as I was able to observe the ripple effects of, for example, an event or a life change from both ends over time. At the urging of the migrant women in New York City to *ipaloob* (internalize) their families' situation, I followed a total of eleven family constellations that included twenty-five members of families in the Philippines. Integrating with these family networks allowed me to track developing and shifting ideas, forms, and definitions of social reproductive labor as well as the changing roles in who was responsible for the various care arrangements in a transnational family. Between 2009 and 2014, I had the privilege of being able to travel from New York City to Manila four times, thus allowing me to not only understand the places in which members of families operated from but also to witness the simultaneity of care work in those places. Throughout the cycle of data collection, analysis, and writing across continents and families, I maintained a hermeneutic of faith and suspicion (Josselson 2004) in the concepts that would surface and disappear, following emotion-evoking events within the family. Different viewpoints of the same incident proved that care was inherently multinodal.

The participation of Filipina migrants in a domestic worker organization called Kabalikat (literally translated as "shoulder to shoulder" in English) Domestic Workers Support Network provided a research community to investigate the institutional processes of migration. Observations and reflections of the women in Kabalikat about their histories and everyday life serve as tools to analyze the institutional processes that shape their decisions to migrate and their subsequent lives abroad. This project's methodology extends the idea of shared experiences, or "dislocation" (Parreñas 2001b), by putting the themes of migration, family, work, and community at the center of the logic of inquiry about the lives of Filipina migrant women while allowing for migrants' participation to guide the direction and conduct of the research. Inspired by principles of participatory action research (PAR), I collaborated with migrants to design the methods of observation, construction of the interview guides, research ventures, analysis and products of the research. During my ethnography, I along with a participatory advisory group—a core of Filipina migrant women from Kabalikat—examined how Filipino migrant men and women wove political and economic institutions into their migration stories to understand how institutions such as the Philippine labor brokerage state were reified and embedded in people's lives. An institutional ethnographic approach (D. E. Smith 2005) allowed me to develop a theory of reconfigured social reproduction as it is produced through the neoliberal political and economic policies exporting Filipino migrants to First World countries, such as the United States.

The design and research process began with the "understanding that people—especially who have experienced historic oppression . . . hold deep knowledge about their lives and experience and should help shape the questions [and] frame the interpretations of [research]" (Torre and Fine 2006, 458). Critical researchers and scholars actively critique traditional forms of research and the often colonial and elite interests they serve (L. T. Smith 1999; Appadurai 2006; Tuck 2008). Although PAR is not the solution to the problematic nature of social scientific research methods (Cooke and Kothari 2001), it offers useful tools for understanding the world with the participation of those marginalized by power. Mapping (Powell 2010), theater of the oppressed (Boal 2000), journal writing, and interview as conversation (Kvale 1996) are all nontraditional qualitative methods used in this ethnographic project that required the participation of migrants and their families instead of relying on me as the solitary researcher. These methods engaged migrants' organic intellectualism and indigenous knowledge of the institutions present daily in their lives and, more importantly, they were integral in identifying the important dimensions of their lives that then became the central facets of this research.

The PAR work in this project was mainly conducted with migrant family members in New York City, as I lived and worked in proximity to them. The migrants contributed to my research by helping to construct the interview guides that I used during my trips to the Philippines. They helped to recruit their family members to the study as well. Their participation encouraged them to reflect on their experience as they critiqued the systems that brought them to their decision to migrate. For example, the recurring theme of family in many interviews was also one of the most sensitive topics for migrants to discuss. With an intentional turn to emotionality in my fieldwork (Mai and King 2009; Kleinman and Copp 1993), I chose to follow the often-intense emotions of migrants when they spoke about their families in guiding the direction of the research toward a study of their families. But it also cautioned me to move forward with care in navigating through their family lives. Migrant family members, especially mothers, only talked about the most painful and intimate parts of their families' lives if and when they felt safe and ready. My decision to follow the emotional patterns in the narratives of members of transnational families was simultaneously methodologically and theoretically significant, as it identified the most salient themes in people's affective realities while also deepening the theories of care work, family, and kinship in the social and political processes of migration and transnationalism.

Before I began field research, I became a volunteer organizer at a local Filipino community center. This role allowed me to build relationships with the migrant community. In the spirit of PAR, early development of this research revolved around strategizing how data collection and analysis could help strengthen Filipina domestic worker organizing in Queens, New York. Group interviews and individual interviews eventually transformed into a community theater program that engaged many of the participants of this study in a year-long process to turn the research narratives into a collaboratively written and produced theatrical play. Although the stage performance and script of the play is not read as text for this book, the group interviews, performance-elicited narratives, and discussions on the theater of the oppressed methods for the theater program imbued the writing of this book. As I have discussed elsewhere (Francisco 2013), the democratization of research through PAR and the theatrical production engaged migrants' critical consciousness and solidarity. Moreover, it informed how I sharpened the arguments of this book. A lengthier discussion about the play can be found in the methodological appendix of this book.

PAR was pivotal in the collection and analysis of my research because it was the compass for writing this book. What follows is a confluence of research participants' analysis of what was important about their lives and my lens as an insider-outsider sociologist. I am not under any illusion that transnational, multisited methods, institutional ethnography (IE), or PAR methodology does not produce an other or otherness in this book; rather, my point in discussing these logics of inquiry here is to contextualize the design of this project and the audiences for which I, as an academic, writer, researcher, activist, *kasama* (comrade), and mother am accountable. I am invested in "working the hyphens" in my positionality, as Michelle Fine writes; working the hyphens means to "probe how we are in relation with the contexts we study and with our informants, understanding that we are all multiple in those relations" (Fine 1994, 72). Thus, as a feminist and transnational researcher, I acknowledge my privileges as a documented Filipina migrant in the United States with a capacity to apply for funding to travel between the Philippines and the United States. However, I also bring my insight as a member of a transnational family who experienced long-term separation from my father when my mother, siblings, and I immigrated and became undocumented in the United States. My family's exchange of service and communication throughout a decade informs how I studied care work within the transnational families as multivalent, multinodal, and multidirectional. With these positionalities coupled with rigorous sociological research, I am working the hyphen between scholar, researcher, transnational daughter, and Filipina migrant to analyze and write about these families' dynamics of care.

I acknowledge that my current documented status and academic position at a university puts me in a very different position from the families in this book; therefore, I prioritize the voices and experiences of migrants and their families to tell a story about their decisions and lives. Throughout these chapters, I retain the Tagalog quotes of the participants of this study to illustrate the epistemological implications of translating someone's story from their mother tongue into English. I collected all of the qualitative data in this book in Tagalog and almost all of the participants engaged in individual and group interviews in Tagalog. The dilemma in translating someone's life story from a language that they feel, think, and identify with is that my interpretation and translation may not capture the whole context or meaning of a story. Thus, to minimize that disruption, I include participants' voices in the text for them and for those who can read Tagalog. Preserving the chunks of conversations in Tagalog is a practice in reflexivity in which I insist to be seen in this text as the person analyzing these stories and co-constructing a narrative for academic purposes.

Finally, a unique contribution of the methods involved in this book is the way that the research design was inherently shaped by the participants of this study, and likewise the ways in which the participants were then changed by their engagement in the research process. The methodological decisions for my research design sought to capture the macrosociological phenomena of globalization and migration in its methodology as I prioritized migrant epistemology and experience. Therefore, this is a book about transnational families but it also yields lessons for political organizing and collective mobilization as a commentary on the embodied relations between the global and the intimate. Migrant women and their families contributed their family histories and adaptations to care work while they crafted solidarities with one another that fostered political participation in a community that would often be counted out of political incorporation. Although many of these women were undocumented and excised from American civic participation, they were still beholden to state regulation and discipline. In this specific context of power and powerlessness, the methods in this research activated their political imagination toward everyday practices of what the anthropologist Aihwa Ong calls "flexible citizenship"—a practice of cultural politics for transnational actors that oftentimes fall out of the juridico-legal status of the nation-states in which they live (Ong 1999). This final note on my methods is an invitation to think beyond this book as the only product of this longitudinal study; rather, it is one of many products.

Who are the Transnational Families?

The migrants in New York City in this project are mostly Filipina migrant women employed as domestic workers. Some were documented and some were not; many of the undocumented people in this study fell out of status. They all experienced long-term separation from their families, chiefly because those who were undocumented chose not to return home because they would be unable to return to the United States to work. They are all migrants working to support and sustain relationships with their families in the Philippines. Recruitment to the study was based on a loose social network of domestic workers in the New York City area that have come together to organize in the Kabalikat Domestic Workers Support Network, which took up campaigns to repatriate the deceased bodies of workers but also to organize support and social gatherings for workers. A second set of participants in this study is the migrants' family members, including but not limited to their children, husbands, partners, siblings, and parents living in Metro Manila, Philippines.

Semi-structured individual and group interviews, or what I call *kuwentuhan* (talk-story in Filipino) elsewhere (Francisco 2013), were the primary method for data collection. *Kuwentuhan* was meaningful because it reflected the social and collective nature of how transnational families exchanged advice and shared stories about their family lives on a daily basis. For families in the Philippines, individual interviews allowed me to gain rapport with family members but it was through *kuwentuhans* that families left behind explored changing forms, roles, and definitions of care. Most of the domestic workers in this study were often cooped up in their workplaces (private homes) six days a week with babies, young children, youth, and adults who did not share their cultural and ethnic background. Many Filipina migrants cherished the days they could eat fried fish and speak in Tagalog or Visaya or their Filipino dialect. *Kuwentuhan*-style interviews allowed migrant workers to talk openly about the stresses at work or the graduation of their children in the Philippines to other migrant women who could relate to their struggles. These methods are key epistemological tools that reflect the social processes that participants engage in daily.

I refer to nonmigrant family members that live in the Philippines as "families left behind" throughout this work to highlight the contradiction between the mobility of one or two migrant members and the immobility of their families in the Philippines. The literature in sociology has claimed that migration and work abroad offer opportunities for income and independence, especially for women, as they are also able to support their children and move into a breadwinner role within their families. However, migration does not automatically mean that women's relative position of power in the family changes. Moreover, it also equates with an automatic social mobility for the family left behind. The class standing of families in the Philippines included in this research ranges from poor to lower middle class. Although migrant women's sacrifices have stabilized most of their families, the increase in their quality of life means being able to keep up with monthly utility and rent bills, tuition fees, and debt repayment and to maintain a limited expendable budget for recreation activities. I am careful not to define class stratification in Philippines with a standard or definition of social class in American sociology, as I argue that the gains of migrant remittances contribute to a growth in what Rolando Tolentino (2010) calls *pakiwaring gitnang uri*, loosely translated as aspirational middle-classness. Given that the Philippines has yet to develop into an industrial society with First World characteristics, the remittances and social class of families left behind can hardly be defined as middle class in the same definition of an American standard. The presence of a migrant family member coupled with the phrasing "left behind" points to the reality of underdevelopment that exists within the migration industry of the country.

The term "migrant" in this book is used to encompass both "migrant" and "immigrant," a demarcation distinguished by how long one stays in a host country. The term "migrant" describes someone who lives abroad but does not foresee permanent settlement. The migrants in this study lived abroad anywhere from two to twenty-five years. No matter how long they had been away, all participants had long-term plans to return to the Philippines. Further, 90% of the Filipina migrants in this study are currently undocumented with no foreseeable avenue of legalization. All of the participants in this study came to the United States legally through tourist, employer-sponsored, family petition, or H1-B visas. However, many of those who are undocumented fell out of status and could not reapply for legal status because of various reasons like costs, inability to renew, or debt bondage from the costs of immigrating to the United States. The term "migrant" is most accurate for members of this group because of these conditions that prevent them from ever feeling like they might belong in the United States or identifying, let alone, becoming an immigrant.

The term "mother" refers to biological mothers as well as women who fulfill a mothering role. Approximately 75% of my research participants have biological children. Without legal papers, many of the women are unable to go back home to see their families. Some women left very young children while others had adult children when they migrated. A majority of the mothers who left their children migrated in the middle of their life course, in their thirties or forties. This is an important point, as many of the women thought they had fulfilled all of their duties prescribed by Filipino culture, as a woman and a mother. With migration, they then had to essentially reverse gender roles to become the breadwinner and remake the meaning of motherhood through migration. In addition to biological mothers, I refer to single women who migrated at a younger age, generally in their twenties, that are supporting their parents, siblings, or nieces and nephews in the Philippines as atypical mothers because they identify their support to their families in the Philippines as a maternal duty. Although this younger generation of Filipina migrant women have not yet borne their own children, they practice mothering like those women who have biological children through remittances. The term "mothers" also applies to othermothers, or whom I call *titas* in this work. They are women who take up mothering duties for migrant friends in their community. Mother, as Pierrette Hondagneu-Sotelo and Ernestine Avila argue, is a socially constructed and historically specific concept (Hondagneu-Sotelo and Avila 1997). In this book, kinship and fictive kin in the transnational context designate Filipina migrant women who engage in transnational mother's work as mothers.

Lastly, the term "worker" applies to all of the participants in this study who are migrants from the Philippines but live and work in New York City. Most undocumented participants without legal papers are working "under the table" in private homes as housecleaners or what the migrants call "paper works," a facetious attempt to professionalize the occupation's name by referring to the use of paper towels, toilet paper, and the like. Most are domestic workers, which can include housekeeping and cooking duties, alongside taking care of children, elderly people, and sometimes a dog or two. The noncontractual basis of employment subjects Filipina migrants to immediate and swift layoffs, wage theft, no access to paid vacation or basic benefits, and no regulation in terms of work conditions and hours of work. Although the historic Domestic Workers Bill of Rights passed in New York State in 2010 (*New York Times* 2010; Greenhouse 2007), domestic workers in this study were only just familiarizing themselves with the legislation and testing out how the law might work on their behalf (Semple 2011). More than half of my study participants are considered migrant workers, as the United States is only one of the numerous countries they have lived and worked in. Typically, no matter what country, the work is still domestic work. The precariousness of work for domestic workers, particularly in New York City, and their experiences of the Filipino labor diaspora are the two key aspects that make migrants intelligible to one another as workers.

Filipina migrants' lived experiences with undocumented status, family separation, and serial labor migration produce a common identification with dislocation in the diaspora (Parreñas 2001b). Needless to say, these terms are fluid. Subjectivities of migrant, mother, and worker are often working in tandem with one another in the identification processes between Filipina migrant women. For example, conversations about unemployment may trigger many of the migrants to identify themselves as workers but also as mothers with a family to support. Other times, people will talk about the strains of being a migrant without acknowledging their experiences as mothers or workers.

Guide to the Book

In chapter 1, I discuss, in the context of historical and continuous labor migration in the Philippines, how the family "relativizes" (Bryceson and Vuorela 2002) who remains in the family and who will take up the work left behind by a migrant family member. I introduce the multidirectional care model of transnational families by highlighting the various forms of care that families left behind enact in the Philippines. I argue that when families in the Philippines take care of themselves and one another, they interpret a thriving family life as a type of care work toward the migrant family members. This chapter also maps out the redefinition or relativization of fictive and biological members of the family in the Philippines in terms of who helps to take up work with the absence of a migrant family member. This intricate network of new care providers and various forms of care work within the local, reorganized version of the family in the Philippines also becomes a form as a contemporaneous stream of care to migrants abroad. Lastly, examining care work as multidirectional allows us to understand how spouses and children continuously challenge and fortify the gendered expectations of who is to attend to care work (Pingol 1999). I argue that differing contexts of masculinity allow for some men in families left behind to break out of patriarchal definitions of manhood or sonhood.

In chapter 2, I examine the most recurrent theme across my research: technology and its role in changing the social relations of separation. The use of technology clearly demonstrated that care work in the transnational family was multidirectional and multimodal. Migrants in New York City prioritized the purchase of technological devices for themselves and their family in the Philippines in order to be present from afar. They sought their children's dexterity in technological use of mobile devices and computer applications to be able to stay in touch. Complementarily, Philippine-based family members were active in the reciprocation of learning a technology, in both the heuristic and figurative senses of the word, toward a new definition of care work across their transnational geography. Depending on the software and internet programs used, like Yahoo Messenger, Skype, and Facebook, families are able to overcome the hurdles of time and space to form new intimacies with various family members. Technology, I argue, is not just a tool for communication; it is changing the roles of who become care providers in the transnational family, shifting gendered responsibilities as well.

Chapter 3 focuses on the concept of communities of care. Examining multidirectional care through migrants' practice of care work in New York City among one another, I argue that Filipina migrant mothers invested in a network of solidarity and strength in and through their experience of reorganized care work with their transnational families. Just as the maintenance of the family from the Philippines is reaching beyond the nuclear members of the family to form fictive and biological kinship networks, these growing constellations are also paralleled in New York City. Drawing from black feminist thought and queer theories, I argue that communities of care are a type of "chosen families" (Weston 1997). As such, I find the political subjectivities of migrant, mother, and worker are queered identities in the American racial and social order and therefore the identification processes in which migrant women in New York take part in is also interpreted as care.

Chapter 4 explores the normative conception of care work as described through qualities of nurturance, love, and warmth in the intimate relationships of family members. However, the work of caring for the transnational family draws from a range of affects, from warmheartedness to reticence. Complicating the emotional narratives of anger, disappointment, and cynicism of children left behind, I find that the affective realities of children in transnational families are wide and fluid, especially when studied over time. Additionally, children still attend to the necessary work needed to keep their families functional despite emotive dissonance, which often triggers a different set of emotions toward the transnationality of their families. This chapter explores the labor of maintaining transnational families in spite of the positive or negative emotional charge of caring. I critique the assumption of the definition of care work based solely on positive emotionality coupled with nurturance. Contributing to the literature on emotions and migration with a specific focus on children, I argue that care work is still work even if family members do not express that work with love. I seek to untangle the idea of care work as nurturing or loving, and present examples where care work is done with contradicting emotions to insist on recognizing the labor in caring.

The concluding chapter recounts the permutations of multidirectional care as a model to examine the care work in transnational Filipino families while linking it to the historically specific developments of neoliberal globalization on migration and family separation in the Philippines. Often the family and the state are construed as separate total institutions and in this last chapter, I situate the family as part and parcel of the vision of a neoliberal state toward integration into a global capitalist economy, and more importantly, the problems in that vision. Lastly, I take up the implications of the methods and arguments of this book on grassroots-organizing and community-building projects among and with migrants. I discuss the possibilities embedded in reconfigured social reproductive labor relations within the family—that the family can be a site to generate critical hope and a point of unity for political organizing for both migrants and families left behind.

In the methodological appendix, I discuss at length the methods and methodology that allowed me to make the arguments of multidirectional care in transnational families. Through the logics of longitudinal, multisited ethnography, PAR principles, and IE, I was able to collect and analyze the stories of migrant women and their families over five years, place the themes that the participants deemed important at the center of the work, and juxtapose the institutions that mediate their decisions to migrate and care for one another from afar. My discussion on methods is an insistence on democratizing science and research methods, as it presents the multiple products of the study, including the implications of my chosen research methods—the potential of research and methods, including mapping, journaling, and theater as research tools for political organizing.

1

Multidirectional Care in Transnational Families

Brother and sister Boyet and Jing exchange high fives and praises for each other about having dinner for their respective children done just in time to call Boyet's wife Tetet in New York City for her birthday. Although Jing's cell phone battery died on her way home, she managed to view her big brother's text asking her to buy some ingredients for dinner. Boyet happened to pass by Jing's son's school only to find out he was sick with a cold. With a sick nephew in tow, Boyet was still able to prepare dinner for his two children when Jing came home with the last ingredients. Right at 8 o'clock, the two siblings managed to get their children fed and ready to sing "happy birthday" to Tetet. The day was a seamless example of kin networks working like a well-oiled machine to step into the vacuums that appear in the lives of families left behind. Not every day is a victory such as this. But for Boyet and Jing, their sibling teamwork made all the difference on this day, and more importantly, for their beloved wife and sister-in-law who remarked, "*Wow, galing! Lahat ng bata, nakakain na at present!* Wow, amazing! All the kids, fed and present!"

Kin networks are the saving grace of the many Filipino families that are struggling to survive in the Philippines. Before migration, many Filipinas mobilized kin networks to support their families in the face of small incomes and joblessness. A majority of the participants in my study living in the Philippines co-habited with one, two, or three other families before they left for the United States. When Filipinas migrate for work, the kin network becomes even more important in keeping the family together and functional. The increased care work in the absence of migrant mothers activates a network of already existing relationships within the Filipino family. Analytically, understanding premigration kin networks is crucial to understanding how migrants' family members absorb postmigration care work. A longitudinal view of the role of the kin network for Filipino families is crucial in understanding that kin care is a longstanding form of Filipino family operations. Through this, we will be able to analyze the adjustment of care work in the event of migration not merely as a consequence of a family member's departure but as a process that includes past experiences.

Part of a historical analysis of kin care in the Filipino family includes the fact that the family has been absorbing the impact of labor migration since the 1970s, when the Philippine state under Ferdinand Marcos's dictatorship turned to labor exportation to generate revenue to combat decreased state social supports. The institutionalization of labor migration in the Philippine political economy currently mobilizes, facilitates, and regulates the outmigration of Filipino citizens as global workers (R. M. Rodriguez 2010; Guevarra 2006b). Therefore, families of those who leave are drafted into the migration industry as they bear the brunt of reorganizing care work in the homes left by the migrants. Given this context, care work in the transnational family abounds in forms and direction, and additionally, the meaning of that care work involves multiple people living in a transnational family.[1] If we accept that care work operates with a multitude of directions with different magnitudes or what scholars have called "vectoral flows of care" (Velayutham and Wise 2005) or a "plurality of care" (E. Graham et al. 2012) within transnational families, we can begin to see the complex constellation of people who are affected by and are actively adjusting to the separation of families.

In the context of standing political economic conditions and the culture of migration in the Philippines, kin view their role of caring for their families in the Philippines as a form of care for their migrant family members even though the migrants are not the direct recipients of care. To this end, the stories in this chapter follow the transnational care work *within* family kin networks to establish how they reconfigure and make meaning of social reproductive labor in and from different places in a transnational arrangement. The unit of analysis in this chapter is the Filipino transnational family, from which I trace the care practices of eleven family constellations with migrant members in New York City and their families in the Philippines. By following care work and its different interpretations from both ends of the transnational family, I track how forms of care are delivered, received, circulated, and reciprocated. This methodological approach assumes that all members of transnational families do some type of maintenance work. Further, the roles that extended and fictive kin play in the transnational family emerge in sketching out the multiple directions of care work transnationally.

The family history prior to a member's migration plays a significant role in the transnational family dynamic in this study. Collecting family history adds nuance to the impact of migration on the family unit and the behavioral changes that occur after a family member migrates. This historical approach assumes that migration is a social process that involves more than the event of departure (Deaux 2009); rather, it begins before and after a family member leaves to go abroad. I found that Filipino families that worked in intricate and extended kin networks prior to migration already had a set of tools to absorb the absence of a family member. Although migration—especially of mothers—can put a strain on a family, migrant women's roles are absorbed and distributed through the extended kin networks that were already there. Moving beyond the paradigm of the nuclear family—the primary family form assumed in past studies of the transnational Filipino family—the Filipino families in this study already worked in an extended care network when they were all present in one place; the migration of a family member thus relied on the activation of that kin network to fill the vacuum of one family member's absence.

I make an effort to decenter the migrant as the nexus of care work in the transnational family and to shed light on a pivotal and unseen form of care work: the extended kin networks as a resource to reorganize care work (Baldassar and Merla 2013; Yeoh et al. 2009). Departing from a common conception of families left behind as passive recipients of care from migrant family members, I assert that family members left behind are enacting varying forms of care work in the Philippines, understanding that their labor benefits their immediate needs and also contributes to the well-being of their family members abroad. To this end, I begin from the assumption that care operates in a decentralized manner where kin networks function as both nurturing and social reproduction entities prior to the migration of any family members. Caregivers in premigration arrangements vary from parents to children to aunts and grandparents. For families in the Philippines, it may seem that absorbing the roles of a migrant member and maintaining the family is simply a matter of filling in the gaps left by an absent family member. However, using a historically rooted, multidirectional care paradigm, I found that families left behind make meaning of absorbing their migrant family members' work as a form of care. In the case of the Garcias, Boyet, his children, and Jing interpret their work as such because they see their work as a reciprocation of their migrant family member's work abroad. Family members in the Philippines consider their absorption of the work that a migrant member once did as an answer to the family member's sacrifice of migration.

Moreover, migrants recognize the work that their families left behind (both biological and extended kin) do to stabilize and regularize life without them as a form of care work. Since migrants' primary reasons for migration are largely to provide their families with opportunities for economic stability, educational avenues, housing, and comfort, they are greatly relieved when they receive good news about the family members they left behind. When families left behind communicate and demonstrate that a migrant family member's work and remittances are transforming the family's life for the better, migrants understand these developments as a repayment—evidence that their families' lives are improving because of their migration. Kin and fictive networks' roles are articulating and understanding their contributions to care work in the transnational family differently as migration and transnationality become social facts of Filipino livelihood and the Filipino family. They are adjusting their families and their transnational care relative to serial and intergenerational migration.

The Garcias: Relativizing the Transnational Family

Teresa, or Tetet, Garcia met her husband Boyet at a college function and they fell in love at first sight. Since then, they have always been sweet on each other. They tell their story of two years of courtship and marriage with giggles and longing looks, even when they tell it individually. In 1980, soon after Tetet graduated college, they moved in with Boyet's family in time for the birth of their daughter Nina. Two years later, their son Michael was born; Brian was born ten years after that. The household also included Boyet's parents, his sister Jing, and her son Max. It was all a financial struggle, but they worked double shifts at a nearby factory making plastic bags. Tetet also managed a small canteen from the side of the extended family house. The household members pooled productive and social reproductive resources, not only sharing income from outside work but depending on one another to care for the children. During some years of unemployment Boyet stayed home and took care of the domestic duties; other years they would all share in child-rearing when each of them had part-time work. As the children got older, the adults started distributing domestic responsibilities. They taught Michael to cook dinners and clean up the house; Nina was in charge of caring for Brian and Max after school. Tetet and Boyet found that their marriage grew stronger with their well-fueled family engine, and they were even able to invest time in religious activities such as Couples for Christ in their church community and to go on dates. They both saw their love and marriage as a blessing, so they always made sure to nurture it through these extra efforts.

Still, as their children went on to high school and Boyet's parents grew older, Boyet and Tetet knew that migration was the only option to pay back their debts, secure their children's future, and care for their elders. Boyet was slow to warm up to this idea: He wanted their children to have two parents at home and did not want to be separated from his beloved wife. Then, in 2000, Tetet's nephew in New York City needed help with a new baby, so she went out on a limb and applied for a tourist visa; it was quickly approved. Before she left the Philippines, Tetet, Boyet, Jing, Nina, and Michael sat down to work out the finances and domestic duties as they had in the past. The differences this time were that Tetet's work would be taking her far away for an indefinite amount of time, and that the older children were now part of the conversation. They all agreed that Boyet would stay home with the youngest children, Brian and Max, while Jing would go to work as a laundry maid. Boyet tentatively accepted all of the responsibilities for the ascribed women's work of child-rearing and domestic duties. Even if he did not understand the full scope of it, he agreed to assume the role without Tetet or Jing around. Although Michael and Nina would be finishing up high school soon, they agreed to continue to live in the family home and help with household maintenance. Less than a week after Tetet's visa was approved, she was on the plane.

A week later, Tetet started to work as a live-in nanny for her nephew's child. She immediately started to remit the kind of money that could put all three of her children through college and pay off some debts. Tetet recalled her first autumn in New York City and what was on her mind:

> *Hindi ko akalain na ganito kalamig, sa September pa lang andami ko ng jacket and scarf na suot tapos nakaka-miss ang Pinas, ang mga bata, si Boyet. Pero sakripisyo lang 'yun, kinaya naman namin. Matagal na kaming mag-asawa ibig sabihin at saka malalaki-laki na 'yung mga bata. Importante din na marunong na siya mag-alaga sa mga needs nila. Sa akin parang kampante na ako doon. Pwede akong makahinga.*

> I didn't know that it was going to be this cold, it was only September and I was already wearing many jackets and scarves; then I missed the Philippines, the kids, and Boyet. But that's just the sacrifice, we carried that burden. We've been married for a long time and the kids were bigger. It was important that

he knew how to take care of their needs. To me, that made me feel secure. I could breathe.

It was a difficult transition, especially because of the distance from her family and the shock of the cold weather. But she knew that Boyet was more than capable of keeping her family safe and happy, as he always had. This capacity to stabilize their lives keeps Philippine migrants like Tetet going in the years they spend away from their families. If you have left everything you hold important and dear, it is a powerful reassurance to know that a trusted person is taking care of your family and that your children can thrive, even without you.

Meanwhile, in the Philippines, the family was going through its own rough transition upon Tetet's departure. Jing remembered her brother's strength at the time:

> Pumayat siya [Boyet] for the first few months, few years. Talagang parang mukhang matanda na dahil naiwan sa kanya 'yung responsibilities. Naging "Natay," nanay at tatay siya. Kaya ina-assist ko siya pero si Boyet ang may dala ng mga bata mostly, gaya ng dati.

> Boyet got so skinny for the first few months, few years. He looked older because he was left with the responsibilities. He became a "MaPa," he was the mama and papa. So I assisted him but Boyet carried the responsibilities mostly, like before.

Jing's reverence for Boyet is a result of the experiences they had in stepping up for one another as caregivers for each other's children in the past. Although Boyet's reaction to Tetet's absence was much more intense, evidenced by his weight loss, Jing insisted that reactivating the sensibilities of caring for his family was just like past times when Boyet stepped up to take care of the children. However, she pointed out that the weight of responsibilities on Boyet completely on his own was heavy and thus Jing's presence in supporting his tasks became part of how Boyet embraced his role as the primary domestic parent. Boyet too remembered this time of transition:

> Napakabigat. Ibig sabihin, 'yung work ng mother hindi kayang isipin ng lalaki. Hindi pwedeng pamacho-macho lang. Dun, na-realize ko 'yung ganoon. Napakahirap, ikaw 'yung magba-badyet, ikaw magluluto, ikaw magbibihis sa mga bata. Laundry ikaw. Lahat. Kahit kakampi kami ni Jing, ang bigat. Pero kailangan gawin, naiisip ko rin na lahat ng trabaho hindi lang para sa mga bata, para kay Tetet na rin. Parang ang pag-aalaga sa mga bata dito, parang kunektado sa pagmamahal ko sa kanya.

It's so heavy. What I mean to say is, men can't fathom the work of mothers. You can't just play macho-macho. That's when I realized that. It is so hard, you are in charge of the budget, you cook, you dress the children. You do the laundry. Everything. Even if Jing is on my side, it's still heavy. But you have to do it. I started to think too that all that work is not only on me, or just for the children, it's for Tetet too. It's like taking care of the children here, it's connected to my love for her.

Boyet was shocked to discover how hard a mother's work truly was. Although he had helped in caring for the children and household in the past, he internalized his duty with much more seriousness upon Tetet's departure. One of the main reasons he did this was because he interpreted his caring for his family as a form of care for Tetet. Boyet's endearing comment about his work for the family as "connected to my love for her" shows that he understands his actions as a way in which he looks after his wife abroad. Additionally, Jing's support gave Boyet the confidence to work through some of his patriarchal logic and move forward with the task at hand, which was to attend to the domestic duties at home and look after his children. Boyet understands internalizing this role and reactivating the old care network to be an extension of his love for Tetet, and thus a form of caring for her.

Photo 1.1. Boyet shows off his clothesline shyly. Photo courtesy of Valerie Francisco-Menchavez.

Boyet's expansion of what counts as care for the transnational Garcia family is echoed in their daughter Nina's understanding of how she contributed to caring for her mother while separated:

> *Hindi ako masyado nagpapabili kasi may trabaho ako eh so kung kaya kong bilihin dito, dito na lang. Lalo na 'yung mga binibili-bili kong kina-adikan ko. So hindi ko na hinihingi 'yun kay mommy. Ayoko na nabu-burden si mommy regarding money kasi ako nagtatrabaho na rin kaya alam ko. Sa'kin it is a way of taking it off her shoulders.*

> I don't ask my mom to buy me much because I work so if I can buy it for myself here, I do it. Especially the things I buy for my hobbies. So I don't ask my mom for that. I don't want to burden my mom regarding money because I work here too so I know. For me, it's a way of taking it off her shoulders.

Nina's comment could be simply interpreted as a daughter growing up and taking responsibility for her own hobbies. However, scholars have established that children in Asian transnational families (J. L. Waters 2015; Alipio, Lu, and Yeoh 2015; Hoang et al. 2015) and even in Asian American immigrant families (Park 2005; Chung 2016; Ninh 2011) have consistently been caregivers in their families. Moreover, children, particularly if they are older at the event of migration, tend to maintain emotional connections with their migrant parents through different avenues (Carling et al. 2012). Nina was already 16 years old and graduating high school when her mother Tetet migrated, which influenced her cooperation in maintaining the family operations and household as homage to her mother's migration. In fact, Nina's financial independence alongside her decision to continue living at home, which means a two-hour commute to her work in Manila, were all part of how she understood her relieving a "burden" from her mother's shoulders. In this way, Nina, Jing, and Boyet all share an ethics of reciprocity (Alipio 2015) in their narratives of stabilizing their lives in the Philippines as an effort to help Tetet. In this family's history, all members described their contribution as a web of care for one another—taking care of each other in the Philippines meant caring for their migrant family member, much like they did before Tetet left. They reimagined their roles and care work relative to their family's new conditions. The different types of care work—from financial independence to domestic duties to helping a brother become self-sustainable—are all in the formula of caring for a family member who has migrated abroad, in this case, Tetet, the wife, sister-in-law, and mother. As Tetet's remittances started to flow back to her family in the Philippines, her family members were doing their best to attend to their immediate responsibilities as a show of respect and reciprocation.

For the Garcias, care work flowed in many different directions. Albeit through different forms and over long distances, all of it was important in maintaining their family life. Their family story illustrates the emotional and practical utility of relativizing the "family" (Bryceson and Vuorela 2002) rather than adhering to an idealized notion of care through proximity and continuous interaction as a basis of family functionality. Deborah Fahy Bryceson and Ulla Vuorela (2002) introduce the notion of "relativizing," describing the process in which transnational families select the membership of the family based on needs, length of separation, and distance, regardless of whether people are blood-related. Transnational families are always adjusting by redefining their family composition by bringing in fictive and extended kin *relative* to their urgent and emergent needs. Scholars of transnational families are in agreement that migrants and their families identify who constitutes family and the roles people play in that unit relative to who is around to attend to the domestic work of the family in the place left behind (Asis, Huang, and Yeoh 2004; Hoang and Yeoh 2012). Indeed, the definition of care for families with members divided by great distances and for extended periods of time must be expansive, as they have limited ways to express care for one another (Baldassar and Merla 2013). Transnational Filipino families continually reimagine and redefine forms of care to adjust to the migration of their family members. These auxiliary forms of care are crucial in keeping the transnational family together. Through a multidirectional care model and in examining family histories, various types of care work become visible as part of the transnational family formation, thus extending the ideas of care beyond in what Pierette Hondagneu-Sotelo and Ernestine Avila call "transnational motherhood" (1997) and what Rhacel Salazar Parreñas calls "long-distance intimacy" (2005b) to include the process in which families construct who is included in the scope of their families and what their roles are.

As the Garcias show us, relativizing has become one way to make meaning of new care arrangements. Boyet's sister Jing is tightly integrated into the postmigration family process as she supports her brother who is caring for the children, which in turn is also a form of care toward Tetet miles away. The elasticity of the transnational family, both in the Philippines and in the United States, relies on relativizing processes, as the labor, services, and acts of care by members in the transnational family are at times done with love and at other times accomplished just because the work of the family needs to be done (Bryceson and Vuorela 2002; Asis, Huang, and Yeoh 2004). This complex web of defining family members *relative* to the current situation is part of capturing the essence of multidirectional care. The process of trial and error in relativizing the family is often interpreted as a type of care work from families left behind to their migrant family member. Remember Boyet's comment about his care for his family as not just attending to their immediate needs but also connected for his love to Tetet and how Nina views her work as indirectly taking weight off her mother's shoulders; these are moments when multidirectional care is being carved out and defined for transnational families. In the following section, peering into the process of relativizing, families left behind explore their roles as caregivers to one another by de-centering their migrant family member as the only person that is in need of care in the transnational arrangement.

"Taking Care of Them Is Taking Care of Her": Decentering Migrants in Transnational Care

The permanence of migration in Filipino family life allows for a truly longitudinal and historical study of the effects of migration on transnational care work. Shifts in political economic pressures and the historical institutionalization of labor export in the Philippines influence Filipino families' coping strategies and the understanding of care work in their transnational contexts. Thus, the Philippines' aggressive and sophisticated institutional organization of migration as labor export (Tadiar 2004; Guevarra 2009; R. M. Rodriguez 2010) can be interpreted as forced transnationality as immigration policy pushes people into labor migration (Bonizzoni and Boccagni 2014; Bernhard, Landolt, and Goldring 2009). Filipino families have been rearticulated across borders since the early twentieth century, primarily through labor migration to different states in the United States (Espiritu 2003; Mabalon 2013). But a key turning point in migration patterns of Filipinos (and consequently the reorganization of Filipino families) was the passage of the Labor Export Policy in 1972 under the dictatorship of Ferdinand Marcos. The new policy catalyzed a sophisticated system of migration management and regulation, pushing a large number of Filipinos out of the Philippines (R. M. Rodriguez 2010; Guevarra 2009). Current rhetoric around labor migration hinges on gender-specific and gender-coded ideals around filial piety and empowerment (Guevarra 2009). Inherent to the state mobilization of migrants is the mobilization of their families to take up the work family members leave behind. Because of the institutionalization and historic embeddedness of labor migration in the Philippines, Filipino families left behind understand their care work toward their migrant family members as multidirectional care in the transnational family.

MULTIDIRECTIONAL CARE PRACTICE
WITHIN THE GONZALEZ KIN NETWORK

When sisters Joan Gonzalez Fernando and Vickie Gonzalez Marquez lived in the Philippines, they resided with their parents, their siblings, their adult children, and their grandchildren in a cramped three-bedroom home. Born and raised in Tondo, Manila, a notoriously rough and impoverished neighborhood, they did not have a choice to live in any other way. When I visited the corner that the Gonzalez clan occupies in their poor urban neighborhood, the first thing I saw was children chasing one another around three older women washing clothes and hanging wet laundry on clotheslines in front of the set of cramped buildings. Joan and Vickie's oldest sister Tita Tina (Aunt Tina) was among the women doing laundry in the sweltering humidity of a July afternoon. She was sitting on a block of wood rubbing soapy clothes together when she recognized me and yelled in Tagalog, "*Hoy Val! Linalabhan ko ang panty ng anak ni Vickie kaya dapat may yakap ako galing sa kanila.* Hoy Val! I'm washing Vickie's kids' underwear so you better give me my hug from Joan and Vickie!"

Joan and Vickie were not in Tondo during my visit. While I was in the Philippines, they were living together in a one-bedroom apartment in Queens, New York. Both are migrant mothers who left their children and their families behind to work as domestic workers in New York City in the early 2000s. In the Philippines, both Joan and Vickie were housewives, relying on their husbands and their siblings' collective income to feed their families and keep their households afloat. When I spoke with Joan in Queens before my trip to Tondo, she said to me:

> *Dati, wala kami masyado. Nawalan ng trabaho yung asawa ko. Ako naman, walang trabaho. 'Yung mga kapatid ko ang tumutulong sa aming utang. Pinatira kami ni Nanay sa bahay niya. As in, anim kami sa isang kuwarto, walang banyo 'yon. Kung kailangan ng banyo, punta ka doon kay Nanay. Ganoon ang buhay namin.*

> Before I decided to leave, we didn't have much. My husband lost his job. I didn't have one. My siblings were giving us money for our basic expenses. My mother let us stay in a room in her house. As in, the six of us in one room with no bathroom. When we needed to use the bathroom we had to go to my mother's side of the house. That's how we lived.

Unemployment and poverty forced Joan's four siblings, their children, and their grandchildren to live together under one roof. Although it was hard to live in an overcrowded house, and the cost of public education was quickly increasing, they traded childcare and chores for little bits of money to pay for clothing, food, and their children's tuition. Both Joan and Vickie described their lives in the Philippines as always intertwined with their experiences of their large family all living together and taking care of one another. Their extended kin would undoubtedly have a role when it came to raising their children, especially in their absence.

Joan was the first to migrate in 2003. Her husband was laid off from his lower management position in a Philippine corporation and, demoralized, he could not apply for new jobs. Her first son had just had a baby, her daughter had dreams of attending a university, and her youngest child was just entering high school. In short, there were many financial demands on her family without a viable avenue of income. Joan decided that instead of her husband looking for a job abroad, she would use his extended family in New York City to look for work. Joan's sister-in-law and her own family pooled enough money to prove that she was financially stable (a stipulation of her tourist visa application) and even paid for an "immigration coach" to assist her in passing visa interviews. She was then approved for a tourist visa and arrived in New York City in 2003, planning to stay, find work, and send money back to all of her family members. With support from her sister-in-law in New York City, Joan found a live-in nanny job for $275 for five days a week within two months of her arrival. Even at only $4.50 per hour for ten-hour days, Joan's income was a promising indicator that she could support her family in the Philippines, if she could just grit her teeth through her loneliness and exhaustion.

Joan convinced her younger sister Vickie to follow in 2005. Vickie, whose husband had tried his luck as a construction worker in Kuwait, was deep in debt and her two children were gearing up to go to high school, which meant an increase in educational costs. Vickie went through the same process of "immigration coaching" but also claimed that she was a businesswoman to secure a two-week tourist visa to New York City. The cost of her immigration coaching, fees, and requirements for the visa was $6,000, pooled together by Joan and her cousin who was now living in New York City. Vickie had her extended family to thank for helping her find a way to go to the United States and also a possible avenue of livelihood for her family.

When they lived in the Philippines with their families, Joan and Vickie stayed at home to take care of the family's collective group of children while other adults in the family held jobs. With Joan and Vickie's migration, they are now the breadwinners while members of their extended family stay home to care for their families. In their years abroad, Joan and Vickie have faithfully sent money back to the Philippines twice a month. Their contributions help support twenty-seven family members: Joan's husband, three children, two spouses, and five grandchildren; Vickie's husband and two children; Vickie and Joan's oldest sister Tina and her three adult children who have a total of four children; Joan's brother and wife and their two children, one of whom has one newborn baby; and Joan, Vickie, and Tina's aging mother. Although some of their siblings in the Philippines still work part-time jobs, most of their responsibilities fall along the lines of keeping families' households together and making sure that Joan's and Vickie's children, along with the other children, have three square meals, money for school, and money to have some fun on the weekends.

Calvin, Joan's youngest son, was only 11 when Joan migrated to New York City. He is now 18. During our interview, he tells me about Tita Tina and the role she plays in his life as well as that of his siblings:

> CALVIN: *Kung 'di kaya ni Ate, tatanungin niya si Tita Tina. Kagaya ng dati, ginagawa ni Mama. Kung hindi alam ni Ate, at least nandiyan si Tita Tina. Oo, Tita Tina. Masaya siya pero of course iba. Iba 'yung aruga niya kesa kay Mama. Kasi, ganito, kung hindi namin alam gawin, amin-amin lang, punta kami sa kanya. 'Yon. Ganyan ang tulong niya sa amin, kay Mama rin.*
>
> If my older sister Melann can't do [chores], it's Tita Tina she goes to. Like when Mama went to her before when she was here. If Melann doesn't know what to do, at least she has someone to go to. Yea, Tita Tina. She's happy to take care of us but of course it's different. Her way of taking care of us is different from Mama. Because it's like this, if we don't know what to do or how to do it and we can't solve it among ourselves, we go to her. That's how she helps us and Mama too.
>
> VALERIE: She doesn't feel like it's too much when you ask?
>
> CALVIN: *No, not really. Sabi niya hindi niya magagawa lahat ng ginawa ni Mama, hindi siya si Mama pero kung kailangan, okay lang. Hindi naman masamang bagay. 'Yan ang pagkaintidi niya na tulong kay Mama.*
>
> No, not really. She said that she can't do everything Mama does and she isn't Mama but when we need help or want help, it's okay to ask her. It's not a bad thing to go to her. This is how she can help.

Calvin acknowledges how Tita Tina thinks of her support for Calvin and his siblings as support for Joan. Calvin views Tita Tina as a reliable person, someone who is available to him and his siblings if they need help. When Calvin talks about "before," he is referring to how the Gonzalez clan worked before anyone migrated. Since his mother's migration, leaning on his Tita Tina feels like a continuation of the relationships they had fostered when his mother still lived in the Philippines. In a way, the care work that is now redistributed among Melann, Calvin, and Tita Tina is a practical move to keep the family together, but it also doubles up as a way to keep Joan's stress to a minimum because she knows that her children and her sister are continuing the way of life they had before her migration. The reorganized care from the vantage point of the family left behind illustrates that activating past kin network practices and habits are an integral part of multidirectional care in the family.

In an interview with Joan, I shared with her how Calvin and Melann saw Tita Tina. She said, "I know that when Tina is there, my heart can rest because I know her with my kids. They respect her. I feel good when she is with my kids." Joan's remarks bring us full circle as she acknowledges how the shifting care work at home gives her some respite even though she still feels the guilt of being away from her family. Joan is relieved at the active relativizing of caregivers in the family and the care work circulating within her family and through her extended kin. Analytically, decentering Joan as the primary caregiver in the family demonstrates a more complex web of care in her transnational family. Emotions like guilt in the migration process are a crucial motivator to act on caregiving for both migrants and their families left behind (Baldassar 2015; Baumeister, Stillwell, and Heatherton 1994; Vermot 2015). Migrants interpret kin care in the Philippines as care for them because they have internalized a Western conception that they have betrayed a moral obligation to always "be with" their children and family. Therefore, the work that Tita Tina and Melann do together becomes a way for migrants like Joan to ease the guilt they have for being away from home.

There are undoubtedly some limitations to having a person like Tita Tina step into the shoes of Joan or Vickie. The power of Tita Tina as the lone adult standing in for both migrant mothers can easily take the agency away from her sisters' children. However, the balance struck in this family, and perhaps many other families left behind, is in the way that children such as Melann and Calvin assert their newfound roles as care providers to one another and their migrant mother. They act on their new responsibilities and invite Tita Tina into their new care configuration. Children left behind are always finding ways to affirm the new meanings of their sometimes unwanted freedom from their migrant mothers. This dynamic of negotiating new and collaborative way of sharing care within families left behind is often mediated with how old children left behind are and the kinds of independence with which they can carry out tasks that are given to them. Still, children left behind are quite inventive about other ways they are deploying multidirectional care in their families in the Philippines, especially with fictive kin such as Melann's cousins Dianne and Zach.

After Vickie left in 2005, her daughter Dianne and son Zach looked to Melann and Calvin as they adjusted to their mother's absence. Melann offered to help out, remembering her own especially hard transition when Joan, her mother, had left in 2003: "Me and Dianne were close but not too close. But when Tita Vickie left, I told her that she could talk to me about anything. Have you read her blog? I told her she could tell me all of those feelings but she can also ask me about how to pick up *padala* [remittances]." Melann and Dianne were childhood friends, but when their mothers migrated, their bond deepened. Sharing the challenging experience of their mothers' migrations meant they shared the experience of adjusting to their mothers' absence. For example, Dianne told me how Melann helped her handle the remittance money.

> VALERIE: When [Tita Vickie] sends *padala*, who pays the bills?
> DIANNE: *Hinahati-hati ko siya, tapos binabayaran ko. Nakukuha ni Lola sa banko kapag pinadala ni Mama. Tapos papalitan niya tapos hinahati ko sa bayarin ng bahay, allowance para sa aming tatlo, tapos, grocery, kuryente, upa, 'yon, lahat ng basic. Pinaghahati ni Mama sa chat tapos ako naghahati para sa mga bayarin. Si Ate nagturo sa akin ng ganyan. Sinasabi niya kung tama ang ginagawa ko.*
>
> I divide it up and then I pay for it. My grandmother gets the money in her bank account when Mama sends money. Then she changes it into pesos and then I divide up per the costs of the house like allowance for us three for the month, then grocery food, then electricity, then rent, yea, everything like the most basic. Mama breaks it down for me over chat and then I divide it up and pay the bills. Ate Melann told me this. I know from her that I'm doing it right.

Melann has played an essential role in Dianne's life since Vickie migrated. When I asked Melann why she felt responsible for Dianne in this way, she replied, "I owe it to my mom and to Tita Vickie. If I didn't take care of Dianne, what kind of daughter would I be? What kind of niece would I be?" Melann understands that "being there" for her cousin emotionally and logistically is not only for Dianne's sake, it is also influenced by the absence of Joan and Vickie: "We have to be there for each other, for them [Joan and Vickie]." Melann's simultaneous mention of her choice to support Dianne—"for each other"—and also as a form of support to Joan and Vickie—"for them"—signals to Vickie that Dianne is never alone in dealing with her absence. Dianne and Melann's relationship allows them to demonstrate to their mothers that someone is caring for them even if it is not their mothers. This partnership between daughters of migrant mothers is a clear demonstration that children in families left behind are constantly crafting care work for one another and for their migrant family members.

In these examples the concept of multidirectional care occurs in several ways. First, among the kin left behind in the Philippines Tita Tina's care work for Melann and Calvin relieves Joan's stresses of being away. Second, Melann's assistance to Dianne through her emotional transition is a horizontal form of care among cousins. Vickie's remittances are sent from New York City to Dianne, and then Dianne redistributes them to her family, the expansive kin network of which Tita Tina and Melann are a part. Tita Tina repays both Vickie and Joan by seeing to it that their children get support in their daily chores. In this "web of care" (E. Graham et al. 2012; Yeoh et al. 2009) there are multiple caregivers in both Manila and New York City and multiple directions in which care is deployed (within kin networks in the Philippines, kin care directed toward migrant family members, migrant remittances to families left behind). The Gonzalez clan shows us that multidirectional care in the transnational family has readjusted to the need of Filipina mothers to migrate for work, even from the same family.

I present this set of multidirectional care to rethink the common formulation of care in the transnational family as chiefly the migrants' responsibility. Although past scholarship has discussed the displacement of care work in families left behind,[2] what is missing is a robust investigation of the way in which nonmigrant family members are caring for one another and then how they interpret that care as a key component in transnationalizing care in their families. Instead of leveraging the care they receive from a migrant family member, for example, withholding emotions to receive a particular outcome (Dreby 2010), overachieving in order to gain rewards (Parreñas 2005a), or making an "immigrant bargain" where children back home do well to return their parents' sacrifice (R. C. Smith 2006), decentering the migrant from the formulation of transnational care highlights the myriad ways that the labor of care in the place left behind continues. Multidirectional care illustrates that work between family members in the Philippines is an activation of existing care networks. Although families also believe that their work is indirectly caring for their migrant family member, it also shows that care is multimodal and continuous.

GENDER SHIFTS FOR MEN: A PRACTICE IN KIN CARE

Boyet and Jing's teamwork is a key example of the role of kin networks shaping gendered shifts in the ideas of masculinity and domestic work. A multidirectional care paradigm can assist in exploring the possible shifts in the gendered expectations of care work in the Filipino family, and in fact, the practice of multidirectional care lays bare the potential for patriarchal logics to be challenged through the participation of kin networks. Echoing the work of scholars who posit gendered ideologies shift through practices of care work, I present examples of local kin cultures linked to global ideologies of gendered division of labor affecting the practices of fathers left behind who are attending to domestic work (Ansell 2009; Hoang and Yeoh 2014).

When Joan and Vickie migrated, Joan's husband Enteng and Vickie's husband Mauricio interacted with the extended kin network in very different ways, thus affecting their adherence to their gendered ideas of domestic work differently. The common narrative around fathers and husbands in transnational arrangements claims that both left behind and migrant men find it hard to build intimacy with their families (Parreñas 2008); rather, they retreat to gender normative logics and disinvest from the domestic labor of their families. Yet more recent studies demonstrate that men left behind are reconstructing their masculinities toward the new conditions of the transnational family, some asserting that fathers' participation in the family produces less behavioral problems in children left behind and greater family cohesion (Pingol 2001; E. Graham et al. 2012; Hoang and Yeoh 2011). Both of these trends are present in my research, but my intervention in this literature is in highlighting the participation of the kin network as a factor in influencing men's participation in care work.

When Joan replaced Enteng as the primary breadwinner, his contributions to domestic work for the family became limited. This instance confirms Rhacel Salazar Parreñas's argument that fathering in transnational families is limited under normative patriarchal cultural logics, specifically in the Philippine culture (Parreñas 2008). Parreñas argues that if fathers do take up nurturing care work (tasks like cooking and cleaning), it is only if their masculine identity is safeguarded. Enteng disavowed nurturing care work out of the shame of having his wife perform the ascribed role of breadwinner. Melann says her father is distant toward them because he feels responsible for the situation of their family separation: "*Lumayo siya kasi guilty kasi siya, kasi kung hindi siya nawalan ng trabaho, kung nag-sumikap siyang magtra-baho, eh 'di nandito si mama.* He is distant because he feels guilty, because if he didn't lose his job, if he did not stop trying to find work, Mama would be here." Melann and Calvin, Enteng and Joan's children, add that their father refused to take up nurturing care work because Joan's migration breached the gender normative ideology of the husband as breadwinner and the wife as homemaker. Historically, Enteng was not close to the Gonzalez kin network because of his provincial dialect and prior conflicts between him and the Gonzalez clan. Upon Joan's departure, he further isolated himself from his wife's kin although Melann and Calvin fostered healthy relationships with their mother's kin. Indeed, Enteng should not be blamed for his distance toward his children; we must analyze men's fathering strategies in the transnational family, taking into consideration both the social controls informed by personal histories and differing ethno-linguistic backgrounds. Enteng did not and could not revise his own vision of masculinity within the new conditions of his family because he did not have support in creating a new identity as a domestic parent. Of course, his own reluctance and disavowal of the role asked of him by his wife's migration did not help his relationships with his children and kin, but because of his historic conflicts with the Gonzalez clan, he also could not use them as a resource to transition into his new role.

Mauricio, Vickie's husband, has a completely different story that is in stark opposition to the narrative of the absent father. Before Vickie migrated, Mauricio was a *jeepney* (type of public transportation) driver, but his pay did not cover the most basic needs of his family. To try to earn more money to support his two growing children and wife, he tried to work abroad as a construction worker and also looked for manual labor jobs in Manila when he returned. Still, even when Mauricio worked sixteen-hour days at different types of low-wage jobs, his salary was not enough. Vickie's migration offered a solution to the family's financial challenges. When Vickie migrated, Mauricio took up the nurturing care work to ensure that his children and their home were as secure as possible. Taking advantage of Vickie's kin network, he learned from Tina—Vickie's older sister—how to cook and do laundry. In my visits to Mauricio and Vickie's family home, Mauricio would explain to me the new strategies he learned to do domestic tasks like cutting vegetables or laundry as if he was acquiring new skills. He was a stay-at-home dad who took pride in his work of getting a shirt whiter than before or cooking a dish better than the last time he cooked it.

The entire Gonzalez kin acknowledged his domestic work by praising his new dishes and joking with him that he'll be the new launderer in the neighborhood soon enough. Dianne, Melann, and Calvin talk about Mauricio in a group interview:

DIANNE: *Kasi ngayon parang wala si mama dapat siya, pinaparamdaman niya naman na kahit wala si mama, nandun siya.*

Because now that Mama is gone, it's just him, he should let us know that even if she isn't here, he is here.

Mauricio was in the room during this interview and the cousins freely shared these sentiments. They were acknowledging his newfound role and in talking about his responsibilities to the family, they affirm him. Mauricio talks about his newfound respect for nurturing duties:

Ngayon ko lang nagawa ang magluto habang naglalaba. Hindi ko naranasan dati 'yun. Noon ko na-realize na ang nanay pala sa bahay, ang trabaho ay mahirap. 'Yun mismo ang naranasan ko, andiyan magbubulyaw ako sa mga batang nag-aaway. Kaya noong umalis si Vicki eh, mahirap pala kako. Pero okay lang, nandiyan sila Tina, sila Mel, tulong-tulong, dahil sa ganoon, kaya ko naman.

It's only now that I've experienced cooking and doing laundry at the same time. I've never experienced that before. That's when I realized that a mother at home, their work is hard. That's what I experienced, I'm there stopping the kids from bickering. That's why when Vickie left, I realized her work was so hard. But it's okay, Tina is there, Mel is there, all of us helping out, I can do it.

Contrary to Parreñas's findings that fathers who take on nurturing work face social disapproval and shaming, Mauricio embraces his public identity as a nurturer. Here, with the help of the kin network and a view of care work as a collective effort, redefinitions of nurturance allow Mauricio to accept and value his new role. Echoing Alicia Pingol's work on masculinities for fathers left behind (Pingol 2001), Mauricio's masculinity as a father and husband adjusted to his role as the sole domestic parent. Kin network and immediate family understand Mauricio's shift as the caregiver at home as complementary to his wife's migration—both transgressing the cultural gender ideology. Kin care and local kin participation in Mauricio's transition, then, is a key factor in this shift: Tita Tina and Melann's support and appreciation for Mauricio affirm his work and new role. Social disapproval eases with new forms of care from new caregivers in transnational arrangements. The collaboration between Mauricio and kin networks enables us to see that fathers are not just deferring to patriarchal norms; rather, they are drawing from all their resources to change their patriarchal ideals and practices. The process of redefining masculinity for men like Mauricio and Boyet is embedded in the context where patriarchal and gendered ideas are either reinforced or challenged, and kin networks have a pivotal role in this process. For men who have taken on their wives' roles as the domestic parent, their masculinity is rooted in how successful they are in that work. While taking up the responsibilities of an additional set of children or another household is challenging, redistributing responsibilities among the people left behind does not present itself as a steep transition if the family's kin arrangement already had experience working together. This continuation of kin care can possibly shift the gender normative framework of men left behind.

Through a multidirectional care model and decentering the migrant to analyze care within the kin network, considering the opposing masculinities of Enteng and Mauricio within the Gonzalez family network establishes that masculinities are always constructed. Mauricio grew into his new domestic role—yet it had an opposite effect on Enteng. The comparison between these two fathers in the same extended family affirms that conflicting masculinities are ever-present in the lives of transnational families (Pingol 2001). The story of Filipinos left behind is not a triumphant one but it is also not a despairing tale. What these stories demonstrate is that masculine identity is constructed both through larger normative social and cultural forces and mediated by local kin interactions. The kin network that shared family responsibilities and upkeep of the house before migration served as the foundation and catalyst for a different sense of manhood for Mauricio to emerge and it is in these situational negotiations where the remaking of masculinities is occurring.

Generations of Migrants: Kin Care Work through the Years of Labor Export

Rita Sancho is a migrant domestic worker living in New York City. She has been away from her family since 1995. She comes from what she calls *isang pamilyang nag-a-abroad* (a family of migrants). In the 1970s, Rita's mother, Remedios, migrated to the Middle East as a seamstress to support her six children as a result of the weakening economy of the Philippines. In the 1980s, as soon as the older children were of age, they also migrated so that their mother could come back to the Philippines. The serial migration in the Sancho family is a common story for Filipino families who rely on migrant remittances for daily costs of living. The long history of transformation of care in the Sancho family highlights the reliance of the Philippines' persistent aggressive labor export industry on recruiting the Filipino family as a site of reorganizing social reproductive labor for profit. Their family history and narrative affirm two aforementioned dimensions in multidirectional care: Shifts in gendered ideas come with the support of family members; and family histories of care become inculcated in the way that kin care continues in transnational arrangements. Additionally, I offer the Sancho family histories to highlight the experiences of migrant women who are not biological mothers yet are still taking part in multidirectional care transnationally. Rita, who is a main character in the Sancho transnational family, does not abandon children in the Philippines rather is an active contributor to family activities.

Rita has no children of her own in the Philippines but she helps support her four siblings, two spouses, four nieces and nephews, and aging mother and father. Rita also has two sisters living in Japan and Israel who contribute to their family home in Quezon City. The Sancho siblings are remarkably close and talk to and with one another with humor and jest, especially about their collective experience with migration. Otherwise, as Rita puts it, "we'd all cry about being apart, instead we laugh." Three sisters, Lara (28 years old), Leslie (34 years old), and Len (43 years old), recount their first encounter with adjusting to a transnational family when their mother Remedios left for Saudi Arabia in 1976 and their father Ignacio filled the roles their mother left behind:

VALERIE: Did your papa step up when your mama left?

LEN: *Oo, si papa? Naman. Naglalaba yan, kasi before pa naman umalis si mama siya 'yun eh naglalaba siya. Siya 'yung taga-laba. Hinahati namin 'yung gawain sa amin, and 'yung mga Tita't Tito namin dito nakatira. Pero nung umalis si Mama, mas pa, sumobra pa kasi siya na 'yung nanay and tatay sa bahay.*

Oh yeah, Papa? So much. He was the one doing the laundry even before Mama left. He was really the only one to do the laundry. Because we had split up chores among the kids and Tita and Tito living with us. But after Mama left, he became a master at it because he was the mother and father at the house.

VALERIE: *Uh-huh. Hindi siya 'yung . . . 'yung naging macho parang ayaw niyang gawin 'yan?* Uh-huh. He didn't feel like too macho to do that?

LARA: *Si papa? Walang kamachohan 'yan! Wala! (Everyone laughs.) Ginagawa na niya 'yun dati! Oo naman, naglalaba na 'yan. Pati underwear namin kahit dalaga na kami, 'yung may mga tinagusan ng menstruation. Ganyan siya, naglalaba tapos si Tita nagpa-plantsa, sa-sabihan kami, "Kayo, kayo, matututunan ninyo 'to rin! Pinapaturuan kayo ni Mama ninyo. Para pagbalik niya, alam ninyo na."*

Oh Papa? He didn't do the macho thing! No way! Not at all! (Everyone laughs.) That was his task in the order of things before! Even our underwear, even when we were in puberty, he washed our underwear with menstruation. That's how he was, while he was do-ing our laundry and our aunt was ironing he would tell us, "You and you, this and that, you're all going to learn how to wash clothes too! Mama would want me to teach you. So when she comes back, you'll know how."

The family history of Ignacio's domestic duties mattered in his ability to assume the hard work of raising six girls and one boy. Lara points out that washing the underwear of menstruating girls is an extreme example of his humility as a father made to shoulder the tasks that might be the domain of a mother. She makes a good point that he was able and willing to do this task because it was part of his domestic mandate even before Remedios migrated. Lara's quick mention of her aunt helping out with laundry should not go unnoticed. As other scholars have established, women kin have con-sistently supported migrant mothers' absence but in this situation, the hand off of laundry and ironing became one way that Ignacio felt affirmed in the role of father left behind. All of this to say that his domestic duties were in the name of making sure his daughters and son were learning the lessons that their mother would have wanted them to know. Ignacio filled in for his wife but in the name of ensuring that she would not be coming back to lazy children but to children with a sense of responsibility to their home and to their family. Ignacio was at once taking up the work of his migrant wife, mak-ing certain that the redistribution of labor among the children taught them how to manage household responsibilities but also it was a way for him to stay true to Remedios's sacrifice.

Taking care of his children was an immediate necessity, but Ignacio's nur-turance work can also be analyzed as care work for his absent wife. Ignacio explained, "Taking care of them is taking care of her." Ignacio's approach to fathering is not restrained by social disapproval or the effeminization of his masculine identity. He willingly took up the ascribed gender roles of his mi-grant wife as he was negotiating his masculinity in relation to the immediate care work he needed to tend to. The local and daily responsibilities to his children provided the basis for a new sense of manhood and responsibility for Ignacio that trumped the constraining logics of Filipino patriarchy (Pingol 2001). And in fact, the support from a kin member, the aunt helping with the ironing, allowed him to continue to make sense of his new masculinity. As Ignacio shows, masculinity is performative and situational (Connell 1998) rather than static, thus allowing men like Ignacio to take up care work as the conditions warrant. Up to the days before Ignacio's dementia compromised his memory, he was still active in domestic duties in his household, never letting go of the tasks he had learned not only as part of his masculinity and fatherhood but also as part of a transnational family.

Across the history of migration in Rita's family, her kin network always worked together to raise one another; intimacy rather than rivalry grew between siblings despite vying for their mother's approval while she was in Saudi Arabia or for their father's attention. In the subsequent migrations of older sisters and finally, Rita, the siblings, whether near or far, incorporated one another into children's lives as co-parents and relied on one another to care for their aging parents. The circulation of care in their transnational family life was a set of practices they constructed over their mother's life course as a migrant and then their migrant siblings' life courses (Wall and Bolzman 2014). Having the experience of creating methods of communication and involvement from their migrant mother, Lara talked about how they kept Rita involved in family affairs in the Philippines by including her in brainstorming ideas for parties and planning special occasions as a form of adjustment to her absence. At first, it sounded like a superficial way of keeping her migrant sister involved. But as we talked, Rita's sisters left behind told me about how she was a central organizer for almost all of their family activities before she migrated, from putting together Sunday dinners to organizing neighborhood fiestas. Therefore, keeping her "in" on these activities at the present was crucial to the family in the Philippines, and in fact, to Rita:

> LARA: *Ayun, ikuwento mo 'yung fiesta noong nagkabulutong siya!* Tell her the story about when Rita had the chickenpox during fiesta!
>
> LESLIE: *Mag-eksena tayo ng fiesta bulutong!* We have to do a flashback to the fiesta of chickenpox!
>
> LEN: (Laughs) *Ang gulo ninyo! Ganito—siya ka-organizer, hindi siya makalabas pero nag-oorder pa siya galing sa kwarto kung anong dapat saan, ano pang bibilhin at 'yung 'di pa namin ginawa.* You guys are crazy! It's like this—Rita's identity is in her love for organizing family

events, but during this fiesta she couldn't leave the room because she was contagious but she was yelling orders from her room to figure out what things needed to go where, what else we were missing, and keeping track of the things that weren't done.

LARA: (laughing) *Ngayon, imbes na bulutong, order galing sa New York! Pati nga color theme, mina-mandohan pa rin kami.* Now, instead of chickenpox, the orders come from New York! She even tells us the color theme of a party.

LEN: *Sa totoo lang, 'yan ang layunin in Rita sa pamilya namin kahit na maliit pa siya at sa ngayon kahit na malayo siya, may importansya ang kanyang mga "marching orders." Malayo man, malapit pa rin siya sa aming big events.* In truth, that was always Rita's purpose in our family even when she was little and even if she's far now, her "marching orders" are important to her. Even if she's far, she's still close to our big events.

LESLIE: *Touching! Kaya we are her soldiers sa panahon ng fiesta. Color theme kung color theme!* Aw, that's touching! That's why we are her soldiers during fiesta. If she wants a color theme, she gets a color theme!

The Sancho sisters recognized that it was central to Rita's identity to be the family event organizer when she was physically with her family to the point that even during a spell of contagious infection, she insisted on participating in organizing the fiesta. So they all make the effort to keep her involved by giving her opportunities to help with the planning of family events. Lara, Leslie, and Len fondly remember Rita's quarantine as a way to reference the role she played in her family when in the Philippines, parallel to the presence she continues to have although she is physically absent from family functions. Rita can perform her role in her kin network from afar because her kin make room for her to participate in the ways that are meaningful for her, especially drawing from their family's past experiences. Whether it is picking out which ice cream to serve or the party theme color, the family ensures that Rita is still integrated in family life, especially in the big events where it may be difficult for her to be absent.

For Rita, the opportunity to help with planning allows her to feel that she has a role in family activities beyond just sending financial support to her family. The role that her family creates for her gives her a sense of connection and belonging: "I'm not physically there but I also feel like I'm not missing. I continue to be there. Like I never left. When they tell me about the day—

what they ate with their rice, what's happening with my nephew Kela, how the ladies planning fiesta are going crazy. When they tell me those things I remember the routine, the things you would miss but you don't because they let you in on it. I am still there." As the Sanchos demonstrate, being part of a transnational family means finding ways to connect across time and space. They elucidate that care is circulated in an asymmetrical yet reciprocal way: Rita's remittances and the intentional work of the Sancho sisters in keeping their migrant sister involved are all part of a care network that continues to build meaningful relationships in their transnational family.

The Sanchos have done this before. Len, the oldest Sancho sister, describes how when the girls were young and their mother was in Saudi Arabia, their mother still found ways to connect with the family left behind: "*Pinadadalhan kami ni mama ng cassette tape sa balikbayan para sabihin kung anong pasalubong ng mga anak niya, darling. Alam niya kung mauubos na ang Tang at magpapadala 'yan 'pag alam niya na ubos na. Pero of course, ako ang reporter.* She would send back a cassette tape along with balikbayan boxes to narrate what imported product should go to which kid, darling. She would keep track of how much orange juice mix we'd drink and send another pack in bulk when she expected us to have no more. But of course, I would be doing the reporting." Rita's mother modeled how to maintain a sense of family despite not being physically together in one place. Len, as the oldest sister, also made sure to communicate the amount of juice mix to her mother as an invitation to keep her involved in the mundane details of the siblings' lives. In this way, Len has been perfecting transnational correspondence from her mother Remedios's ledger of juice to Rita's color themes; the purpose is to keep them involved in the daily routines in the Philippines in a meaningful way.

In the Sancho family's case, multidirectional care has been honed through the cycles of migration within a plurality of family care configurations. In the 1970s, Ignacio and the siblings ensured that they communicated and made room for an absent mother, Remedios. At one point in the late 1980s, Rita and Len migrated to Israel at the urging of one of their siblings who had been living there for some time since both Ignacio and Remedios had health issues and jobs in the Philippines were hard to come by under martial law. The responsibility of caring for their parents shifted and even if Rita went ahead to New York City and Len headed back to the Philippines after their attempt at making a life in Israel, siblings at home kept tasks available for migrants to participate in the care of ailing Remedios or for major family events. Lara and Leslie took turns making phone calls to their migrant siblings in Israel during unexciting times in the Philippines. Lara remembered, "*Trabaho 'yan usapin boring 'pag walang nangyayari dito! Pero go lang!* It's work talking to them when there's nothing happening! But we still did it!" Lara and Leslie took on the bulk of the work, paying off the debts for the family home and caring for Ignacio and Remedios when four of their siblings were abroad. It was a heavy responsibility but they persisted as they had the experience. Leslie reflected, "*Parang basketball team lang yan, one player in, one player out pero winning pa rin ang goal namin. Pamilya pa rin kami.* It's like a basketball team, one player in, one player out, but our goal is to win. But we're still a family." In this analogy, players in and out refer to the migrants that have come in and out of their family in their history, and the winning part is about keeping a family life meaningful.

In a sense, their family's multiple and serial migrations have adapted to the wills of a neoliberal political economy that requires at least one or two of them to continue to live and work outside the Philippines. Therefore, their multidirectional care is a commitment to reorganizing care work to withstand the test of serial migration. Still, they so aptly demonstrate the creativity in the work of multidirectional care as they reference their past experiences of separation.

Finally, in this discussion of multidirectional care practices, I want to focus for a moment on Rita as a sister, daughter, and aunt who is active and involved in multidirectional care in her transnational family. The narrative of the biological mother sending money to her biological children is dominant in the literature on transnational family and care work. However, the kin network is central to the transnational family form. Not only is it key in filling the absence of a migrant woman in the family and place left behind, but Rita represents many migrant women who take their roles as kin much like how biological mothers of children see their responsibilities to their families. We need to expand the definition of mothering into the practice of social reproductive labor that sustains transnational family operations. Although migrant sisters, daughters, and aunts do not support biological offspring, their commitment to sharing mothering responsibilities with their sisters who have children makes their contributions to the transnational family integral to their own multidirectional care ethic and to the stabilization of their families in the Philippines. Below, I include the perspective of migrants in deciphering if the care within their family networks left behind affects them, but I am also intentional in incorporating the stories of migrant daughters, aunts, and sisters, along with mothers, to continue analyzing the function of migrant kin in the transnational family.

But Do Migrants Care?

Philippine-based families interpret multidirectional care within their kin networks as a form of care for one another *and* for their migrant family members. Migrants, whose family histories I completed through multisited ethnography, admitted every little bit of help matters when separation from family starts to add up in years. Tetet, Joan, Vickie, and Rita all underscored that knowing that their families were doing well in spite of their absence became a sort of continuing comfort for them. But, in general, does every migrant see family stabilization in the Philippines as reciprocal care work toward them?

There was a set of migrant women in my participant pool whose families in the Philippines I was not able to interview. Although I was not able to reach these migrant women's families, I continued to investigate how they interpreted forms of care circling back to them from their families in the Philippines. In this section, I bring migrants back into focus to capture the diverse and asymmetrical ways in which multidirectional care is received and understood. Migrants interpret their families' achievements as an integral form of care sustaining their narrative of sacrifice and absence, a reverse direction in care remittance from the place left behind to the person abroad.

JANESSA, LORIE, AND BETTY:
PRIDE AND RELIEF AS RECIPROCAL CARE

Janessa Velez is the second youngest of five siblings born to parents who worked as peasants in a province in Central Luzon in the Philippines. Janessa's parents quickly found out that raising five children through growing rice was nearly impossible. They moved to a nearby city where Janessa's mother worked as a laundry woman and her father worked as a driver. In her urban poor upbringing, Janessa was no stranger to work. She and her siblings took care of one another as they grew up, and they all pitched in with their mother to do laundry by hand.

> *Naawa ako sa kanya kasi talagang 'yung kamay niya sobra ng binabad. Halimbawa kapag binibisita ko siya ng naglalaba hawak ko ang mga kapatid ko, kapag tinitingnan ko siya naiiyak talaga ako. 'Pag nakikita ko siya my god 'yung nilalabhan niya ang dami, talaga mga ilang pantalon. Gusto ko siyang matulungan, kaya ginawa ko lahat talaga para makatulong sa kanya, sa kanila.*

> I felt so bad for her because her hands looked like they soaked in water for too long. When I would visit her with my brothers in my arms, when I looked at her I wanted to cry. When I saw her, my god, the amount of laundry she had

to do, really like so many pairs of pants. I wanted to help her, that's why I've done everything I can do to help her, help them.

By taking on the care of her siblings, Janessa performed horizontal care work:

Lahat ng mga neighbor namin natutuwa na sa akin. Hindi ako 'yung tatamad-tamad na kakain na wala namang itutulong. Ako mismo magsasabi kung ako na maghuhugas, ako na magluluto kasi kung hindi ko gagawin hindi kami kakain Val, alam mo 'yun. Minsan binibitbit ko 'yung kapatid ko o kaya sinasabihan ko 'yung kapatid kong bunso, "Ikaw huwag kang tatamad-tamad tumulong ka naman, mahiya ka naman!" Ginaganun ko siya. Para makakain kami. Kasi 'pag nakita mo si Mama, gusto ko talagang tulungan siya. Pero 'di ko sinasabi 'yan sa kanya, ako na lang. Sabi ko sa sarili ko, wala naman tumutulong sa kanya, ako na.

All of my neighbors looked at me like I was a good kid. I wasn't that lazy girl that would eat and wouldn't help out. I myself would announce that I would wash the dishes, and I would cook because if I didn't do it, we wouldn't eat, Val, you know that? Sometimes, I had my brother on my hip or I tell my youngest sister, "You, you can't be lazy, help out around here!" That's what I would tell her. Just so we could eat. Because when I see my mama, I really want to help her. But of course I didn't tell her, I just kept it to myself. I said, no one is gonna help her, I'll just do it.

From an early age, Janessa learned that everyone in the family has to pitch in, that parents are not the sole caregivers. Janessa carried this lesson into adulthood. When she finished college and went back home to help her family, she had the opportunity to become a domestic worker for a wealthy family that lived in the same province. Janessa saw the opportunity to earn a wage as an extension of her duties as a care provider in her family. She says, "*Kaya nga sinakripisyo ko 'yung 2000 hanggang 2003. Ang hirap magluto, maglinis, magluto, maglinis. Pero sabi ko, tutulungan ko sila kahit maliit lang ang sahod.* That's why I sacrificed for three years from 2000 to 2003. It was a really hard job to clean and cook and clean and cook. But I said I'd help my family, I'll take care of them even if I only make a small amount of money." Janessa made a sacrifice, going from college student to domestic worker, but she frames her efforts as part of her role in maintaining her family's overall well-being.

Then, in 2003, a friend of the family who was getting too old to work abroad offered Janessa's mother a job as a domestic worker for a Filipino diplomat in Canada. Janessa volunteered to go instead; unlike her older siblings she had no children. She explained to me why she chose to migrate:

Ang concept ko lang kasi ay matulungan ko 'yung mama ko, na ayaw ko na siyang maglabada, 'yung ganoon. O kaya 'yung para maiba naman 'yung buhay namin kasi 'yung mga kapatid ko, nabuntisan, 'yung isa naglayas. 15 years saka namin siya nakita. Kasi hirap na hirap kaming lahat noon, alam mo, alam ko na ito ang magagawa ko, 'yung masipag dati, ngayon ako na 'yung nagtatrabaho at nagpapadala.

My concept is because I would be able to help Mama, and I didn't want her to do laundry anymore, you know? Or, so that our lives would change because my siblings had run off to have kids and get married. They were all having such a hard time, you know, and I knew this is how I could continue on being the helpful kid I was then, but today I'll work to send them money.

Janessa views migration as a contribution to her family's betterment. Her experience as a caregiver when she was younger shapes her role as breadwinner in adulthood. The shared caregiving operation within her family has informed Janessa's decisions to take up paid work in her adult life.

Janessa had been living and working abroad for nearly ten years when I met her. She told me that it is satisfying to send money home:

Kahit mga kapatid ko umiiyak 'yan. Kasi kahit mga kapatid ko tinutulungan ko rin sila. Alam kong wala naman silang mahihingian ng pera. Kaya ko ginagawa ito sa inyo hindi ako nanghihingi ng kapalit. At least masaya ako na natutulungan ko sila. Gumagaan ang loob ko 'pag alam ko na nag-aaral ang mga pamangkin ko. Nabayaran ko na 'yun. Kaya sabi ko sa kapatid ko, tapusin na 'yung papel ng lupa para maumpisahan na 'yung business tapos ok na ako nun. Asikasuhin ang pagpapagawa ng bahay para sa atin, kay Mama. Bilihan ko din sila ng kaunting lupa, kahit installments. Kahit mabagal ang pagbabayad, Val. Ok na sa akin 'yun, sa amin na 'yun.

Yeah, even my siblings, they cry. Because even my siblings, I help them. They don't have anyone else to ask for help from. I told them that I send money back because I know they don't have anywhere to turn to. I left, but I'm not asking to pay me back. I'm happy to know that I can help take care of them. I feel like they give me my sacrifice back when I know my nieces and nephews are able to pay for tuition and finish school. I finished those payments. That's why I tell my brother, I told him to help finish the papers for our farm to help start our business because then I'll be okay. They take care of the house I want to build for my family, for my mama. And I even pay installments to get us a farm. And making payments on house and lot or land is progress little by little, Val. I'm okay even with that, it's ours now.

Janessa identifies these milestones—finishing school, buying a house and lot, making installments on farmland—as steps toward stabilizing her family's finances. Echoing her objectives when she migrated, she effectively changed her family's life opportunities by providing them with financial support to open doors to education, home ownership, and possibly a business opportunity. Scholars have likewise shown that Mexican and Jamaican transnational families interpret such shifts in quality of life as a result of migration (D. E. Smith 2006; Stephen 2007; Foner 2005); based on stories like Janessa's, these shifts in living standards result as well from the attentive work of families left behind.

The reciprocity that produces feelings of satisfaction and relief in migrant family members like Janessa is facilitated by the commitment of the family back home to transform the remittances into practical life improvements. Janessa could keep sending money back to the Philippines and end up feeling cheated if her *padala* (financial support) didn't amount to any improvements for her family. Families left behind, therefore, play a crucial role in converting care in the form of remittances into a better life at home. By demonstrating that support from abroad "changes lives," families left behind are providing reciprocal care to their migrant relatives. Janessa says, "Building the house makes me feel like I can be proud of myself. By building the house they showed me that they're okay, and I feel good about that."

I asked Lorie, a 34-year-old domestic worker in New Jersey, what her biggest accomplishment has been since she left the Philippines in 1996. She replied that it was to support her parents, siblings, and siblings' families. "Both of my brothers graduated college. Even if I wasn't able to do that. I bought a house for my parents. It's important to me that they include me in the decisions of what happens in the house or what courses my brothers took. Because I know they are taking care of my sacrifices." Lorie walks us through what types of opportunities opened up for her parents and brothers because of her work abroad. Her parents had both worked in the Philippines to make ends meet while her four siblings took care of one another. Lorie had dreams of finishing school but she was the first to receive an opportunity to go abroad for work and so she went with no hesitation. Lorie expresses pride that her sacrifice resulted in her brothers graduating college. She tells me, "I'm so proud of them. I'm proud that I can do that for them."

Despite the time and distance between her and her family, she continues to feel closely connected to them. This is facilitated in part by the fact that her family actively invites and acknowledges her opinion on important matters.

Lorie also told me that they didn't always follow her advice. Still, she believes that college diplomas, new homes, and similar accomplishments are her family's way of caring for her. Lorie views her brothers' graduation as the ultimate reciprocity for her migration. She said, "If my sister or brother had the opportunity before I did, they would have gone. I would've made them proud." Lorie acknowledges that migration was an investment in family, and her intersubjective turn in the interview highlights how care comes not only from her sacrifice but also from her siblings accomplishing what she could not.

Betty is a 56-year-old mother of four. She lives in Queens, New York, and is employed as a domestic worker. When I met her, she had been away from her children for four years. When her husband died and the savings ran out, she relied on her older children to take care of their younger siblings. When she could no longer support her family on her income as a government worker, she decided that she might fare better as a migrant worker. She retired from her government job (which she had made a career out of) and applied for a visa. She was easily approved because of her numerous work trips to countries like Canada. Betty explained to her children that her retirement meant that this trip would be more than a work trip. Her migration would ultimately be the family's new source of income. Betty stated:

> I have to explain to them that I'm not coming here to enjoy because this is New York. It's really a sacrifice for me. My daughter said that they would be like orphans when I leave. When I left, when we were in the airport, she was crying and weeping so much. It was so much that I almost couldn't leave. But we all had to sacrifice. And they understood, especially when they saw the difference financially. When they didn't have to take loans for school, when they didn't have to stand in line to get a promissory note, things like that [that had been] really hard for them.

Betty did all she could to ensure that her children understood that her departure would secure their education and their future.

When Betty left, three of her four children were already young adults. But her youngest daughter was only 9 years old at the time. The older children were capable of taking care of the youngest child, but Betty was nervous about leaving her children "all alone." She didn't have extended kin to rely on so she hired a domestic helper in the Philippines to attend to her children's needs. The hired help wasn't there long. Betty explains, "Last April, the housekeeper left them. I asked them, 'Who will take care of the house?' You know what they [the children] said? 'We had a meeting, us four. We decided that we'll

share the chores.' So that I could save. See? This is how they take care of me."
Like the families discussed above, her children understood the necessity of
addressing the housework, and they also know that by pitching in to help
one another they help their mother both financially and emotionally. Betty
interprets her children taking care of one another as a form of taking care of
her. Betty understands this sort of reciprocity as a form of care toward her
because it is one less thing for her to worry about. She also takes comfort
in knowing that her children are taking responsibility for one another. This
dynamic helps migrant women like Betty know that the sacrifice of migration and distance is not for naught.

In this section, I have discussed how migrant women make meaning of
multidirectional care. In Lorie's and Janessa's cases, the opportunity to migrate
in turn supports a wide constellation of family in the Philippines. Often family members who have no children choose to migrate, under the assumption
that it will be less hard for them to separate from their families and that they
will be able to concentrate more on their work abroad. Although this may be
true, Lorie's and Janessa's stories illustrate that migrants who are not mothers
also experience isolation and distress as a result of migration. Like migrant
mothers, migrants who are daughters, sisters, and aunts look to their families
back home for nurturance and an affirmation that their decision to migrate
and be separated from their families is not in vain. Ultimately, their roles as
care providers in their kin networks before they migrated continued from
afar. Complementarily, their kin are also engaged in multidirectional care
for them as well.

Janessa and the other women featured here all experienced reciprocity of
care when their family members left behind stepped up to care for one another. Even if the care work coming from the Philippines did not manifest
in financial ways, the stories of families and their migrant family members
show that different forms of care count. Those that internalize and frame
their family members' migration as sacrifice try their best to make good on
that sacrifice. Whether it is through finishing college or taking care of one
another, these demonstrations that life in the Philippines not only progresses
but becomes better is proof for the migrants that their sacrifice has value.
This sort of care formula is evidence that care work is multiple in providers
and directions.

As noted earlier, these migrant women demonstrate how migrants experience multidirectional care. Instead of feeling isolated as a result of the family
left behind pitching in to take care of one another, migrants take comfort and
consolation in the achievements of family members back home. Whether it

is buying a house or earning a college degree, these accomplishments allow migrant family members to justify their sacrifice and to confirm their role in improving the lives of their families back home.

Conclusion

Tetet shared one of her proudest moments in the ten years she's been apart from her family: "*Nung nagsarili na si Jing. Alam mo, parang gumaan ang loob ko nung sinabi niya na malaki na ang mga bata at pwede na sila ni Max tumira sa sariling bahay malapit sa amin. 'Di sa ayaw ko na magsama-sama kami, gusto ko lang na kayanin niya gawin ang gusto niya.* When Jing went out on her own. You know, a weight was lifted from me when she said that the kids were grown up already and she and Max could live in her own home near us. It's not that I didn't want them in the house, I just wanted her to do what she wanted to do." Multidirectional care is apparent in the family history of the Garcias: they showed that the already existing care network their family functioned under was reactivated upon Tetet's departure as the

Photo 1.2. Tetet's remittances financed two homes on the same street in this new housing development where her family and sister-in-law live a few doors down from one another. Photo courtesy of Kevin Brian Gonzales.

Boyet and Jing sibling team attended to the new conditions of their extended family. Tetet also felt relieved even if she lived and worked in New York City; while she sent money back home she understood her family's reciprocation through the stabilization of their family life in Manila. Tetet's comment highlights the fact that Jing's achievements could also be celebrated by Tetet as part of her accomplishments as a migrant. I bookend this chapter with the Garcias' story because they show that through the application of a multidirectional care model, we are able to decenter the migrant in the formula of transnational care and bring to the surface the role of kin networks in the transnational family.

In a rapidly relativizing (Bryceson and Vuorela 2002) transnational family arrangement, alternative forms and organization of care coming from kin networks in the Philippines is important to understand how care is circulated in a transnational family. In contrast to a narrow definition of care work solely as financial remittances (E. R. Rodriguez 1996), the care work of families left behind cannot be financially calculated in the same way as money wired from one place to another. The care work of anyone outside the nuclear conception of the family, "the unpaid and more intimate dimensions of transnational lives, in particular of 'kin-work' and caregiving are often overlooked" (Baldassar and Merla 2013, 8). Therefore, decentering the migrant and instead calling attention to family members in the Philippines performing various acts of care contributing to a migrant family member's well-being is a crucial part of multidirectional care. In contrast to earlier studies on transnational Filipino families, which represent families of migrants as passive receivers of care from their migrant family members abroad, I argue that families left behind are active agents in the circulation of care work in the transnational family from the places left behind. Although some scholars have argued that care work from immigrant children (Park 2005) or families left behind (Parreñas 2005b) are often governed by the logics of consumption, these stories of kin and children left behind seen from a wider lens of multidirectional care highlight that care work can be detached from the utilitarian formula of "give some to get some." Rather, studying the circulation of care within families left behind and deploying that care toward migrants is about focusing on the work done to fulfill the immediate needs of family members but also sustaining emotional relationships that can include repaying a migrant's sacrifice of leaving. This argument builds on the emergent field of study on children and migration that emphasizes the agency of children in sustaining the life of their families—an explicit departure from conceptualizing children, and in extension family and kin left behind, as mere attachments to the experience of adult migrants (Dobson 2009; Huijsman 2011). Additionally, the agency from the place left behind magnifies the fact that migration does not halt life. In fact, life for families left behind is full of agency and innovation when it comes to care work.

Given the expansive kin networks of Filipino families, the families of migrants interpret the renegotiation of care work to make up for absent family members as a progression of past roles. Premigration kin networks that share in care work are critical to the ongoing maintenance of the family after migration. Family members left behind view their roles as a form of care for migrants. The roles that kin take on are often compensated with financial support from their migrant members. Yet, as the above narratives show, the care work equation is much more complex than a simple exchange of money for domestic labor. The concept of multidirectional care in the transnational family embraces the horizontal exchange of care from nonmigrant family members to their migrant counterparts simultaneously with the care work *within* nonmigrant families in Manila. Reorganizing and taking up the work of maintaining the family is at once caring for physically present family members, but it is also a form of care for those who are abroad. By including a picture of the transnational family prior to migration, we gain greater insight into the family dynamic postmigration. This added component gives a long view of "doing family" and reveals how the transnational family cannot be isolated from the event of migration; rather, it should be studied as the process of migration unfolds. Adaptation to migration cannot be fully understood without decentering the migrant, considering a family's history of care work, and thus opening up the possibility of simultaneous flows of care work within kin networks.

In regard to gender roles, scholars have theorized about how fathers are absent from caregiving roles, clinging to patriarchal ideals in a world that has sentenced them to an emasculated life of unemployment and underemployment or taking up ascribed women's work (Parreñas 2008). However, the development and renegotiation of masculinities for men left behind are often varied and conflicting. Some fathers adopt a strict patriarchal logic because they believe that the transgression in the normative gender ideology—their wives' migration to assume a breadwinner role—strips them of their masculinity. However, a multidirectional care lens focuses on the role of kin networks and local cultures of shared domestic labor in assisting in the transition of fathers and husbands' sense of manhood. It is easier for fathers to take up a greater role in maintaining the household and raising the children postmigration with support and affirmation of kin. Of course, even the best of fathers in transnational families still feel the stigma of the reversal of gender roles even though they have more sources on which to draw their value (i.e., kin, children, migrant counterparts) to combat that stigma. Still, this dialectic between patriarchal logics and daily social conditions is proving to be productive and illustrative of how masculinities are tethered to both local experiences and global processes. Kin contributions to care work in the transnational family remain heavy as they are also helping fathers left behind; their roles becomes key in understanding the fluidity of masculinities within the transnational family.

Lastly, tracing transnational Filipino family histories adds new detail to the history of migration in the Philippines. As demonstrated by the Sancho clan or Vickie and Mauricio, family history shows how care work grows and evolves as a result of migration. More importantly, the histories become an index of the effects of neoliberal immigration policies gone wrong. Historical excavation of reorganized care work with husbands and wives switching to try their hand at working abroad or siblings migrating to take turns to support their families demonstrate the discrepancy of migration as a form of national development. As the journey of migrants illuminates much about migration and globalization, the lives of the families they leave behind highlight their innovative resilience and reworking of care arrangements in the transnational context.

2

Skype Mothers and Facebook Children

Manila

It's humid today. July is rainy season in the Philippines. I'm a bit nervous about being in Barangay 50, a neighborhood in Manila notorious for petty crime and theft. Dianne, Nanay Vickie's daughter,[1] hurries me through the bus terminal and reminds me to hold on to my purse. We arrive at Vickie's home. While it is small, it has such high ceilings that Vickie's husband Mauricio has had room to build a makeshift flat out of plywood to divide the tall space into two stories, with stairs on the side. Zach, Vickie's only son, is sitting in a corner next to the door on the first floor, at the computer with a fan blowing directly on him. The fan does little to battle the heat and humidity so we all sweat. I sit down, a bit dizzy from the hurry and travel, while Dianne sits right next to me smiling. We are meeting in person for the first time, but we have been chatting on Facebook for almost six months. I touch her shoulder and ask her how she's doing. She answers, "Okay naman. I'm okay." Dianne is 16 years old, 5'4" with long black hair and she dons a light pink shirt with an "I Love New York" logo with blue jeans.

Vickie told me Dianne is rather shy but I find she is just the opposite. She sits next to me and immediately starts a conversation with me about her mother. I hurry to get my recorder but miss recording the beginnings of our conversation about her Facebook conversations with her mom about our upcoming visit. She assures me that everyone in her family, in both Manila and New York City, has been looking forward to my visit.

In the beginning of our conversation, Dianne doesn't tell me about teenage love or high school drama. She's still just a kid and the biggest real thing that has happened to her is her mother's departure in 2008. All she asks is how her mother looks and what she does for fun. Ten minutes into our kuwentuhan *(talk-story), I ask her about what has changed about her relationship with her mom since she left. She replies, "Best friend ko siya. Gusto ko siyang alagaan. She's my best friend, I like taking care of her"; her eyes well up and tears start to run down her cheeks. "Pwede kong sabihin sa kanya, kahit ano. Pati nga blog ko pinapabasa ko sa kanya. Para alam niya, na kahit malayo kami, pareho pa rin. I can tell her anything. I even have her read my blog. So she knows that even if we're far away from each other, it's still the same."*

I nod. I'm surprised that she has opened up to me so quickly since this is our first in-person meeting. I think maybe it's because I know her mom so well or maybe all of our online chats have helped me gain her trust. At that moment, the Skype phone rings and Dianne says, "Ok lang, o, dito na siya. It's okay, because she's here now." I'm again surprised. I'm confused about what she means. But a couple of moments later I understand because Nanay Vickie is now on Skype. Tito Mauricio, Nanay Vickie's husband, a strikingly tall man with an apron on, calls us to the table to

Photo 2.1. Portable computer set up in a home in Manila, Philippines, complete with computer, speakers, mic, camera, printer, and fan. Photo courtesy of Valerie Francisco-Menchavez.

have dinner. Everyone has a place around the table and they make sure to leave a space in between me and Dianne for the computer. They angle the portable computer table with a webcam to face the dining table and the awaiting dinner, sour shrimp soup, crab, and meatballs, all of Vickie's favorites so that Vickie, all the way in New York City, can join us.

New York City

It's a chilly November Sunday and I'm happy to be inside. I have just arrived at the flat that Nanay Vickie, Nanay Joan, and Ate Teresa share in Queens, New York. It takes me about five minutes to peel off my winter layers. The three of them live in the attic of a house, with two "bedrooms" separated by collapsible screens. Joan and Vickie, the sisters, share one bedroom and the other is for Teresa, who only comes home on the weekends because she works as a live-in domestic worker during the week. They keep their place neat and the first thing I notice is the four boxes stacked on top of each other, almost touching the ceiling, waiting to be sent back home for the holidays.

Nanay Joan and Ate Teresa are at the market, and Nanay Vickie invites me to sit down and eat lunch. We start our kuwentuhan, *our third, over sour shrimp soup and rice, Vickie's specialty. She waits until I set my recorder down. I ask her to tell me what is hardest about being separated from her family. She replies, "Hindi ko maasikaso 'yung kanilang pag-aaral or igabay sila. That I can't help them with their studies or guide them in their everyday." She starts to cry when talking about her daughter Dianne, who will be going into her first year of college in a month. Her pain is twofold. Not only does she miss her daughter, but Nanay Vickie's employer just moved away so she is unemployed. She is hard on herself as she says, "Kung wala pala akong trabaho, 'di doon na lang ako. If I don't have a job anyway, I should be there."*

After talking for an hour and a half, I hear the sound of dishes being washed and I have the urge to wash my own plate as it has been sitting in front of me for so long. I ask Nanay Vickie to pause for a second and I proceed to the kitchen—but find the kitchen empty and start to wonder where the noise is coming from. So I pop my head back into Nanay Vickie's room. She is looking into her computer corner, complete with a mic, speakers, camera, photo printer, and charger. When she refreshes the screen, I discover that Skype has been on the whole time we have been talk-storying. The clinks of utensils on plates were sounds from someone washing dishes in the Philippines. I ask Nanay Vickie if I have intruded

Photo 2.2. Filipina migrant in New York using Skype to communicate with her family in the Philippines. Photo courtesy of Lorena Sanchez-McRae.

on the time that she and her children were supposed to talk. She says, "Hindi, naka-on lang 'yan. Gusto ko lang marinig sila kahit hindi nila ako kinakausap, gusto ko lang na alam nila na nandito ako. *No, it's just on all the time. I just like to listen to them even if they're not directly talking to me, I just want them to know that I'm here."*

In this transnational vignette, my field notes describe the main paradox in this chapter: the use of technology for communication to build intimacy toward closer relationship building under the conditions of long-term separation through migration. This chapter echoes the aim in this book to scrutinize the reorganization of the family under the neoliberal condition, which includes rapid advancements in technology and also systematic outmigration of people from developing countries like the Philippines. Filipino transnational families navigate these specific developments in neoliberal globalization by creatively sustaining their relationships through new technologies but under circumstances not of their choosing—engineered flows of labor migration that separate families for extended periods of time. The context of new technologies and labor migration is crucial; interconnected parts of neoliberal globalization engender the affective realities and care work demonstrated by Vickie and Dianne. Since the Philippine labor brokerage state regulates and maintains a $25 billion per year labor migration industry by recruiting and exporting Filipinos as migrant workers globally (Chipongian 2016), scaffolding this lucrative migrant export industry is a secondary and almost equally profitable industry of communication technology (i.e., phone cards, roaming mobile telephone services, etc.). Filipino transnational families rely on these technologies to ease the sacrifice, guilt, and hardship they face as they are separated indefinitely. In what follows, I offer a critical analysis of these technological dynamics in the care work of transnational families in the larger historical and political economic trajectory of capitalism that forces families to be separated to begin with. But still through a multidirectional care model, families are utilizing the technologies that are bound up with their condition of separation to craft intimacies specific to their transnational lives.

Social media platforms such as Facebook and video-conferencing applications like Skype offer transnational families new ways to stay connected, easing the strains of long-term separation. Computers and smartphones allow them to communicate frequently and inexpensively in real time. As the vignettes above demonstrate, it also offers them a different way to relate to one another. Technology gives families who are separated over time and space new ways to explore and create intimacies through new digital lives and relationships. Early on in my research, before the popularization of Skype and other video-conferencing applications, I asked migrants and their family members about the hardest thing about being separated. People in New York City and Manila often answered in tears with a common thread:

"*Hindi ko sila nakikita.* That I can't see them."

"I can't see them grow up."

"I can't see Mama's face."

"*Hindi ko alam ang hitsura nila,* I don't know what they look like anymore."

Comments like these narrated the sadness in failing to see or witness the physical growth of family members. Migrants who migrated while the internet was still nascent technology are particularly attuned to how technology has changed the dynamics of the transnational family. Carmie, a 60-year-old migrant mother who has been abroad for more than two decades, says, "You know, internet is magic. It's a magic because before when you write letters it takes months before they receive it. It's the internet that keeps us together. Cam to cam. When I'm not online for two days they worry. So we always talk on Facebook, Yahoo." As technology and communications platforms advanced in leaps and bounds throughout the longitudinal research period of this project, it was apparent that technology changed how family members who are separated relate to one another. Most notably, today's technologies offer unprecedented visual and aural access in real time.

Care work and intimacy between transnational family members are mediated by the advancement in communication technologies, specifically examined here, Skype and Facebook. New care providers, patterns of care work, and forms of care emerge through particular technological venues. Although technology brings new possibilities of supporting relationships over long distances, it also sometimes hinders relationships through its "all seeing eye" character. Transnational family members are impressive in their ability to stay connected through technology, and yet these strategies are only possible in fact because they are necessary in a world where families are forced to be separated to sustain their livelihoods. My aim is to examine, in the frame of multidirectional care, how technology is transforming the relationships in transnational families and how under the neoliberal condition they are transformed.

A Short History of Migration and Technology

Innovations in technology do not exist outside the political and economic conditions that produce them, so it is worth looking back at how transnational families communicated prior to the advent of the internet. Migrants have and continue to sustain relationships with people back home through letters, cassette tapes, landline phones, mobile phones, text messages, and, more recently, emails and internet-based applications. These technologies serve both emotional and practical purposes for transnational communication in the lives of migrants and their families left behind. Still, the frequency and types of technology engender different types of transnational relationships. For example, people interpret relationships with their families left behind quite differently when their only communication consists of infrequent letters over years; it is an entirely different relationship when they stay in touch daily in real time through computer or smartphone. In a historical study of early European immigrants' epistolary relationships with families left behind, David A. Gerber posits that although letters affirmed immigrant ties to the Old World, relationships through this technology were limited to communicating practicalities and formulating plans for future reunion or extended separation (Gerber 2001). Letters from early transnational communities expedited the exchange of information and resources about migration on practicalities of travel and settlement (Foner 2005). This type of correspondence transmitted sensitive information about remittances, costs of living, emergency situations, and shipment of parcels and goods (Wyman 1993). The pragmatic purpose of this communication represents a limited form of intimacy compared to different methods that developed as communication technology advanced.

Historically, Filipina migrant women also relied on letters as their primary form of communication with family members back home. Letters were breaths of fresh air between long periods of time without contact that would inform migrants of how remittances were spent or how a sick family member was doing. Still, the infrequency of this type of communication left migrants feeling isolated and detached from their families. In the late 1990s, mobile phones introduced the entire world to a quicker and more direct form of communication. Compared to a landline phone, the mobile phone let people call more often and more cheaply. Family members both abroad and at home could initiate and return calls at their convenience. The mobile phone substantially changed the quality of relationships for families separated by migration (Horst 2006; Madianou and Miller 2011; Reynolds and Zontini 2006). In the illuminating studies of Jamaican transnationalism, Heather A. Horst and Daniel Miller argue, the mobile phone eased formalities of remittances and communicating emergency situations (Horst and Miller 2006). Now family members could gain a more accurate picture of situations at home and abroad; they could communicate about the sacrifices of migration in unprecedented ways.

While the mobile phone gave both migrants and family members comfort in knowing they could get in touch at almost any time, such access to one another's daily life continues to give way to surveillance and harassment. Migrants demand to know daily movements of spouses, while children and relatives left behind stress their need for more and more financial support (Riak-Akuei 2005). Additionally, the cost and maintenance of the mobile phone becomes another burden for the transnational family. Scholars have found that although mobile phones have allowed more quality communication between transnational families, ambivalence about constant communication remains (Madianou and Miller 2011). In her research on Mexican transnational families, Joanna Dreby found that phone calls alleviated some of the strain of separation, but they also brought up feelings of shame and guilt for migrant parents who were not able to see their young children grow up (Dreby 2010).

The Short Message Service (SMS), or text messages as they are more popularly known, developed alongside the mobile phone. In the Philippines, a majority of Filipinos from different class backgrounds had access to prepaid phones for the sole purpose of texting. Long before texting was popular in the United States, Filipinos found texting to be a cheap and viable form of communication with people both near and far. For migrants, text messages presented a more covert and private way to communicate with families at home or friends nearby. Text messages on mobile phones can be received at any time without migrants having to physically interrupt a workday or conversation to receive information or communication (Lan 2006). The cost of texts, their brevity, and their ability to distribute information widely and quickly contribute to a more rapid updating system for migrants and their families back home. Texts are also used for more colloquial and conversational exchanges like jokes, poems, riddles, and personal messages (Horst 2006; Lan 2006). In fact, text messages' rapidity and frequency are equally as important as the content for transnational communication (Licoppe and Smoreda 2005). Text messages allow separated families to exchange daily banter, helping them to feel closer despite the long distances.

The onset of the internet in the late 1980s changed transnational life along with everything else. For migrants, the virtual world intensified what the aforementioned communication technologies already provided. Migrants and their families in the late 1990s and early 2000s managed separation through unreliable phone calls, gifts, and remittances (Dreby 2010). Migrant parents sent gifts of clothes and toys that were age-inappropriate or no longer fit growing children, the time difference making it difficult for them to provide anything but financial support for their children. In contrast to the Mexican migrants at the turn of the twenty-first century, these mothers can offer their children much more than financial support and gifts. The internet has provided more ways for migrants to stay involved in the transnational activities of their families positively and also ambivalently (Madianou 2012). The internet has facilitated a host of different uses for migrants and those left behind and for their transnational life more generally. It has facilitated support for hometown associations (Levitt 2001), political campaigns (D. E. Smith 2006), and cultural diffusion (Vertovec 2009). The internet's entry into the lives of people who live in a transnational context accurately describes the simultaneity in which they live, together yet apart. Yet, the nature of technology is that of rapid advancement. The swiftness of changing internet interfaces and computer communication technologies parallels the changing dynamics of social relations produced by them. Even by the time this book is published, major communication shifts will have already given way to new forms of social media, interactions, and relations.

The remainder of this chapter examines how technology—the internet in particular—shapes intimate relationships among members of transnational families. If letters informed migrants about issues of the family left behind in a delayed manner, thus shaping the relationships of transnational family members, Skype and Facebook update migrants abroad in real time, producing different types of interactions and relations.

Skype Mothers: Presence and Surveillance

Rapidly developing video conference applications such as Skype, Gmail video chat, Yahoo Messenger video chat, and Apple FaceTime enable family members to be virtually present in one another's lives. The visual register on these mobile and desktop programs is a new window into the lives of family members who are separated. Although scholars argue that technological interaction often makes it difficult to create and maintain intimacy (Pea et al. 2012), I find that the conditions of long-term separation and the specific characteristic of undocumentation that are ascribed to many migrants in this study leave transnational families with few options for building meaningful memories with each other. Video-conferencing technology, at times, becomes the only viable option for literally seeing their families whom they are physically away from for years at a time. Although the visual register of these technologies is a special feature that may enhance relationship building in families, the key aspect of undocumentation for migrants in this study makes this "face-to-face" interaction even more unique given that they are unable to return to their families indefinitely as a result of the broken immigration systems that push them to illegality (Abrego 2014). The migrant mothers in New York City I interviewed managed their absence in Manila by being present online for communicating with and monitoring their families back home. As Vickie's story shows, although she cannot touch her quickly growing children, she can at least see them face to face on a daily basis and join them for something as basic as dinnertime.

Video conferencing changes how migrants relate with their families and loved ones at home. Seeing a face on a screen produces a sense of integration and presence. Even if Vickie is away she is still present through technology. She tells her children, "*Bukasan ang online 'pag dating sa bahay.* Turn on the internet once you get home." Her presence through Skype adds another dimension to her participation in the maintenance of the family at home in Manila. Since Manila is exactly twelve hours ahead of New York City, Vickie's children get home from school just as she's getting ready for work. Other women I interviewed also kept themselves apprised of daily activities through Skype sessions. Some indicated that they wanted to be "in the room" even if the children were just getting ready for school. Anne, a migrant mother, says, "I just like hearing them move around" about her four sons who would get ready for middle and high school in the morning in Manila just as she was winding down her day in New York City. Anne was perfectly fine with her sons not talking with her as they clanked bowls for breakfast and hurriedly readied bags for school. As they were getting ready, Anne would also busy herself with dinnertime rituals of cooking rice and other household chores. She would ask them about their homework or bus fare. Anne's sons would shout out their goodbyes as they headed out the door. As her home in Manila quieted down, her husband would appear in the Skype window to update her on his day's activities. Quickly thereafter, Anne would retire for the night. Seeing and "being with" family members through mundane processes was not an especially involved project of keeping up a conversation. Skype's ability to bring the transnational family in the same room through their computers was more important than actual conversations. Anne's comments about liking the sound of her sons getting ready point to the affective reality that "being with" is more than conversations; it includes feeling integrated in the everyday lives and processes of families in the Philippines. For her youngest son Buddy, a 12-year-old tech-savvy boy, turning on Skype as he woke up and calling his mother in New York City became his dutiful task. And although Buddy didn't always talk to his mother as he wiped sleep from his eye, the gesture of setting up Skype and calling was a form of multidirectional care work he invested in every morning for his mother. He knew that it mattered to her to even hear the family get ready in the morning.

The actual practice of seeing family members through video-conferencing apps allows migrants and families left behind to work together to produce relationships that foster meaningful integration into one another's significant family milestones. The Sancho family's practice of technology and fostering intimacy demonstrates how Skype is a multidirectional mode of care that is often facilitated by both migrants and their families left behind and that creates possibilities for building intimacy for both groups on different ends of the transnational family spectrum. The six siblings are more like best friends than siblings. They joke around with a scathing sense of humor in a way that only loved ones can, using street slang to insult one another with laughter following shortly after. From their mother's migration in the 1970s to their diasporic family that places half of their siblings in Israel, Japan, and the United States, they all share the understanding that they have to work at sustaining their closeness even if they are apart. They do this in name, giving godparent responsibilities to one another so that they have parenting ties to all the children in their family regardless of what country the children live in. Their transnational family relies on Skype to make animate these nominal relationships.

Rita immigrated in 1992. She was a single woman in her mid-twenties who left to support her aging parents and the nieces and nephews in her family. In a staggered pattern, the Sancho sisters migrated for work to take turns as family breadwinner. Rita, unlike some of her sisters, never made it back to the Philippines to live. She settled in New York City, got married, and bought a home with her husband in New Jersey. Still, her relationship with her siblings hasn't changed. Leslie, Rita's sister closest in age, is a single mother who lives in the family house in Metro Manila. Leslie tells me that Rita has a special affection for Leslie's son Kela, as he was the first child born to the group of siblings. Rita provides primary financial support for Kela. Leslie describes how the webcam allowed Rita to become integrated into Kela's life as he grew up:

> 'Yan ang drama dati. 'Yung voice tape, (dramatic voice) boses lang, eh ngayon, hi-tech na. Pero kasi ang problema dun, hindi mo mavi-visualize, mavi-visualize 'yung bata, ang maganda ngayon, nakikita mo 'yung bata lumalaki, sa internet 'di ba? Kahit papaano.

> That was the drama back then. The voice tape (dramatic voice) only her voice, but now, it's high tech. Because the problem back then is you couldn't visualize, visualize the kid, what's nice today, is you can see the kid grow up, on the internet, right? At the very least that.

Leslie notes that the webcam allows Rita to *see* Kela grow and therefore, she might not feel as alienated as she had before when she could only send her voice back home or only hear Kela's voice. "*Kahit papaano.* At the very least that" suggests that communication with Rita is a reciprocation, a sort of payback in exchange for Rita's migration and continued support for Kela. Leslie is engaging in multidirectional care through Skype; she understands that communication through this visual interface allows Rita to stay up-to-date and therefore reassures her that her nephew Kela is doing well. As Leslie notes, technology now allows Rita to see Kela in real time, to *see* her beloved nephew grow taller, bigger, and more mature. A long-term serial migrant like Rita once clung to the memory of the face of her nephew the last time they saw one another; now Skype allows her to not only cling to the memory of his face but to see it again and again as he grows. Skype helps Rita feel close to Kela but it is also a particular type of intimacy building between Rita and Leslie. Rita's role and desire to see Kela grow is particularly special to Leslie, as she can build her relationship based on her real-time relationship with Kela. Often it is on Leslie's phone that Kela and Rita are chatting; Leslie is often interjecting side comments and jokes on their conversations. In this way, facilitating daily conversations with Rita is a form of care through Skype, but it is also a way to sustain the bond between the sisters.

Seeing the faces of families left behind makes a difference in how migrants transition into separation and their new lives away from their loved ones. Rose migrated in 2003, leaving her husband and four children when the children were 1, 2, 5, and 8 years old. Her youngest son JJ was just an infant when she had to quickly pack up and leave with her employer, a diplomat who was moving from Manila to New York City. Now JJ is almost 10. Rose has been away for most of the formative years of her children's lives. She remembers the first years of her duty as a domestic worker for a Philippine diplomat:

> Kasi nandoon ako sa diplomat noon, kasi almost two years din ako nandoon na may trabaho tapos wala naman akong laptop wala naman. 'Di ko sila makita katulad ngayon, kung hanggang ano lang tawag, phonecard, text ganyan. Nung first year ko dito siyempre gabi-gabi akong umiyak.

> Because I was with the diplomat then, because I was with them almost two years working for them then I didn't have a laptop, nothing. I couldn't see them like I do now, it would only be through calls, phone cards, text, like that. My first year here, of course, I cried every night.

Rose's first job in the United States was marked by abuse, exploitation, and isolation, which I return to in a later chapter. She endured difficult work conditions because her employer withheld her passport, causing her immigration paperwork to fall out of legal status. Her undocumented status led her to believe that making claims about better wages and work conditions or better quality of life was out of the question. She thus surrendered her ability to communicate with her family in her first two years in the United States; she could not even get a laptop computer for herself with her hard-earned wages. She sent all of her wages back to her family so they could purchase a complete computer with camera and mics so that one day they could use it to communicate with her. It was important to her to "see" her children, understanding that "seeing" them meant talking with them through a webcam. Her statement privileges webcam communication over phone calls and texts because it allows her to *see* them and for them to *see* her. In Rose's case, she is unable to return to her family until they all finish college—her ultimate goal in migrating. Until then, the visual register of the webcam is often the only thing Rose has as a way of being with and keeping up with her children.

For children left behind, the visual register of Skype also legitimizes their relationship with their migrant mothers even if they have spent most of their lives separated; seeing their mothers on video-conferencing apps gives them an authentic connection to them. I asked Rose's two youngest children, Grace and JJ who were 11 and 10 at the time of the interview, about using Skype to talk to their mother:

> JJ: *Dati po telepono, ngayon mas Skype.* In the past, telephone, now more Skype.
>
> GRACE: *Nanibago nga po kami noong makita namin siya kasi ang taba niya! (laughs)* We were shocked when we first saw her because she was so chubby! (laughs)
>
> JJ: *Tumaba siya eh!* (laughs) She got chubby! (laughs)
>
> GRACE: *Payat kasi, ang payat kasi niya noong umalis siya dito. Tapos payat na maitim.* She was thin, she was thin when she left here. Then, she was thin and dark skinned.
>
> JJ: *Ngayon pumuti!* (laughs) Now she's white! (laughs)
>
> GRACE: *Pumuti siya.* She got lighter.
>
> JJ: *Sabi nila ng mga friend niya dito tumaba eh tumaba tapos puma, pumuti sabi ng mga friend niya dito.* Her friends here said that she got fat, eh fatter, then, whi, whiter, said all of her friends here.
>
> GRACE: *Marami nang changes.* Lots of changes.
>
> JJ: *'Lagi niyang tinitingnan 'yung height naming apat. Kung gaano na daw kami katangkad, tapos 'yung ano 'yung head tapos 'yung ano lagi talaga niyang binabantayan 'lagi 'yung height namin.* She always looks at our height, us four. How tall we're getting, then measuring our heads, then um, she always keeps track of our height.
>
> GRACE: *Parang ano, gusto niya makita kung gaano kabilis kaming lumaki. Sabi ko nga, gaano siya kabilis tumaba? Para lumaki tayong lahat, sama-sama! (laughs)* It's like um, she wants to see how fast we are growing. I told her how fast are you getting chubbier? So we can grow together! (laughs)

In this conversation, JJ and Grace remember when their family transitioned to regular use of webcams. They note that seeing their mother for the first time surprised them and her appearance was the first thing they spoke about. Of course, JJ's and Grace's memories of their mother's physical appearance when she left are probably an amalgamation of pictures from the past and stories from other family members. In their recollection of this transition to webcam technology, they deemed it important for me to know that they knew the difference between their mother then and now. Their comments on how chubbier or lighter she became during her time in the United States intimated that they know their mother in a much more corporeal sense than if they were just talking on the phone like before. Further, the story they are telling about physical growth in height and weight includes dimensions of family life that, in the past, would likely not come up through phone or letters. Tracking height or weight becomes a sign of a physical closeness, an intimacy that the distance of migration could not allow before. Now, because of the visual register of mobile and computer cameras, the ability to see one another means families can have a physical connection that migration and separation took from them.

Rose could not see her children grow taller and bigger before the popularity of Skype and especially as she suffered under deep isolation from an exploitative employer. However, after sending her wages back home and prioritizing the purchase of technology she strove to escape from her diplomat employer to seek a new job that would enable her to continue working but also be in constant contact with her family. "*Kailangan ko silang makita, kaya ako tumakas.* I needed to see them, that's why I escaped," Rose remarked about changing her situation. "*Parang 'di lang hanggang pera ang nakikita nila, mukha ko rin.* So that it's not just money they see, it's my face too." Seeing her children through webcam became tantamount to the financial remittances Rose sent back to her family. She interprets her contact with them through Skype and a webcam as part of her maternal responsibilities, but the fact that she could see her children made her motherly duties more urgent.

Grace's last comment about growing fat and tall brings this point home; the visual component of the webcam lets transnational families experience corporeality in a way that they could not before. Because of Rose's undocumented status and her inability to go home and see her children for more than nine years, this type of technology means more than just a way to keep in touch. Skype and a webcam assisted Rose in fulfilling her mothering role from afar, but it also calls on JJ and Grace to interact with their mom so as to affirm that she is fulfilling her parental tasks. Grace's remark that "we can grow together" provides insight into how a child interprets the role of Skype in maintaining a relationship to a mother from far away. She offers togetherness as a new way to think about reciprocal care, with each family member doing their part in creating the intimacy they desire from one another.

Video-conferencing apps and webcams bring migrant family members into rooms where day-to-day affairs are ongoing. Leslie discusses how the webcam opens up a whole new world for migrants and their families left behind:

> Pero ngayon, parang nandun sila sa internet, Skype, kahit wala silang sinasabi, 'yun na ang trend ngayon. Naka . . . naka-mic lang sila, parang lang nili-live nila 'yung . . . kagigising lang nung bata, nagho-homework, nagluluto si Tatay.

> But now, they're there on the internet, Skype, even if they aren't saying anything. That's the trend now. They . . . they're on the mic, and it's like live. They see us live, when the kids get up, when they're doing their homework, when Dad is cooking.

Leslie notes how banal life becomes consumable, even an enjoyable part of transnational family life. Being "live" on the webcam invites migrants to be around, close, and present even from afar. Maya, Rose's eldest daughter, says:

> Noong simula noong nakaka-chat naman namin siya sa webcam 'lagi naman kaming nagkikita parang ganoon na rin parang 'lagi na rin siyang nandito.

> When we started chatting with her on the webcam, we always see each other. It's like before, it's like she's always here.

Streaming someone else's daily life "live" lets family members in the Philippines imagine that their migrant family members can experience the mundane as if they are "here," as Maya states. As migrants watch, witness, and take part in the daily happenings in their homes, trust, closeness, and familiarity form the foundation of their intimate relationships. This social process mediated by technology is an aspect of multidirectional care, given that both families left behind and migrants are engaged in time, energy, and choices to go "live." These quotes provide the affective background that motivates transnational family members committed to turning on their webcams and interacting, actively or passively, with one another on Skype. But surely, this type of integration requires a decision and choice to let migrant members into daily life practices in the Philippines.

Vickie talks about the feeling of closeness and integration she feels with her family in Manila because she can be online:

'Pag naka-online kami, alam mo 'yung lahat nangyayari, sa araw-araw. Nasisi-yahan ako 'pag alam ko na araw-araw na gumagawa sila ng rebyu o nakikisama sa isa't isa. Parang nakikita ko sila matured. You believe in yourself that you are not a fail as a mom.

You know when we're always online, you find out what's going on, you start to know what's happening every day. It makes me feel better when I know every day they are doing homework and taking care of each other. It's like I see they're maturing. You believe in yourself that you didn't fail as a mom.

Vickie likes to set up her webcam when she gets home from work and keeps it on as she does chores around her apartment in Queens. Her webcam doesn't necessarily need around-the-clock attention, but by being signed on she makes herself available. She watches her children doing homework or listens in when her daughter Dianne makes breakfast for her brother Zach; she watches as if she were right there with them. I asked Dianne about her mother's online presence and she answered,

Everyday naman nag-o-online. Minsan 'pag mag-isa ako okay lang basta ka-chat ko siya. Binubuksan 'pag gumagawa ng work niya, gumagawa ako ng work ko. Pagka may work siya, every day time dito tapos night doon. Ngayon kasi wala siyang work kaya every day at every night kausap namin siya.

Everyday we're online. Sometimes when I'm by myself, I just chat with her. She turns it on when she's doing her work and when I'm doing my work. When she has work, every morning here and night there. But now, she has no work so now we talk to her in the day and night.

The frequency of interaction through webcam between Vickie and her family in Manila mimics her physical presence in their home. Because of her ability to stay present with, integrated into, and knowledgeable about the family's daily routines, the family bonds appear seamless. Of course, being present through webcam—the very connection—relies on having the parties at each end sign on. The very action of turning on Skype is a form of multidirectional care that Dianne and Zach participate in, as they know that being present on the webcam gives Vickie a feeling of relief. Maintaining Skype sessions underscores the importance of simultaneity as Vickie and her family, actually and figuratively, let one another into their daily routines even as they are occurring thousands of miles apart. Logging on and even passively interacting with one another may seem like a trivial act of service for one another, but the "being with" even on Skype is a bridge that separated family members treasure.

Yet, the ability of migrants and families left behind to see one another online also produces an affect of surveillance: The daily use of webcams means someone is always watching. In her provocative work on Jamaican transnational families, Heather A. Horst found that mobile phones allowed migrants to stay involved in the day-to-day affairs of their families, but that communication also always relied on the watchful eye and self-reporting of the voice on the other end. Similarly, migrants often use the webcam to ensure that families back home aren't spending their hard-earned money on lavish things or are doing work around the house. Families left behind can find that sort of surveillance exasperating. The cousins Dianne, Zach, Melann, and Chris, children of Vickie and Joan, discuss how they sometimes find reprieve from their mothers "watching" them:

VALERIE: *Anong sinasabi ninyo sa kanila 'pag bukas ng online?* What do you tell them when they first get online?

DIANNE: *Ah, 'yung reporting namin? Minsan . . . hindi kumpleto . . .* (laughs) Oh our reporting, you mean? Sometimes, incomplete?

VALERIE: What do you mean?

ZACH: *Kailangan may konting pagtatago!* (laughs) There's gotta be some secrets! (laughs)

CHRIS: *Like minsan, ano umm . . . pupunta ka sa ganito o tamad ka, so may konting ano 'yun, na sabihin gagawa ka ng project. Minsan hindi ka gagawa ng project. Ituro lang ang webcam pababa ng konti!* Like sometimes, um . . . when you wanna go somewhere or you're just lazy, just say you have a project to do. Sometimes you don't work on the project. Just point the camera a little downward!

DIANNE: *Uy! Hindi ako ganun!* (laughs) Hey! I'm not like that!

MELANN: *Uy! Lahat tayo ganun!* (laughs) Hey! We're all like that!

Children here, just like children in families that live under one roof, create strategies to evade their parents' gaze. Although the cousins' mothers live thousands of miles away, the game of cat and mouse still continues. When Skype becomes surveillance, computer technology eases anxieties for migrants abroad, but it can trigger anxieties for families left behind as well.

Video-conferencing apps and cameras on computers or smartphones give transnational families an unprecedented way to be present on a daily basis. While the frequency of communication is not so different from traditional communications such as the phone, the visual interface of this type of technology mediates the type of care that results from it. If the cameras cover the basics of keeping up with daily activities and even disciplining the household, Facebook makes room for a different type of relationship building.

Facebook Children: Boundaries, Friendship, and Intimacies

Transnational families are using social media platforms like Facebook (before that, Friendster and Myspace and now Instagram, Snapchat, etc.) to stay abreast of one another's daily activities and interests. On this type of application, families exchange emotional care work through their online interactions, as well as practical and useful skills about how to use the very media through which they communicate. When family members tutor each other on the ins and outs of Facebook, the exchange actually helps foster intimate familial bonds. For example, Rose keeps in touch with her eldest Maya, 14 years old at the time of this interview, through Facebook. Rose had been living and working in New York City for almost a decade; Maya lives in Manila. When I talk with Maya, she tells me about how Facebook brings her and her mother closer:

> *Tinuturuan ko siyang gumawa ng Facebook account kasi nga mayroon libangan 'yung games sa Facebook. Tapos nung natutunan niya na ang marami, tinuturuan din niya ako kasi ano para daw, ano, magkalaro kami sa games. Kasi 'yun din daw 'yung nagpaluwag sa kanya.*

> I taught her how to make an account because then she'd have something to bide her time with, the games on Facebook. Then when she learned a lot more, she taught me, because, um, so that, um, we could play games together. Because that's what helps her feel better.

In this case, the first type of care work circulated is technological advice. When Maya uses the term *nagpaluwag,* literally translated as to ease or provide comfort, the exchange of skills through Facebook is an expression of care work that Maya and Rose exchange. Maya's initiation of this skill share and Rose's instruction of Maya on new game strategies become the basis for further intimacy. Maya interprets the gesture of teaching her mother how to log on to Facebook not solely as a utilitarian act but also as a form of care toward her mother who may be feeling lonely. By correlating *nagpaluwag* and emotionality, Maya recognizes that this skill share operates on dual levels of practicality and care work.

Children who are friends with their mothers on Facebook are allowing their mothers to come into a social part of their life that mothers might not have been privy to if they were physically in the same vicinity. Many daughters of migrant mothers, inadvertently, let their mothers in a little too much. Maya says:

> *Noong tinuruan ko siyang gumawa ng account sa Facebook, nilagay niya 'yung picture ko para matutunan niya lang. Tapos 'yun, doon siya nagsimulang mag-tanong kasi picture ko lang 'yung ginamit niya, ang daming nagco-comment, na ang dami daw may crush sa akin. So ganyan kaya nagtanong siya na may boyfriend ka na ba kasi sa Facebook pa lang daw ang dami nang nagtatanong, paano pa daw kaya pag ano, sa totoo.*

> When I taught her how to make a Facebook account, she put my picture up just so she could learn it. Then, that's when it started, she started asking because my picture was the one she used and a lot of people started to comment on it, she told me that there were so many guys who were crushing on me. So then, she asked if I had a boyfriend because if on Facebook so many people were asking about me, what more in real life.

Maya had not anticipated the repercussions when she let her mother post a picture of her. She did it as part of a technological exchange of skills and care. However, when the unintended consequence of her mother asking around about her personal life backfired, she realized that sharing this digital platform let her mother into topics that she would have preferred to keep private. Later on in our conversation, Maya yields to the platform's sometimes invasive qualities:

> *'Pag pinag-usapan namin ang mga crush crush na ganyan, nakakahiya nga kay Mommy, pero kasi nakikita niya na sa Facebook. Sasabihin ko na lang.*

> When we talk about crushes, I sometimes feel embarrassed with Mommy. But because she sees it on Facebook, I just tell her anyway.

In her realization that Facebook invites her mother into dimensions of her social life that she would have preferred to keep private, Maya learns to accept the consequences of social media. By "just telling her anyway," Maya surrenders to the fact that the site will eventually show all the social parts of her life to her mother. Maya accepts this as a part of building a relationship with her mother, who hasn't been around for almost a decade. Facebook offers both Maya and her mother an unprecedented forum for sharing their daily lives. Indeed, Maya is not the only one adjusting to the intimacy that Facebook offers. Rose says,

> *'Pag nakikita ko ang mga bagong pictures, parang shini-share nila sa'kin 'yung bagay na 'yon. So feeling ko, pwede ko silang tanungin tungkol sa mga status updates nila sa Facebook.*

When I see new pictures, it's like they are sharing those things with me. So I feel like, I can ask them about their status updates on Facebook.

Here, Rose expresses gratitude for feeling like she is a part of her family's life in the Philippines. Photos on Facebook continue while phone calls and emails also help Rose feel more connected despite the distance.

At other times, letting your mother in on your social life on Facebook can become as cumbersome as having her around to remind you of your chores. The site encourages people to perform social life digitally. Therefore, all of the things you share on the site are available for comments, literally and figuratively. Friends and family can comment on status updates and mobile uploads of photos the moment they are posted. Dianne, Vickie's 16-year-old daughter, discusses her mother's commentary:

> *Actually nag-away kami . . . (laughs) kasi nag-comment siya sa mga post ko eh . . . ako kasi post lang ako post. Tapos sinabihan ko siya, "Ma, huwag ka ngang comment ng comment!"*

> Actually, we got into a fight . . . (laughs) because she kept commenting on all of my posts, cuz me, I just post and post whatever. Then I had to tell her, "Ma, don't keep commenting and commenting!"

> Valerie: *Anong sabi niya?* What did she say?

> *Wala lang. Okay lang daw, sige hindi na nga sabi niya. Pero sabi ko sa kanya, piliin niya lang, hindi 'yung lahat! (laughs)*

> Nothing. She said okay, she won't do it anymore. But I told her, just choose some things, not all of it! (laughs)

As this case demonstrates, children do not wholly surrender their lives to their mothers and families on Facebook—they can draw boundaries. Facebook offers options to limit who sees what—but those choices can shut migrant family members out of the picture entirely. Althea is 23 years old. She has been separated from her mother Olivia since she was 2. For Althea, fostering a relationship with her mother through Facebook is tricky:

> *Me, I don't think about it. I just post. And then one time sabi niya sa'kin, dahil dun nakita niya . . . parang nakikita niya yung hitsura ko. Pangit, uy payat-payat mo mukha ka ng adik ganyan, ganyan. Sawang-sawa na ako sa suot mo! Malaswa! Kaya hindi ka nagustuhan ni ganito! Ganyan, ganyan. Hala! Parang feeling niya siguro napaka-ano ko . . . 'yung dahil dun sa technology nakikita niya rin. Kaya ngayon, kunyari 'pag magpo-post ako, umm . . . kunwari naka-suot ako ng ano ng tama . . . tinatago ko na lang para hindi na niya makita.*

Me, I don't think about it. I just post. And then one time she said, because of what she saw . . . like she saw what I was wearing. Ugly, I'm so skinny, I look like an addict, like this and like that. I've seen you wear that before! How improper! That's why this person doesn't like you! Blah, blah. You better watch it! I think she feels that I'm so . . . but it's because of the technology that she sees it too. That's why now, when I post, um . . . I pretend that I wear something nice . . . I hide other things from her so she doesn't see.

The quality of the relationship between Althea and Olivia is strained, in part of course because they have been apart for most of Althea's life. The judgmental and then guarded interaction they have on Facebook reflects a lack of trust offline and also exacerbates their prickly relationship. Social media sites such as Facebook allow for a relationship between migrants and their families left behind, but one that is heavily mediated by what Erving Goffman calls "impression management" (Goffman 1959). As privacy settings on a Facebook profile are adjusted to show what one wants the world to see, these intentions are filtered through the types of relationships transnational family members want to foster in their digital friendships.

Facebook helped the members of transnational families to foster friendship. While a migrant is abroad, decades can pass. Sites such as Facebook give families the option of sharing daily life and give migrants a way to stay abreast of the changing dimensions of family life back home. Melanie is a migrant mother of three who migrated in her mid-fifties when her children were in their teens and shortly after her seventeenth wedding anniversary. At the time of our first interaction, she had been separated from her husband and children for about two years. From my repeated visits to Melanie's family home in Olongapo, Manila, and her apartment in Queens, I knew that the family understood Melanie's migration as a family decision given that Melanie's two youngest children had aspirations to go to college after high school. This shared understanding of Melanie's sacrifice provided a basis for the family to find specific ways to continue building their relationships through various communications technologies. Melanie learns more about her 15-year-old son Brian:

'Yung bunso ko naman naging active sa Facebook, dun ko lang na-find out na magaling siya, 'yun bang hidden talents niya. Nung maliit siya sumasayaw siya pero ngayon nagpe-perform talaga na! Nagsasayaw! Ina-upload niya 'yung video! Cumo-comment ako parati, lahat sila artist, magaling mag-sketch. Kung makikita mo 'yung ano ni Brian eh, magaling mag-sketch, mag-drawing.

My youngest son he started being active on Facebook, that's when I found out that he's good at, you know, his hidden talents. When he was small, he used to dance but now he really performs! Dancing! Then he uploads the video! I always comment on it, all of them are artists, they're good at sketching. If you could see Brian's stuff, eh, he's good at sketching, drawing.

The "hidden talents" of her son Melanie finds out about through Facebook helps her feel connected to him. When he posts his artwork or dance videos, Melanie can view and comment on his activities. She provides a form of care by supporting him through Facebook. Similarly, he is caring for her by making these posts visible for her to view and comment on. This relationship becomes the fodder for their conversations over Skype or through text messages. Although the digital interaction may seem commonplace—just one person viewing another person's life through social media—these details are immensely important to a family separated indefinitely. The details allow members of the family to feel that they are in the "know" about each other's lives, even if it is about mundane things like dancing and hobbies.

Another example of a family striving to share the banality of everyday life with one another is Rutsi's relationship with her children. Rutsi migrated in 2000, leaving her children when all three were in grade school and only just forming their own likes and hobbies. They are now in high school and exploring different hobbies. Rutsi learns about these activities from Facebook:

> Sa Facebook, nakikita ko 'yung mga pictures, 'lagi 'pag may mga pagka-proud ka. Proud na proud ka! Lalo sa mga achievements ng mga anak mo. Magiging proud ka talaga. Lalo 'yung ikalawa ko na nag-join siya ng modeling ba tapos nasakay siya sa taf five! Masaya talaga ako nun! Gwapo talaga anak kung gumaganun siya. Tapos umm ang bunso ko active sila sa sayawan! Eh active talaga silang tatlo sa sayaw-sayaw. 'Di ko alam pala na lav na lav nila ang sayawan!

> On Facebook, I see the pictures, and I can always feel proud about something. Very proud! Especially because of my children's achievements. You'll really be proud. Especially my second child, he joined a modeling competition and landed in the top five! I was so happy! My son's really good looking if he got up there. Then, um, my youngest, active in dance! Well, all three of them really like to dance. I didn't even know that they loved dancing!

Rutsi discovers from Facebook that her son aspires to be a model and that all of her children love to dance. By sharing on Facebook, the children give Rutsi a glimpse into their lives. She reads their posts as things and events that her children think are important accomplishments in their everyday lives. Thus, she is able to view and consume what is important to them.

The surveillance aspect, while sometimes bothersome to children left behind (like Maya, Dianne, and Althea), is highly desirable for migrants. The feeling that you are sharing your every move with your friends and family in the Philippines gives migrants a sense of connection, healing the isolation they often feel as migrants. Photos and updates of family members in the Philippines on the social networking site give migrant women access to their families that they cannot achieve through phone calls or letters. Instead of feeling like their connection to their family back home is merely financial, migrants use social media to get to know the people that they are supporting.

Lorna, a 54-year-old woman, originally immigrated to New York City with a plan to stay for just two years. Since she had no children, she ended up staying for five years in order to support her niece, who is taking up nursing, as well as her ailing mother. The telephone is the most regular communication technology that Lorna used, but recently she has been using Facebook to talk with her niece. She says, "I'm the cool *tita*. Because I'm friends on Facebook with her, I know about her boyfriend *na* because she changed it to 'In a Relationship.' Before her mother even knew. I tell her, it's okay to have boyfriend but you also finish your studies. I'm paying for that, you know! (laughs)." In our conversation, Lorna prides herself on her ability to know a very personal part of her niece's life. Lorna feels like she has a more meaningful connection to her niece. As a result, her financial support for her niece's nursing school education isn't just an isolated deposit of money but an investment in someone's holistic future—a friendship, a more human connection.

Social media networking sites depend in large part on users to continuously post photos and status updates. Constant updating allows all members of a transnational family who are connected as "friends" to observe and, to a certain degree, participate in each other's lives despite distance, time apart, and even different time zones. Migrants in New York City post status updates, reporting on how they are doing, whether they are working late, or whether they are in the Hamptons for the summer and cannot be contacted by phone or video chat. Melanie states:

> Sa Facebook, mga kumustahan lang pero ina-update ko galing ako sa trabaho. 'Gaya ng isang beses, sabado kasi. May date night sila Priscilla [boss ko] so umuwi ako, ano na 11:30 p.m. Nag-update ako para alam nila na 'di ako maka-katawag. O 'pag nasa Hampton at madalang lang ako maka-computer, update ko para alam nila na humihinga pa ako (laughs).

On Facebook, we ask each other how we're doing but I always update when I'm coming from work. Like one time, on a Saturday. Priscilla [my boss] held a gathering at night so I went home at 11:30 p.m. I update so they know I can't call. Or if I'm in the Hamptons and I can't use the computer much, I write a status update so they know I'm still breathing (laughs).

Melanie uses Facebook to keep her family abreast of her daily movements. She likes that Facebook keeps her whereabouts and activities known to her social network, which includes her family. In addition, migrants use Facebook to share their lives outside work. In a group interview with four migrant women, Vickie says:

> *Ay naku, 'di ko pa na-upload 'yung mga pictures galing sa Cherry Blossom. Sayang 'di makikita ni Dianne 'yung napuntahan natin bago siyang pumunta ng iskul!*

> Oh man, I haven't been able to upload the pictures from the Cherry Blossom festival. It's a shame that Dianne won't be able to see where we went before she goes to school!

Melanie replies:

> *Ah, ako ina-upload ko 'yan, automatic 'pag dating sa bahay. Para naman makita nila na kahit konti may kabonggahan naman ang buhay.*

> Oh, me, I upload it automatically when I get home. So, at least, they see that there's some flare in life.

This conversation between migrant women reveals how important it is to them to share their lives outside work on Facebook. They feel that portraying their lives as made up solely of work would be inaccurate. They also want to share information about their days off, excursions, and social gatherings to assure their families left behind that they are faring well.

Brian, Melanie's son, speaks jokingly about one particular interaction he had with his mother on Facebook:

> *Brian! Nakita mo na ba 'yung mga picture ko? Mag-comment ka naman. Tuwing ako 'pag nag-like ako, bakit ni-like mo lang, nasaan 'yung comment mo? Tapos nag-comment ako, "Ma, ang cute mo." Bakit ang ikli ng comment mo? (laughs) Sabi ko, "Ma, ano bang gusto mong comment ko, magco-copy paste ako from the internet tapos ipa-paste ko na lang!"*

> Brian! Did you see my picture? C'mon and comment on it. And when I "like" it, why did you only "like" it, where's your comment? (laughs) Then I commented, "Ma, you're cute." She says, "Why is your comment so short?" I said, "Ma, what do you want, I'll just copy and paste it from the internet!"

The ability to banter back and forth in real time fosters intimate familial relationships. The ability to communicate multiple times a day gives a new dimension to transnational relationships. And it is important for Melanie and other migrants like her not only to upload photos of her life in New York City but to know that her children and husband see and comment on the photos. In turn, Brian says, "I comment because I like to see what she does when she's not working. With or without the pressure." Brian's more serious tone in this follow-up comment highlights how important it is to him to see what his mother does and to keep up with her as well.

Family members in the Philippines are equally attentive to their Facebook profiles, uploading photos of family outings or other events that their migrant family members might be interested in. It is a type of care work that invites migrant family members to partake in occasions such as graduations or birthdays or events as simple as a Sunday dinner. Dianne says:

> *Ina-upload ko kasi natutuwa siya pagka lumalabas kami together, kaming tatlo. Nakikita niya na may kaya na kaming kumain sa labas. Nati-treat niya kami. Pinapagalitan si Papa ni Mama 'pag ayaw niyang sumama sa'min nga eh! (laughs)*

> I upload [pictures] because she's happy when we all go out together, us three. She sees that, now, we can eat out. Her treat. She even gets mad at Papa when he doesn't want to come with us! (laughs)

Dianne, with her father and her brother, sees to it that they mark these outings for her mother Vickie. It is important to the family that Vickie can see that they have fun and are enjoying their lives despite her absence and because of her sacrifice. Facebook's photo albums give Vickie a chance to see her family enjoying the fruits of her labor. Families will often "tag" migrant family members even though the migrants aren't actually in the photos. Tagging communicates to migrant family members that they are still present in those important milestones and that the family unit they are investing in is intact.

Reciprocal photo sharing is another way that families can include one another in special events and occasions. Rose's two youngest children, Grace and JJ, describe the process of sharing and uploading photos:

> JJ: *Kahit paano, nakikita namin ang picture niya. Lalo 'pag nasa snow! 'Yung mga jacket niya!* At least, we see her picture, especially when she's in the snow! And when it's cold! All of her coats!
> VALERIE: Oh yea! (Everyone laughs)
> GRACE: *Tapos kami din magsha-share sa kanya.* Then we can share pictures with her too.
> JJ: *Shared din ang pictures namin, para lagi niyang nakikita. Kunyari na pumunta kami sa okasyon tapos 'yun ano nagdadala si Papa ng*

digicam, tapos picture picture, tapos 'yun ia-upload namin tapos
ipapakita namin kay mama para malaman ni mama kung ano ang
ginagawa namin ngayon. Tapos 'yun na nga minsan nag-okasyon
din siya pinapakita din naman niya sa amin.

We share pictures so she can always see us, like when we go
somewhere or an occasion when Papa brings a digicam then we take
picture picture! Then after we upload so we can show Mama so she
knows what we did today. And yea, sometimes, when she has different occasions she shows us too.

Carrying a digital camera or taking photos on their phones on special outings and uploading the photos to Facebook, Rose's family shares experiences
with their mother that she would otherwise miss. And although telling Rose
about their family trips on the phone could be satisfying for both parties, the
immediate availability of the photos gives Rose a semblance of simultaneity.

Still, the instantaneous quality of Facebook doesn't always translate into
positive outcomes. Heather A. Horst and Daniel Miller found that frequent
contact through mobile phones gave families back home additional opportunity to cajole their migrant members into sending more money and goods,
and quickly too (Horst and Miller 2006)! For Rutsi, seeing her children's talents on Facebook isn't enough to offset such demands and get her to check
her account daily:

Ino-open ko lang 'pag ano paminsan-minsan. Hindi na talaga ako nag-i-stay
kasi SUS! Ang daming nanghihingi. Mabi-bwisit ka lang. "We know that you're
living a good life in New York can you sponsor us?" Aba ba mahirap na 'to!
Tapos may iba akong estudyante na ang nanay nila, "Uy andiyan ka na pala sa
New York bil'han mo naman ako ng eyeglasses ko para remembrance." Pagka-
sunod, "Mam birthday ko na." Hala! Nakikita tayo sa Facebook eh kaya hindi
ko masyadong ginagamit na ang Facebook.

I only open [Facebook] sometimes. I don't really stay on it because GEEZ!
So many people want stuff from me. Gives me a headache. "We know that
you're living a good life in New York, can you sponsor us?" Oh, no, that's too
much! Then, I have this student, and their mother approached me, "Hey,
you're in New York, please buy me some glasses as a remembrance of you."
Next, "Ma'am, it's my birthday." Whoa! We are being watched on Facebook
that's why I'm not always on Facebook.

Rutsi's Facebook experience, with friends vying for attention and financial
gifts, is more akin to harassment, creating unwanted pressure. While Face-

book provides opportunities for friendship and intimacy among far-flung family and friends, it also allows those left behind to proposition migrants for additional benefits.

Facebook connects transnational families in much the same way as it connects friends and families who live in close proximity. What makes Facebook interactions among transnational family members important and unique for the participants in this study is the fact that more than 90% of these families have not seen one another in years. Migrants in this study are largely undocumented so long-term separation is the modus operandi for their families. In the transnational context, technologies like Facebook and Skype are not just tools of communication or instruments to bide the time in what Hosu Kim has called "virtual mothering" (2016). Rather, they are often the *only* thing families have to develop and maintain relationships. "Being with" other family members, abroad or at home through Facebook or Skype, collapses the time and distance that they cannot recover by simply flying across state borders or commuting an hour by car or train. Facebook is a simple way of feeling like lives are being lived simultaneously and together, no matter how far apart or how long since those lives have existed in the same home.

Conclusion

As noted at the beginning of this chapter, the very development of technology lauded by the family members in this study was made possible by neoliberal globalization and the specific migration in this era—systemic-induced labor migration and massive illegalization of migrants in destination countries. Technology, as a part of global capitalism for profit, has transformed communication and information into a fetish commodity—a natural, matter-of-fact aspect of migration (Fuchs 2009a, 2009b). Filipino migrants and their families hold technology up as consolation to their difficult life situations. Further, the Philippine state—the very architect of the multibillion-dollar migration industry—also praises (and profits from) the fact that technology can keep transnational families together.[2] This fetishism has blunted critiques of the systematic and lucrative export of people. Marxist scholars of communication and technology argue that the use value of media technologies enabled global communication, creation of culture, and exchange of information for capital circulation (Manzerolle and Kjøsen 2012). So even though new media technologies provide constant communication and connection for migrants and their families left behind, the technology industry necessitates the separation of family members. And as families in a transnational arrangement use video technology to organize practical matters such as remittances, the technology industry is not only facilitating the continued flow of remittances from abroad but is also normalizing migration as a form of sustaining Filipino families.

The Philippine labor brokerage state can and often does co-opt transnational families' creative adaptations to their conditions of separation; it is a structure that relies on family separation for the profit of a few. In many ways, different technologies such as air transportation and financial systems are assisting in the accumulation of profit for the Philippine nation-state's economy and ruling elite. The coupling of the global demand for migrant workers and globalization's technological advances has pushed Filipinos out into more than 150 countries all over the world with the promise that they will still have frequent contact with their families through Skype or Facebook. Although advocates of globalization celebrate the mobility of migrant workers and their ability to stay in contact with their homes left behind, these laudatory logics must be contextualized in the same neoliberal conditions that have pulled desperate migrants from their families, homes, and communities to then be able to use technology to retain the very bonds they had to leave behind.

The stories featured in this chapter are reminders of the pressures of globalization: People make creative use of what they have, yet they also often have no other options than to make the best of what they have. Families' use of technology to maintain familial bonds is both remarkable and depressing: Families' opportunity to innovate is mediated by the fact that they have to be apart to do so. Yet, these various virtual activities are understood as forms of care work, thus defining some members of the transnational family (i.e., children) who are not traditional care providers as contributors to multidirectional care through the use of technology. For example, both migrants and families left behind are using technology to do a range of care work—from keeping people abreast of current events to teaching one another how to use the various computer technologies. Both migrants and those left behind actively teach one another about the newest applications and software. This exchange is not only practical but also builds emotional connections among separated members of the transnational family. Still, in an effort to combat adultism in the studies of migration and transnationalism, I want to highlight the dexterity of children left behind in the use of technology and their contribution to their families through sharing their skills and interpreting these contributions as care (Alipio, Lu, and Yeoh 2015; J. L. Waters 2015). The exchange of information and communication opens the door for continued conversation, relationship building, and intimacy development as an expression of care work (Baldassar and Merla 2013; Aguila 2011).

Technology opens up a unique potential for friendships, intimacy, and closeness for the families featured here. The exploration of computer communication technology and resulting exchanges illuminates the ways in which transnational families are engaging in multidirectional care work. In this case, the visual component of the webcam allows for a different type of care work to be exchanged by both migrants and families left behind. The act of turning on a webcam and maintaining a live feed that connects households in New York City and Manila integrates far-away loved ones into everyday life. This is part of a transnational formula of multidirectional care. These technologies encourage the development of intimacy and friendship between separated family members. Among my participants, I found that the visual register offered by services such as Skype gave migrants and those left behind equal opportunity to interpret their digital face-to-digital face sessions as care for one another.

Still, the limits to this form of intimacy are also bound up with its possibilities; surveillance from migrant family members abroad and families left behind often mitigates what types of information is shared over social media or video conferencing apps. Also, technology can aggravate already strained relationships in the transnational family. At both ends of the transnational family, participants expressed discomfort and frustration with the amount of monitoring that Facebook or Skype allows. Particular technologies serve specific purposes and limitations that depend on the needs of family members (San Pascual 2014). The different ways members participate in this virtual care circulation are useful in understanding the multidirectional care in the Filipino transnational family. And although not all engagements with technology are pleasing, the asymmetrical reciprocity maintains the circulation of care work in separated families.

We need to see these strategies in multidirectional care through technology as a contextualized use of globalization's tools—tools that are part and parcel of the rubric of capitalist globalization—to deal with the conditions of labor migration. The adaptive use of technology mediates the difficulty in the separation transnational families experience. However, the contradiction remains: Becoming Skype mothers and Facebook children is the result of the condition of long-term separation for families who would otherwise choose not to be apart.

3

Communities of Care

Marisol Antonio was the oldest of five siblings raised by parents from the peasant class in a rural province in the Visayas, the central region of the Philippines. As the eldest daughter, she was used to taking care of others in the family. As she and her siblings grew into adulthood and had children, she expertly juggled the family household budget for daily needs and special occasions, such as birthdays and holidays. She never did anything for herself, though. Everything she did, even migrating in 2007 at the age of 47, was for her children and her extended kin; for Marisol, going to New York City felt like the right decision. She did it all in the name of providing for them. After all, she was the oldest. Expenses were rising for her family: Her parents were ailing, her four children were heading to college, and her eighth nephew had just been born.

Upon her arrival, Marisol adjusted quickly to the subway system and the snowy winters, but the isolation crippled her heart. She rented an attic in the home of a Chinese family and spent her days off alone. She tearfully remembered, "*Mag-isa ka lang, araw-araw. Punta ng trabaho, alaga ng baby, balik sa bahay, kain doon kain dito. Nakaka-miss 'yung ingay ng maraming tao sa bahay. Nawala 'yung sense ko na may kamag-anak ako.* You're alone, day in and day out. You go to work, take care of the baby, come back home, eat here or there. I miss the noise of people in the house. I lost that sense of family." She broke this monotony by spending some time on the weekends in a neighborhood in the borough of Queens with so many Filipino migrants that it almost felt like Manila. Some of the domestic workers lovingly called it "Queenila." The stretch of three to four blocks on Roosevelt Avenue in

Queens was home to Filipino restaurants, remittance centers, small grocery stores, a Catholic church, and a community center. This hub of Filipino institutions was a frequent destination for many Filipino domestic workers to meet, eat, socialize, and spend their days off. Even in the worst of weather, migrants would find a way to congregate in Queenila. For domestic workers new to the country, the city, and isolation, this neighborhood offered respite from the pressures of their everyday lives.

In an effort to get out in the world, Marisol signed up for a computer class at the Filipino Community Center in Queenila where I volunteered. Many Filipino domestic workers took advantage of the computer classes, as well as health and legal clinics among other services. Sometimes they went just to *tambay*, sit and chat with other migrants visiting the center. There, Marisol met Rose, a Filipina mother younger than her; they bonded over having four children, even having the same numbers of boys and girls. Marisol also hit it off with the Gonzalez sisters, Joan and Vickie; their brash humor and quick tongues made their conversations fast, furious, and funny. They all became members of the Filipino Community Center's network for domestic workers, Kabalikat (shoulder to shoulder) Domestic Workers Support Network. Shortly thereafter, the four would hold regular, open, rotating karaoke Sunday gatherings at one another's homes where they cooked food from their provinces and sang American pop songs and original Filipino music for hours. After a few months of karaoke and computer classes, Rose, Joan, and Vickie had coaxed Marisol to celebrate her 50th birthday at a nearby Filipino restaurant. Later, reflecting on that day, Marisol said,

> I never thought it would be a big thing. I mean, they helped out a lot like, for example, Rita did my invitations, Rose and Tetet bought some decors. And umm, Vickie and Joan they they they just volunteered like we can cook *lumpiang isda*. That's amazing like, who can I call for things like this? I don't have family (starts crying). But you can really rely on Kabalikat; they are the family I don't have here.

Marisol is so accustomed to taking care of others that she was completely taken aback when members of Kabalikat threw her a party. Their simple gestures—making invitations, decorations, and familiar food—re-created the very thing that she missed the most, family. Especially for women who did not have much history as friends, who did not even speak the same dialect, the bond was fierce: As Marisol said, "They're more than friendships, more than a network of friends."

New migrants, like Marisol, were often shy upon their arrival to the Filipino Community Center, wary of telling their stories or asking for help because they did not want to be perceived as vulnerable or ignorant. Still, while providing services or participating in events assisting new migrants, other Filipino migrants would informally step forward to offer support and stories of their own experiences. This moment of reaching out would then produce an easy, flowing conversation that could last for hours. In Marisol's case, these conversations would become the foundation of lasting relationships. In different contexts, I would later learn that some migrants would start conversations with any and all Filipinos they crossed paths with for the simple purpose of connecting to fellow *kababayans* and countrymen—an extension of patriotic care, perhaps. Carmie said, "I just see another Filipino and talk, talk, talk as if we know each other for a long time. Even in subway stations I can see some nannies, some caregivers and they take pictures and they invite you to be in the picture, ask you, 'You're a Filipino? Come on! Take a picture with us!' As if we know each other for a long time, that's because of our special bonding. We want to feel love from another Filipino." These moments of immediate familiarity would spawn friendships and connections with Filipino migrants that were sometimes beneficial and sometimes disadvantageous. Yet, these connections were forged in Queenila—feet in Queens but heart and mind always referencing Manila. In the Filipino Community Center, inside the ethnic enclave, migrants felt safe in connecting with other migrant women through their experiences in New York City and simultaneously their transnational lives. I wondered about the basis of these relationships: What did care work within migrant communities mean for the migrant women who found connections based on their experiences as migrants and domestic workers, yet also with their identities as transnational family members? How do these processes of identifying with one another in a community work to tap into their many common experiences of gender, work, race, and migration?

Marisol's story of friendship and fictive kinship highlights the nodes of migrant womanhood, motherhood, sisterhood, and work on which Filipina migrants built communities of care. This chapter turns to the peripatetic community of migrant women who construct a permutation of multidirectional care within the bounds of their new home, New York City. I draw my analysis strictly from fifty individual qualitative interviews and group interviews or *kuwentuhan* (Francisco 2013) between domestic workers in New York City. A majority were women, hence the usage of "Filipina" in the rest of the chapter when referring to participants. I deepened my analysis of the care work circulated in migrant communities through a year of monthly workshop meetings with domestic workers and community members who co-wrote, co-produced, and co-starred in a play, *Diwang Pinay: Kasaysayan ng Kababaihang Migranteng Manggagawa* (Spirit of the Filipina: The Story of the Woman Migrant Worker). The composite play was about the experiences and lives of Filipina migrant workers in this study and was staged in March 2011 at the City University of New York, Hunter College. The script produced from the theater program drew from the individual interviews I collected from 2009 to 2011, and different qualitative material collected during the community theater program, such as *kuwentuhan*, domestic workers' journals, and field notes from the monthly workshops (see the methodological appendix). Women were 95% of the participants in this program that utilized theater of the oppressed methods (Boal 2000) to create a cultural production that was composed of the group's narrative experience of migration, motherhood, and paid domestic work.

In this chapter I introduce a concept I call "community of care," which is a form of reorganizing care horizontally, *from* migrants *to* other migrants informed by their transnational familial context. In the previous chapters, I've discussed the ways care has been circulated within transnational family units. In this discussion of multidirectional care, the key distinction I make is the exchange in care beyond the transnational family to fictive kin created abroad. Although the people in this chapter are living and working in New York City, they actively draw from their subjectivities as transnational family members and migrant workers to build a "community of care." This concept highlights the direction of care within migrant communities as a necessary form of work that maintains the migrant family members of the transnational families. Drawing from queer theories on kinship, I argue that this horizontal care among migrants is configured socially rather than biologically (Bailey 2014). In contrast to a vertical kinship structure wherein the biogenetic kin and therefore heteropatriarchal lineage takes primacy, communities of care rely on the subjectivities produced by the liminality of migrancy, undocumentation, and precariousness as the social sphere in which they care for one another.

Migrants are crafting these pockets of care as they are at the intersection of race, class, and globalization. The American racial order, the Filipino labor diaspora, and the Philippine labor brokerage state—these are the contexts in which immigrants have reformulated care in their transnational families and in their relationships with fellow migrants. In their interviews, migrants told me that experiences of isolation as migrants and workers in New York

City were the most salient categories in their transitions to the United States. Isolation was informed, principally, by the contemporary American racial order that segregates immigrants as the current racial "other." In New York City, immigrant identities are lauded and disciplined simultaneously, which can be dehumanizing and fear-inducing. For example, this tension can be seen in the informal labor market, especially for undocumented immigrants: Migrant labor is needed to support New York City's economy, but those very jobs are also easily expendable, not to mention some of the most precarious occupations in the city (Sassen 1999; Chang 2000). This contradictory political background informs how Filipinos understand their identities as migrants and domestic workers, often mired in anxiety and insecurity. Indeed, New York City is a traditional and contemporary port of entry for the world, and thus a place where immigrants form the bedrock for the city's economy (Foner 2005). Yet, after the tragedy of 9/11 and current national anti-immigrant sentiment, New York City continues to be a highly securitized zone set up for immigrant raids, detention, and deportation. Many migrants know that their work is essential to their employers, who work long hours at multinational corporations and financial firms, but they also doubt the security of their jobs and carry fears of deportation. These conditions shape how Filipinas engage with employers and also engage with one another as precarious workers.

Isolation coupled with experiences of migration and displacement from their homeland forms an integral part of the migrant experience in the Filipino labor diaspora. These are key components in the migrants' building of and participation in communities of care. Filipino migrants' global migrations and consciousness often inform their conception of a "global imagined community" (B. R. Anderson 1991; Parreñas 2001c). The common transnational geography establishes a platform for Filipino migrants to recognize one another as people who have moved through a series of displacements: first from the Philippines to labor destinations around the globe, then from other diasporic locations around the world, cities like Hong Kong and Rome, and finally, to New York City. Some migrants' experiences in migrant communities elsewhere in the world before they migrated to New York City shaped the way they engage with migrants in their current community. Because of stints in places with large Filipino migrant worker populations like Israel, the United Arab Emirates, and Singapore, I discovered that the Filipina women were well versed in the Filipino cultural value of *pakikisama*, or building relationships with other Filipinos under the same circumstances. Their stepwise migration (Paul 2011) from prior destinations and eventually to the United

States provides a migratory milieu from which they draw on to build their networks. Migrant women scaled their global imaginary to their local communities to participate in a network of care in New York City.

This community of care is indubitably imbued with the migration rhetoric of the Philippine labor brokerage state often depicting migrants as *bagong bayani* (modern hero) (R. M. Rodriguez 2002). Joan says, "*Sabi ng gobyerno bayani ng araw 'yun e, 'yung umaalis. So ang ano ko is . . . ini-encourage nila. Kasi 'yun ang pinakamadaling paraan para magkalingkod ng pera di ba? Ang problema lang is, hindi nila inaalagaan ang tao pagkalabas ng bansa. The* government said back then that the people migrating were heroes. So what I mean is . . . they encouraged it. Because that's the quickest way to make money, right? The problem is, they don't take care of their people when they leave the country." Comments such as these demonstrate migrants' critique of displacement resulting from the role of the Philippine state in inducing Filipino labor migration as it disperses 10% of its population as laboring citizens all over the world. Displacement within a global imagined community—migration between global cities with high Filipino immigrant concentrations—shapes migrants' interactions with one another and their ability to rearticulate care within their networks. These dynamics are not simply "immigrant social networks" (Hagan 1998; Waldinger and Fitzgerald 2004; Portes 1995). They are far more than a constellation of contacts and exchanges in social capital or a swapping of resources.[1] Rather, immigrants initiate and circulate care through communities of care as they draw from their transnational identities and experiences as migrants in New York City.

From My Transnational Family to Our Migrant Community of Care

Migrant women in this story transformed their form of care within their community from devastating circumstances to a distinct type of network, drawing from their experiences as transnational mothers, sisters, daughters, and aunts. In this chapter, some of the narratives come from members of the Kabalikat Domestic Workers Support Network, a group composed primarily of Filipina migrant workers. Kabalikat was born from a humanitarian campaign to raise funds to help repatriate the remains of a deceased Filipina domestic worker, Fely Garcia, to her family and home in the Philippines (Francisco 2015a). Garcia was found dead in her apartment closet in the Bronx in April 2007; there were signs of foul play, and the community pressed for a thorough investigation. Yet the Philippine Consulate and the

New York City Police Department quickly closed the case. Filipino American community organizations and what was then an informal program of Filipino domestic workers meeting at a community center in Queens demanded that the Philippine government, at the very least, bear the cost of returning Garcia's body to her family since community members felt these institutions were shirking their responsibility for a formal investigation. A community-based memorial service for Garcia drew hundreds of Filipino migrants and Filipino American community members from New York and New Jersey, while hundreds of Filipino migrants employed in other parts of the world, including Filipina domestic workers in Hong Kong, signed petitions in support of the campaign. At a meeting for Garcia, Joan, who had visited the Filipino Community Center only twice at that point, said:

> *Naku, anong mangyayari sa mga bata? Yan talaga ang kinakatakutan ko, kung may mangyari man sa'kin, God forbid. Ang iniisip ko parati ay ang mga anak ko, paano na sila kung hindi ko sila mapadalahan. Anong mangyayari sa mga anak niya?*

> Oh no, what will happen to her kids? That's exactly what I fear, if something happens to me, God forbid. All I think about is my children, what'll happen to them if I can't send money back. What will happen to her kids?

Immediately after Joan made this comment, a flurry of side conversations exploded among the migrant women, who talked about their own families and their fears about if something tragic like this happened to them. With their own families in mind, they felt the urgency in Garcia's case and the intimately private matter of a death in a family became the concern of the migrant women working to get Garcia home. Garcia's lonely death rendered visible the violence of a global care economy that requires migrants to perform the labor of care while simultaneously uprooting them from familial and other networks of care for themselves, especially in tragic situations. This group of migrants transformed into a community of care as they referenced their own transnational families as they volunteered for funeral tasks, as they would for their own family members in the Philippines.

Migrant women quickly transformed the networks for this community of care into a complex formation with more functions than the initial political organizing around the public issue of Garcia's victimization and death. After migrants in the campaign won the repatriation fees to send Garcia's body to her family from the New York Philippine Consulate, additional grassroots fundraising brought two of her sons from Manila to retrieve their deceased mother's body, as well as another public memorial. This latter effort signaled a unique dimension in the collective action of the migrant women; it demonstrated that although the political issue of state abandonment took primacy in their organizing, the women connected to Garcia through their shared identities as migrant mothers. Sending for Garcia's sons was more than just claiming the repatriation fees as a campaign victory for the organization; it was also building communal intimacy within their newly formed group as a sort of transnational condolence to Garcia's family. "*Kung ako ito, gugustuhin ko na ang aking pamilya ang sumundo sa akin.* If it was me, I'd like that my own family would pick up my remains," said Lorna, a domestic worker involved in the early campaign organizing. The intersubjectivity that the domestic workers demonstrated for Garcia revolved around their identification processes (Hall 2003) with one another as members of transnational families. Confronted with the reality of Garcia's precarious life, many of these women not only saw a possible fate for themselves, but a sadder reality for the families they would leave behind. In this way, Kabalikat women were strengthening their ties with one another even in the face of exploitation and precariousness.

Migrant women who led the campaign finally formalized their group into an organized collective, Kabalikat, which worked to provide job leads, housing matches, and social activities to Filipinas in New York City—in short, to alleviate their isolation. Kabalikat members began to meet regularly with each other and with extended circles of friends and contacts to build the organization, and also share in one another's familial victories and challenges. They worked to create a community that was an extension of acts of care and service they performed for their own transnational families. Migrant women built these networks of care using Filipino cultural traditions of fictive kinship and *bayanihan* (camaraderie) because of the marginalization and other difficult circumstances they experienced. Parallel to other women-centered networks in communities of color (Stack and Burton 1993) or queer kinship structures (Manalansan 2005), Filipinas in Kabalikat used their community of care as a "social language by which [they] experience[d], express[ed], and frame[d] loss" to make meaning of Fely Garcia's death and the collective power they built because of it (Eng 2010, 88). Their stronger ties became a resource to counter the tropes of powerless, vulnerable, and sometimes suicidal migrants produced by the Philippine state and circulating in the American social imagination. More importantly, these networks were formed to help women face their daily conditions in stride.

In Carol Stack's pioneering ethnography of African American women and their families in the late 1960s, *All Our Kin*, she effectively argued that the tropes of African American women as "deviant, matriarchal and broken" (Stack 1997, 22) come from an ideology of American racism that pathologized African American communities during a time of segregation and discrimination. As the US government sponsored scholars to publish reports like "The Negro Family: The Case for National Action" (1965), or what's more popularly known as the "Moynihan Report," to underscore the lives of single mothers as deviant, Stack wrote about the African American kin network that proved to be a crucial resource for the communities they served. With simple exchanges of goods, food, and time for child-rearing, this homosocial community of African American women created stable networks for kin "folk" to swap the resources that were missing from their lives. In the conditions under which African American kin networks are forcibly produced in state-abandoned communities with unemployment and lack of resources, kin are as important as the people that build domestic networks for "child-keeping." Patricia Hill Collins's concept of "othermothers" (Collins 1995) emphasizes the centrality of fictive kin in African American communities in the 1970s as a holdover from African traditions. Care is not solely the task of biological mothers, or "bloodmothers," but as a responsibility of a women-centered network. I make this comparison to point out that Kabalikat, as a community of care, is more than what sociologists have called "immigrant social networks"—a social web of resources utilized by migrants for the purposes of assimilation and acculturation (Massey 1999; Portes 1995). Rather, it is a community of care established in and through the racialized and gendered experience of being modern-day servants and transnational family members.[2]

Although women migrants in this study do not share the daily and proximal responsibilities of collective child-rearing, as their children are in the Philippines, they had a deep understanding of one another as bloodmothers and othermothers who supported families in the Philippines. Whether they had biological children or not, women migrants identified with one another on the basis of their maternal filial obligations back home. Gloria, a 34-year-old single migrant, supports one older sibling and her child and two younger siblings going to college in the Philippines. She said, "I feel for other migrants here. Even if I'm not a mother. I'm still doing mother duties by sending money to my niece and my young brother and sister. I am their mother because I have this responsibility to them. Same with the rest of us, kids or no kids." Sharon, a 56-year-old mother of four adult children in the Philippines, says, "*Lahat kami naging ina. As long as nagpapadala ka, kahit may anak o wala, ina ka. Inaasahan ka.* We all become mothers. As long as you send money back, whether you have kids or not, you're a mother. They depend on you." This sensibility of mothering, albeit from afar, became an axis in which the community of care operated, as the responsibility of migrant women to their families was always at the forefront of their minds. These comments and the effort of Kabalikat in bringing Fely Garcia's sons to attend her public memorial echo the ideas of collective care in the women-centered networks that Stack and Collins write about. The community of care created fictive filial connections to both Garcia and her family, just as many of them create those links to one another.

Care With or Without Papers

Investment in a community of care increased because many of the women were undocumented and the uncertainty of their stays in New York City or their return home to the Philippines was a consistent reminder to sustain networks that were more than just an exchange of resources. Consider what happened when one of the mothers and leaders of Kabalikat, Bernadette, lost her son in the floods after a severe typhoon ravaged the national capital region of the Philippines. Kabalikat responded with organized relief efforts, and individuals in the group sought to care for their grieving friend. They attended to Bernadette's mental and physical health through daily visits to her home and workplace, bringing food and offering novena prayers for a week. When Bernadette did not improve, a few Kabalikat leaders talked with Bernadette about her desire to go back to the Philippines to mourn her son with her family. Bernadette knew that she would not be able to come back to the United States to work because she had overstayed her tourist visa, but she felt the best decision was to go home. The women who faithfully came to Bernadette's aid after her son's death also made sure they pooled together some money so she could also have some cash to sustain her in her first months back home. Bernadette's close friend Lorna, a 53-year-old migrant woman in New York City without biological children, said, "Even though I don't know the loss of a son, I know the burning desire to be with my family at times like this. I wanted to be home with my mother when she was very sick. This is what I have in common with Bernadette. I am giving what I can to Bernadette because in my heart, I've lost a son." Here Lorna assumed the role of othermother to the deceased son of Bernadette, not through child-keeping but by contributing resources to send Bernadette home to be with her deceased child. Lorna and Bernadette activate fictive kinship in their participation in the community of care, but their connection is unsettled by the uncertainties of immigration status and their familial obligations. Bernadette leaving the community of care reminded the women in her network about deep, shared experiences they had as migrants, mothers, and women.

Many migrant women see their tenure in New York City from a sojourner perspective because of their undocumented status; thus, it informs their participation in communities of care. Ties to one another were always predicated on their concept of time as finite given the conditions of raids and deportations in New York City during the years of this study. Additionally, time literally equated with money to many migrant women, thus influencing women's ability (or inability) to participate in the community of care. Betty, a 42-year-old mother of three children in a province in Central Luzon, says:

> *Kasi 'pag illegal ka it was uncertain kung ilang years ka pa. Naiintindihan 'yan ng mga Ate. Hindi ako parati makaka-attend. Although may goal ako na after graduation nila uwi na 'ko, kagaya rin nila. Maybe another two years more na pag-save para pwedeng makabalik pa. Alam na nila 'yan ang kundisyon ko pero di nila ako pababayaan kahit ganun pa man din.*

> Because if you're illegal, you're uncertain about how many years you have left here. The *ates*, older sisters, understand that. I'm not able to attend every event. Although I have a goal that I'll go back after the kids graduate, like them. Maybe another two years and I'm able to save, I can go back. They know that those are my conditions but they won't turn away from me even if that's the case.

Betty works three jobs: one full-time job as a nanny four days a week and two part-time cleaning jobs (on the weekends and on the nights after nannying). She's known as a "slippery fish" because, at times, no one can get hold of her. Still, many of the women call her to go to church on Sundays and attend Kabalikat events. When she does appear at an event or a birthday party, many of the women shout in glee upon her arrival and joke with her about how many jobs she now has. Betty does not feel isolated from her community of care because of the common understanding that the women fully understand why she works so hard and so much. Betty measures the moments of her undocumented status and her work as the primary breadwinner like the grains of sand in an hourglass, counting out the time until she can go back home. Meanwhile, belonging to a community of care that acknowledges these circumstances allows her to invest in this type of horizontal care work when she can.

Migrants choose their communities of care in and through their identities as diasporic subjects. Martin F. Manalansan examines the transnational lives of Filipino gay men living in New York City in his groundbreaking book *Global Divas*. In this study, he argues that although friends and lovers take the form of "chosen families," gay men do not equate their families of choice with their biological kin (Manalansan 2003). For Filipino gay men, friends or *barkada* (peer group) would be a social network for support during transitions, such as migrating or coming out as gay. In many instances, migrant women in this study embody this dynamic: They are women who have built their chosen families abroad. Migrant women engage in an identification process (Hall 2003) to link their diasporic experience as the basis for forming chosen migrant families in New York City, like queer Filipino migrant men. For "global divas" (Manalansan 2003) and "servants of globalization" (Parreñas 2001b), "the meaning of the family . . . contains notions of continuity and persistence and at the same time the translation and transformation of relationships" (Manalansan 2003, 101) specifically under the conditions of the political and economic milieu that drives thousands of migrants to leave the Philippines. Migrants choose their fictive kin on the basis of understanding the stakes of (undocumented) migration, a type of global and diasporic sensibility (Manalansan 2006).

Domestic Worker Solidarity in Communities of Care

Migrant women build relationships of reverence and care as *titas* in situations when others are in dire need of assistance, while relying on their shared experience as domestic workers. Janessa, a 30-year-old migrant, found Kabalikat when she was in crisis: After finally escaping from the exploitative diplomat who had brought her to the United States, she was terrified of even moving around the city on public transportation.

> *Ah 'yung Kabalikat? Kasi sa simula kaya ako nakapasok diyan, sila Tita Vickie ang nagyaya diyan sa akin. 'Di ba noon nga takot nga akong maglalabas. Tapos takot akong kumuha ng passport and everything kesyo nga huhulihin ako, 'yung mga ganoon. Pero noong nakilala ko nga 'yang grupo na 'yan. Dati hindi pa ako nagpapapansin, trabaho lang ako. Pero sabi ni Tita Joan, baka matulungan ka niyan, na makakuha ka ng passport. Naano rin ako kasi totoo talaga 'yun kasi habang nagpupunta-punta ako nalalaman ko na kung sino'ng mga lawyer, kung sino'ng malakas sa consulate, 'yung mga ganoon. Sige nga sabi ko parang okay. Ayun kaya naglakas loob akong sumama sa Kabalikat kasi hindi*

naman sapilitan na sumali ka eh. Nasa sa'yo 'yun eh kung gusto mo. Kaya ako minsan sasabihin ng iba, ano 'yun binabayaran ba kayo? Kasi minsan may mga Pilipinong ganyan na sasabihin na binabayaran ba kayo? Sabi ko it's your decision kung gusto mong pumunta o hindi. Porke pumupunta ka diyan araw-araw linggo-linggo babayaran kayo, you don't have to. Kumbaga 'yan, grupo lang siya. Alam mo Val, naging mga nanay ko na 'yan, mga tita ko na 'yan. Magka-edad naman sila ng mga kapamilya ko sa Pinas! (laughs) Huy, huwag mo sabihin sa kanila 'yun, gulpihin pa ako! Pero pupunta ako lingo-linggo kasi sila na ang aking pamilya, 'yan ang kapalit, 'di pera.

Oh Kabalikat? I started Kabalikat because Tita Vickie invited me. Remember, in the past I was scared to go outside. Then I was scared to apply for a new passport and everything because I thought I'd get caught, like that. But when I met that group . . . before I never really got involved, I just worked. But Tita Joan said that they might be able to help me get my passport. I started to think about it because it was true because when I started going, I found out about lawyers, who are influential at the consulate, like that. So, I said this is okay. There, that's how my spirit got strong when I was part of Kabalikat because they didn't force you to join. It's on you, if you want to. When others say, do they pay you to join? I say, it's your decision if you want to go or not. Just because I go every day, every week, doesn't mean they pay me. You don't have to go. It's a group. You know, Val, they've become my mothers, my *titas*. They're all the same age as my mom and aunts in the Philippines! (laughs) Hey, don't tell them I said that, they'll beat me up. But I go week after week because they've become my family, that's what I get in return, not money.

Kabalikat's community of care helped Janessa leave her home and socialize again; like Vilna Bashi's hub-and-spoke network model (Bashi 2007), Joan and Vickie form a hub that spokes, like Janessa, can depend on for resources. Through Joan and Vickie, Janessa had the opportunity to meet other women in the organization and find the legal resources she needed. Still, the latter part of Janessa's quote speaks to something more than a simple acquisition of resources or social capital; the return she gets from the group comes in the form of care and relationships. The women in Kabalikat, like Vickie, take the place of her mother and aunts in the Philippines: As a *tita*, or what Collins describes as "othermother," Vickie is a fictive mother for Janessa in this women-centered immigrant network. Janessa's last comment references her relationships with other women migrants as symbolically equivalent to those with her biological mother and aunts in the Philippines. But why does she identify those women as intimate fictive family members? Exploring Janessa's experience as a domestic worker can shine a light on her understanding of a "chosen family" (Weston 1997).

Janessa's story of exploitation was one of the worst I heard during my fieldwork. From a rural province in the Philippines, she was hired by a Philippine diplomat to be a nanny for his children in Manila. Janessa endured a frightening range of abuse from her employer's family: deplorable living conditions, brutal work hours, unlawful sexual advances, and threats to her family's safety if she was not deferent.

> *Ang dami-dami mong ginagawa tapos 'yung tutulugan mo ang tigas, sa sahig. Walang kama, sa closet lang. Nagtiya-tiyaga ako kasi sila ang amo ko wala akong mapupuntahan dito. I don't know but my back is hurting!* I do so much but I sleep on a rock hard floor. No bed, just in the closet. I just grit my teeth because they are my employers and I had nowhere else to go. I don't know but my back is hurting!
>
> *Tapos 'yung aabusuhin ka sa trabaho, walang off, lahat ng trabaho sa'kin.* They would abuse me at work, no off, all the work by myself.
>
> *Sometimes nagta-try siyang magbukas ng baño na he knows I'm inside and he pretends na, "Oops I didn't know you're there!" He's also coming in with only his underwear on. Paano mo 'di alam, eh naka-on ang shower?* Sometimes he tried to open the bathroom door when he knew I was inside and he pretended that he didn't know I was there! He's also coming in with only his underwear on. How could you not know if the shower was on?
>
> *'Yung ganoon ngang banta na papa-pulis ako, 'yung pamilya ko sa probinsya.* Threats that they'd call the police on me, on my family in the province.

Janessa worked for the Filipino diplomat for five years before she escaped. She organized her escape with the help of other Filipina migrants, stashing her clothes and belongings with them little by little on her daily visits to the park. She lived in a state of fear in the year right after she escaped. "*Tumatago talaga ako, it's true kasi natatakot ako baka makita ako at hulihin ako. Talagang takot na takot ako hindi ako bumaba doon sabi ko sa alaga ko.* I hid because I was afraid they'd see me and catch me. I was so afraid that I didn't separate from my charge." After her escape, Janessa avoided speaking to her family for a year as she worried that any contact would put them at risk. She felt scared and alone. When she finally mustered enough courage to talk with people, she began to build relationships that helped her heal the wounds of abuse. Janessa began to open up about her difficult past because of the informal sharing that happened in Kabalikat meetings and in small group interactions. Often these discussions were about migrants' naïveté when it came to their jobs as domestics. For example, Anne laughingly recalled her first experience with cleaning a bathroom: "The boss told me to look for the 'comet' before I clean up the bathroom. In my mind, I was thinking of the comet in the sky! Then finally after some days, I asked her about what comet is and she showed me the brand of toilet cleaner called Comet!" These initial exchanges about worker struggles were often accompanied by boisterous laughter and tears of joy. Migrant women like Anne invited the likes of Janessa to then share the experiences that were more grim and trying. This community of care was able to embrace the hardships as well as the silly stories of workers navigating a world of domestic work.

After meetings where migrants would share the experiences they had in the workplace, many migrants continued to fortify their relationships by spending time together outside Kabalikat. In a group interview with Janessa, Joan, and Vickie, they reflected on what it was like to nurse Janessa back into stable mental health after her escape. Vickie said:

> *Takot na takot siya, kawawa. Isang beses nag-taxi kami pauwi, nadaanan na-min itong Roosevelt, sa takot ni Ja kailangan kaming huminto kasi naihi siya sa takot. Pagsakay niya ulit, iyak ng iyak, yinakap ko at sabi ko, anak kaya pa, nadaanan na natin lahat 'yan.*

> She was so afraid, poor thing. One time, we took a taxi home through Roosevelt [a Filipino enclave in Queens] and Ja was so scared she pulled the cab over because she peed herself because she was so scared. When she got back in crying, I held her and said, daughter, you can do this, we've all gone through this.

The fictive kinship between Vickie, Joan, and Janessa is rooted in their shared experience of trauma as migrant domestic workers. As migrants away from their own families, they lean on one another for strength, support, and assistance. Like African American women and their kin or other communities of color who work as domestic workers in the United States (Dill 1988; Glenn 1985), the basis of the community of care with this group of women is their experiences of work while extending support to one another. Vickie explicitly labels Janessa as *anak* (daughter), explaining that this type of support is as much about worker solidarity as it is about developing intimacy as fictive kin. Redeploying what Carol Stack and Linda M. Burton call "kinscript" (Stack and Burton 1993), the women here are creating a community of care that reflects intergenerational care in politically and economically constructed circumstances—in this case, migration and separation from biological kin.

Even more importantly, this fictive kinship is an act of choice in recognizing shared struggles and forging new relations based on sustenance and healing.[3] Developing a relationship with some semblance to motherhood and daughterhood is not about replacing their blood relatives. Rather, it is about the conditions under which they find themselves as marginalized migrants and workers. The story of Rose, a mother of four who came to the United States working for a Philippine ambassador, is an example of a migrant suffering from wage theft, exploitation, and abuse and whose näiveté was taken advantage of. She recounted her experience:

> *Noong sinabi ng ambassador sa akin na sumama ka sa'min sa New York, sabi ko, "Wow New York? Magkano suweldo?" Sabi, "Ten thousand pesos," akala ko malaki na iyon. First time ako talagang nag-abroad, wala ako experience work abroad. 'Pag dating dito ibinigay na suweldo is 200 dollars a month for twenty-four-hour live-in nanny and housekeeper. Na-realize 'yung 200 dollars a month hindi pala 'yun enough na padala and pabili ng basic necessities, 'di nga kaya bumili ng phone card to communicate with my family. Kayod ang trabaho. Nung nakausap ko ang mga ibang nanny sa pick up sa school, gaya nila Rita, naisipan kong tumakas. Natatakot ako kasi ambassador sila eh, I know they have power. Pero alam ko na kahit paano, mapapagkatiwalaan ko sila Rita at ibang tutulong sa'kin tumakas. Sila ang naging parang pamilya ko na pwede kong iyakan or kausapin tungkol sa lahat. Kasi alam nila ang bigat ng pagiging alila sa amo.*

When the ambassador said, come to New York with us, I said, "Wow, New York? How much will they pay me?" He said, "Ten thousand pesos," I thought that was big money. It was the first time I went abroad with no experience at all. When I got here they gave me $200 a month for a twenty-four-hour live-in nanny and housekeeper. I realized that $200 wasn't enough to send money back to my family much less buy a phone card to communicate with my family. I worked my fingers to the bone. When I talked to other nannies during pickup at school, like Rita, I thought about escaping. I was scared because they were the ambassador, I know they have power. But I know, if anything, I could trust Rita and the others to help me escape. They became my family that I could cry to or talk to about anything. Because they understood what it was like to be a slave to an employer.

Rose admitted that her inexperience led her to accept a job that she knew nothing about. However, as she realized the degree of exploitation she was enduring, she turned to other domestic workers like Rita as confidantes. Her treatment of Rita "like family" was based on trust she felt for her and other domestics who could understand the frightful conditions. Although there were other migrants Rose interacted with at church and on the subways, she chose to confide in fellow domestic workers and trusted that they could help her to escape from her employer. Rita and other women from Kabalikat did not share the experience of exploitation with Rose, but they did understand the desperation she felt. In a group interview remembering that time in their friendship, Rita said, "Rose was so strong when she chose to leave. She did not know us very well, all she knew was that we understood what it's like to work like that and that she wanted to get out of her situation. That was enough." This issue of trust is so embedded in a common experience as domestic workers and the solidarity demonstrated by migrants like Rita and Rose, so much that they became one another's hope, or in what Rachel Brown calls "coalitional consciousness" (2016). Rose reflected about her escape and said, "*Tinuring ko silang kapatid sa aking pinakamababa na panahon. Sila ang tumulong sa akin, hinahatid ko sa kanila ang aking kasangkapan and damit paunti-unti sa mga after school. Hanggang nakatakas ako at sila ang naghanap ng pabahay at bagong trabaho.* I treated them like my sisters during my lowest times. They helped me, I took my things to them little by little during school pickup until I was able to escape and they were the ones who helped me find housing and work." Perhaps during these times, migrants might turn to anyone as they are searching for rescue and help, but in this community of care, Rose and Rita so aptly illustrate that the solidarity they act on is on the basis of their status as domestic workers framed by the possibility of fictive kinship. As Kath Weston notes in her innovative study of GLBT chosen families, the notion of family "is not fixed, for GLBT people or anyone else . . . [Families] are multiple and emerge from historically changing conditions" (Weston 2005, 134). This framework applies to the Filipinas in this community of care wherein the changing conditions for them consists of treatment as exploitable workers and as vulnerable migrants. Therefore, their chosen migrant family, like queer chosen families, is a product of a political choice to see one another as possible allies and trustworthy friends.[4] In fact, the fictive kin built in and around the conditions of Filipina migrants are reinscribing the ideas of care in their transnational family in their homosocial community and the political and economic conditions they live out daily.[5] They are at once appropriating the language and practices of sisterhood while creating new kinscripts based on the types of care they need as migrants, workers, and mothers and sisters abroad. I deploy the term "queer" in describing how the Kabalikat women create their community of care based on the shared experiences of displacement and endurance through Cathy Cohen's "broadened understanding of queerness . . . that recognizes how numerous systems of oppression interact . . . to regulate the lives of most people" (1997, 441). And much like queer kin, migrants' community of care calls into question the natural and biological basis of kinship by enacting a practice of care in relation to migration, transnationalism, and precariousness.

Texture of Care Between Migrants

Communities of care are not void of in-group conflicts. Immigrant networks often supply migrants opportunities to stabilize their lives, but they can also constrain one's choices based on the expectations and mores of a particular network (Portes 1995). Denise, like other migrant women, told me she hesitated to join circles of Filipinas because of the plague of *tsismis* (gossip) that is characteristic of Filipino communities: "Ay, I don't want to be involved with them because all they do is *tsismis* and I don't want to be part of the drama." Indeed, group criticisms sometimes articulate conservative norms and discipline migrant women about their gendered duties or moral obligations to the transnational family (Dreby 2009). Yet some migrant women said that *tsismis* is absorbed in a different way within their community of care where it not only operated as a disciplining form of group communication, but it also had a quality of preserving the fortitude of migrant women as transnational family members. When *tsismis* was spread about one member within their networks and from outside, many of them resorted to defending fellow migrants to people who might be labeling one's behavior as outside "good mothering." The fictive kin ties translate into a line of defense for migrant women who were experiencing similar situations at work or with their families to combat traditional cultural expectations of motherhood and womanhood hoisted on them by other migrants in their locales (Constable 2014; Park 2017). It is generally accepted that networks inform immigrants' decisions to migrate (Grasmuck and Pessar 1991), and how they find jobs in their destinations (Foner 2005), secure housing (Hagan 1998), and maintain transnational links to the homeland (Schiller, Basch, and Blanc-Szanton 1992; Levitt 1998). Social capital within immigrant communities is exchanged through these networks, often impacting new immigrants' settlement experiences and ability to adapt to their new homes. The deep intersubjectivity within these networks challenges the static notions of motherhood and attempts to shift migrants' perspectives of one another to more accurately reflect their daily conditions.

Brenda, a 36-year-old mother of two small children and wife of a husband back in Manila, said, "When it comes to being a good mother, I don't think

I am that because I am far away from them. Maybe I am a good mother in a different way like being a provider, but not in a traditional way. So when you see other women doing the same here and you talk to them about their kids so even if they judge your actions they know we are under the same stresses." Brenda refers to the bonds she has built with other women in her community of care who share transnational family responsibilities with her as tempering the stigma she may otherwise feel about the "traditional" definitions of motherhood. Between Kabalikat women and the women involved in their communities of care, the fictive kin relationships built inside a community of care are based on their migrant experiences of care in their transnational family.

Members of the fictive or chosen migrant family go well beyond exchanging resources to take responsibility for the events and emergencies in one another's lives. Joan, a member of Kabalikat, said the group "is a big help" in combating isolation:

> [Kabalikat] *sa mga nandito na nag-iisa dito, lalong-lalo nag-iisa ka. Kasi 'pag nag-iisa ka walang pupuntahan e, lalo sa ganitong ah . . . ganitong panahon. 'Di ba? Meron nga nagsabi sa'kin na very down ka, wala kang mapuntahan mabuti na lang may Kabalikat. At least punta sila kahit wala, meron silang makakausap, ganoon. Para kayong magkakapatid.*

> [Kabalikat] is a big help for those who are alone here, especially if you are alone. Because when you are by yourself you have nowhere to go, especially when it's this [winter] season. Right? Someone told me once that [during the winter] you get very down, you have nowhere to go, it's good that there is something like Kabalikat. At least, they'll all come even if there's nothing, you'll have someone to talk to. Like sisters.

Joan, like many women migrants, suffered from isolation during her transition to the United States. As a mother of three and a grandmother of four, she was never alone when she lived in the Philippines. Her own children, grandchildren, sisters, and brothers lived close to her in Manila and always surrounded her. She remarks that coming to the United States alone was hard but *being* in the United States alone is even harder. The unusual winter weather coupled with isolation left Joan feeling lonely and sad. Her decision to reach out and join Kabalikat reframed that feeling of vulnerability; she identifies group members as "sisters," signifying that companionship and conversation are critical to building relationships.

During our conversation, I asked Joan to talk about how having friends can help during times of need. She told me:

At least you will have someone to hold on, hold on you. 'Di man dumating sa puntong ganoon, 'yun lang may makausap ka na iba, na hindi bata o hindi 'yung mga bata. Nadagdagan 'yung friends mo. Kahit sabihin mo na hindi kayo close, 'pag dating mo dito parang close ka na rin (laughs). Kahit matagal na kayo 'di nagkita, 'pag nagkita, parang, ay, ang close close na. Malaki ang naitulong. Parang shoulder to cry on. Home away from home. Family away from family.

At least you will have someone to hold on, hold on you. Even if it doesn't get to that point [of an emergency], at least you have someone else to talk to that's not a child or your children. You have more friends. Even if you say that you're not close, when you get here, it's like you are close (laughs). Even if you haven't seen each other, when you see each other, it's like, hey, it feels like we are so close. It's a huge help. Like a shoulder to cry on. Home away from home. Family away from family.

As Joan explains, the situation does not have to be so dire for her to see the benefits of having a community of care that she treats like family. She feels isolated in most areas of her life; at her workplace she spends all day with a child. Her remark about talking to someone that's *not* a child—let alone her own child—demonstrates that talking with other women migrants is a welcome break from the monotony of her life. She goes on to analyze the closeness she feels with other members of Kabalikat, signaling the significance of this fictive kin for her. To combat the seclusion of work and being away from her biological family, Joan invests in her fictive "sisters" to share moments of vulnerability, joy, and just being able to take one's mind off the daily grind. When migrants come together to share their journeys, they recognize one another as resources and as persons who identify with their experiences as migrants, domestic workers, and transnational family members, thus forming a community of care.

Conclusion

Studies on "immigrant social networks" often reify the impetus for migration and therefore the development of social networks in immigrant communities abroad. There is much to be uncovered by denaturalizing the reasons why immigrants identify with one another and how those conditions contribute to building an immigrant social network. For example, experiences of adapting to a new country, or the hardships of losing a low-paying job and then having to accept an even lower-paying job, or not being able to see one's family for years are all significant experiences that become nodes of intelligibility for migrants. Migrants collect experiences as new migrants, precarious workers, and migrant family members even before they engage or are invested in immigrant social networks. Migrants in this community of care use their networks to do more than exchange social capital that abets their ability to adapt to their new home in New York City (Kasinitz, Mollenkopf, and Waters 2004).

Bringing together concepts in queer and black feminist theories with the sociology of immigrant social networks reframes the flow and forms of care within social networks of migrants because of the conditions of neoliberalism and migration. Concepts of the "chosen family" and "othermothers" along with the literature on immigrant social networks agree that the functions and versatility of networks are central in the lives of marginalized groups. Yet, research on immigrant social networks operates from the assumption that networks are developed on the basis of identity, membership, and acquaintance in a migrant community, whereas queer and black feminist theories offer an examination of macroconstraints that shape identifications. Specifically, analyses of queer chosen families and black fictive kinship offer a critique and examination of the political and economic conditions that drive disruptive change among marginalized communities while communities foster creative responses of resilience. These theoretical frameworks, or what Roderick A. Ferguson calls "queer of color analysis" (Ferguson 2004), disrupt notions of biological kin and the centrality of a heteronormative family in the examination of migrant networks in mainstream sociology of immigration, as it puts the non-normative family formation as the standard. Therefore, I apply this structural analysis to the migrant communities here; the circulation of care within a migrant network is extended to a homosocial, non-nuclear, nonbiological definition of family and care. Communities of care unsettle neoliberal discourses of migrant labor as they both affirm the trauma in the migrant experience and constitute an intimacy that queers the "ideological and fetishistic basis of the home and the biological family" (Bailey 2014, 496).

The migrants in my study, the majority of them women, relate to one another through different exchanges of social capital, such as circulating job opportunities, advice on work, and money lending. However, migrants also pull from their analysis of the labor brokerage (R. M. Rodriguez 2010) and the redefinitions of social reproductive labor circulated within their transnational families to inform their social network. Instead of the event of migration as a starting point in creating and investing in a social immigrant network, migrants reach back to their premigration stories and ongoing transnational experience of migration to sustain communities of care. Offering a different analysis of immigrant social networks, I argue that the communities of care in this study are engendered by the political economy of labor migration. The circulation of support and constraint that the women in these communities of care experience is not just based on knowing a veteran migrant or moving into an immigrant community, but on their precarious situations as migrants, workers, and migrant family members. The political economy of labor brokerage, displacement and isolation as a migrant, conditions of low-wage and unstable work, and long-term separation over long distances are the neoliberal conditions under which communities of care are formed. The intimate labor of migrant women in their transnational families and in their paid domestic work produces a liminal zone where they produce care for everyone but themselves. This liminality is generative—this horizontal caring for one another is not just informed by the reconfigured care in their families and paid work, but it is political and subversive. It calls into question the biological and sexual basis of kinship, allowing for strong ties to be tethered to the practice of communing and care.

Lorna, a single woman who left behind her siblings and her mother in the Philippines, replied to my question about why migrant women built such deep and intimate relationships by saying, "Maybe because of the camaraderie, the care. That's all. Sense of belongingness because we're the same. We can understand each other, we share laughter." It was clear to me in my time among these women that their communities of care are not only about helping out in harder moments, but also about sharing joy. As I re-listen to the recordings I made of our conversations, I regularly hear laughter accompanying the booming karaoke music and crooning voices in the background. Interviews were often interrupted by people inviting us to pick up another plate of *alimango* (steamed crab) and *pancit* (Filipino noodle dish). There was always time to talk about someone's new boyfriend and joke about how domestics become divas with heels on the weekends. While *tsismis* (gossip) may be annoying at times, it is an important part of the collective life of domestic workers (Lan 2006, 171). These moments of teasing, banter, and laughter are just as important as the struggles—all of these elements produce what Martin F. Manalansan calls "diasporic intimacy" (2005, 148). Although these migrant women come to their subjectivities as migrants, workers, and mothers in different ways, they are nonetheless still bound up in the in-betweenness of home and abroad, framed by the precariousness of life under neoliberal globalization. The simultaneity of working and living abroad and still participating and staying present at home is an experience that is particular to diasporic subjects. This in-betweenness, produced by interactions among migrants, is characterized by a geographic consciousness and diasporic imaginary. The knowledge of the diaspora is a migrant worker's lived experience; it is as Rita says, *iisang istorya*, or the "one story" that migrants share no matter what stamps they have on their passports. In this way, they subvert the binary narrative of assimilation to the United States while pushing back on the sojourner trope of migrant labor; they are so brilliantly laying bare the inherent contradictions of neoliberal migration.

As has been argued by black feminists and queer scholars, families for migrant women are as much chosen as they are given, they are as much fictive as they are biological, and they are as much homosocial as they are heteronormative. These scholars remind us that communities, including biological and fictive kin, have always circulated care in response to the gaps created by the reduction in state support, historical and colonial violence, social prejudice, and diaspora. The conditions under which families are chosen, expanded, and maintained are in part the products of marginalized people's creativity and resilience. Migrants in this study have lost their choice to be with and care for their biological families in the way they prefer. However, they actively choose their new families in a new place.

Still, Manalansan's sentiment about a "cautionary hopefulness" (Manalansan 2003) regarding migrancy and mobility is important, in that migration can superficially improve a family's income but not their quality of life. To reiterate, the reconfiguration of social reproduction is the context under which communities of care are produced. Social immigrant networks don't just crop up whenever and wherever immigrants land—they are a transnational phenomenon, beginning with the material changes in family lives and fortified by the global imagined community that is inherently part of any immigrant's life. Communities of care thus speak to bigger shifts in social reproductive care, where care has been reorganized from the local place left behind and evolves into different forms and arrangements in the diaspora.

The peculiar, yet normative, characteristic of migrant women in this study is the distance between them and their families, which frees them from traditional, unpaid women's domestic work (e.g., laundry, cooking, cleaning, child-rearing, etc.) within their own biological families. Although they still perform care work through remittances and technology, the majority of their everyday reality is that they are a group of women who are childless mothers, motherless daughters, and sisters without siblings when they are not at work. Therefore, the responsibilities for care among Filipino migrant fictive kin look different from those in African American families whose fictive kin often take up mothering duties such as child-rearing and babysitting. With the Filipinas in this study, care work between migrants is a horizontal kinship that toggles between migrant sisterhood, motherhood, and friendship. They establish these connections as othermothers or *titas* through their transnational experience in multidirectional care and solidarity as domestic workers. A quick scan of who is in the streets and restaurants of Queenila shows migrant women arm in arm and talking about their days over a hot Filipino meal. Even for a day or two they can feel as if they are back in Manila, even if their feet are in Queens.

4

Caring Even if It Hurts

Althea and Olivia

Althea told me that she was not close to her mother—that is, not like other girls and their mothers. At the time of our first conversation, Althea was 23 years old, living in Manila with her boyfriend's family. Although all she wanted to do was work, she was trying to finish college, her mother's dream. If she were to discontinue her education, her mother would stop sending monthly remittances from New York City. And her mother would know immediately, having appointed aunts and cousins to track her progress in school. Althea had tried to escape from their surveillance, moving out of shared residences and transferring schools, but they always caught up to her. It seemed that she could never get far enough away from her mother's watchful eye.

Although Althea acknowledged that her mother's migration has helped her live a more comfortable life, providing shelter, clothing, food, and education, she lamented the costs of those comforts. In her twenty-three years of life, she has only seen her mother for a total of eight months: Olivia came home between contracts for overseas work in various countries for a month at a time when Althea was 2, 6, 8, and 13; two months when she was 15; and the last time when Althea was 18. These few days at a time did not make up for the years of absence. She says, "I mean, I'm not that close with my mom because when your mom is far, you don't . . . it's like you don't feel a natural sense that she's your own mama. Not like with other moms who live close to their kids and they're glad to be together. Because your mom is right there.

We didn't get along." Ever since Olivia secured a temporary visa to the United States and then stayed beyond it, she has not been able to come back home; if she left her job and the United States, she would not be able to return to New York City to work at a reliable nanny job. Even though Althea did not express a loving emotional attachment to her mother, she teared up in gratitude for her mother paying her bills diligently. So Althea made sure to call her mother once a month like clockwork.

Olivia's side of the story started with an account of the biggest sacrifice she made: migrating abroad for work when Althea was only 14 months old. (Althea's father left soon after he found out about her pregnancy.) Olivia remembered being devastated when she had to leave her baby girl, knowing that if she stayed in the Philippines, they would live in poverty. Olivia said that she pursued any and all opportunities to work abroad, knowing that earning a living abroad, though painful, would be the only way to provide a better future for her daughter. Olivia believed that she made the best decision she could for Althea.

Olivia admitted that she has been disappointed in her daughter's decisions as Althea grew into adulthood. She was hurt that Althea kept lying to her about transferring schools and moving in with her boyfriend's family. Olivia turned to her sister, nieces, and nephews to keep an eye out on Althea. She instructed them to report Althea's daily actions and movements to her and to disburse Althea's monthly allowance only when she obeyed Olivia's rules. Feeling betrayed, Olivia gave Althea an ultimatum: Remittances and financial support would cease if Althea dropped out of college. Overall, Olivia expressed her regrets about migrating, wishing that she could reverse her choice so that she could be on better terms with her daughter. "*Sana nga, malapit pa siya sa akin. Pero ginawa ko ang kailangan gawin para sa aming dalawa. Kahit na 'di kami nagkakasundo, pamilya pa rin kami.* I wish we were close. But I did what was best for the both of us. Even if we don't get along, we are still family," says Olivia. She still sends money bimonthly; pays for basic necessities like rent, tuition, and food; and plans to go back to see Althea as soon as possible.

* * *

Althea's and Olivia's stories are mired with hurt feelings and betrayal. The only cohesive thread in their family narrative is a feeling of bitterness both from abroad and the place left behind. Althea and Olivia disappoint each other, harboring feelings of resentment and distrust; yet they both still attend to one another's needs for care, almost more diligently when under great pressure and stress. This mother-and-daughter transnational dyad continues to do care work in their family despite their churlish manner with each other, whether it's Althea's phone calls once every third Sunday of each month exactly at 8:00 a.m. Eastern Standard Time or it's Olivia's bi-monthly remittance to pay for Althea's rent, utilities, and food expenses. Both Althea and Olivia base their comments about their current relationship on a romanticized idea that being "close" is the only way of being mother and daughter, their internalized understanding of an ideal mother-daughter relationship blinding them to other social reproductive aspects of their relationship.

In this chapter, I tell a story of emotional strain that travels on the circuits of multidirectional care just as the care work that is undergirded with love and warmth. I explore the emotionality in care work specifically during trying times of anger, guilt, and disappointment to illustrate that a family works through the pains of their transnational relationship through learning, and a continuation of the social reproductive labor in caring from afar. Like in Althea and Olivia's experience, one story of betrayal triggers another's story of lashing out, from daughter to mother and vice versa. Like any other parent-child dyad, they navigate those difficult periods with the added challenge of separation. The emotional attachments in their transnational family are based on the existing emotional distance and intensified by the ongoing physical distance. They must figure out how to manage the emotional strain of their relationships from afar. For Althea and Olivia, finding out how to trust one another transnationally means redefining what types of communication and connection they can and want to maintain, continually negotiating the terms of intimacy by forging new connections and meanings of how to be in their family.

Migration predictably creates emotional distance in transnational families,[1] but even under these difficult conditions people still take up care work. If we define care work solely as nurturance and warmth,[2] we miss other types of labor that continue to keep the transnational family afloat. It is easy to hear resentful narratives of children or migrant parents outraged at spoiled children left behind resulting from migration and separation. Yet family interactions can be dysfunctional and painful even when members live under the same roof, in the same city, or in the same nation. These social interactions can be produced and triggered by separation, but transnational families still continue to maintain essential family operations, like communication and bill payments. Regardless of bitterness and hurt or emotional strain, families are still attending to the labor of care from afar. Nonetheless, many familial relationships suffer under long-term separation (Parreñas 2005a; Dreby 2010). Whole families have spent part of their transnational lives in blame and confusion, feeling indignation and resentment, enduring disappointment and betrayal. Still, these types of emotional distance characterize moments and temporary periods of time in a family's history, not its entirety. Indignation is not the only way in which transnational families describe their whole lives together. In fact, it is during these times, they still attend to the work of "doing family."[3]

It is absolutely true that children left behind feel abandoned and migrant parents feel taken advantage of, but children also finish school in honor of their parents' sacrifice and parents buy expensive presents to express their pride in their children's accomplishments. This chapter attends to the affective contradictions that live in the bodies of children left behind and migrant parents far away. It follows families moving in and out of growing pains, some faster than others. Because care work travels multidirectionally, strain too follows those circuits of care. And yet, families under emotional distress or disappointment can still attend to the labor in caring. The stories here actively pull apart the idealized notion that care work always comes from nurturance, love, and warmth.[4] The work of sustaining the transnational family must happen whether members feel gratified or good about that work. For transnational families, periods of emotional strain are compounded by separation over long periods of time and long distances; at the same time transnational family members continue to perform acts of care despite contradictory emotions.[5]

A methodological note about this prickly discussion about emotional dissonance in transnational families: A distinguishing factor about this study is its longitudinal approach to studying transnational families as a unit and with each family's history as context. Past scholars have shown that families left behind, children especially, have harbored feelings of resentment against their migrant parents (Parreñas 2005a). However, a long-term approach to understanding the dynamics of care and emotions in transnational families demonstrates that strain is one part of negotiating their lives apart. Often those ill feelings are tempered by time or resolved, which gives way to new understandings of one another given the distance between family members. Scholars have argued that different ages and the context-specific construction of childhood shape the experiences of children left behind and how they understand their social world as a part of a transnational family (Hoang and Yeoh 2015; Huijsman 2011; Ní Laoire et al. 2010). Since I approached the study of emotional strain in transnational families longitudinally, I demonstrate that children's understanding of emotional strain changes throughout the time they are navigating their family lives transnationally. Although this chapter centers on the troublesome relationships between migrants and their family members—with children, in particular, addressing the ebbs and flows in transnational families is not to minimize the stress undergone by migrants and families left behind; rather, it is to show the work or social reproductive labor that goes into the maintenance of the transnational family even under exasperating emotions. And more importantly, these narratives highlight the agency of children left behind who are engaged in the labor of care in their context of separation while negotiating the transnational affect of their families, growing in their understanding of transnationalism as they mature and acquire lessons in multidirectional care.

The emotional turn in this chapter is a step toward scholars' call to center emotions as an analytical lens in which to study the process of migration (Mai and King 2009; Vermot 2015; Boccagni and Baldassar 2015). The vantage point of children and their emotion work is absent in the literature as often the affective realities of children are simply descriptive rather than analyzing young people's labors in contributing to their transnational families (Dobson 2009; J. L. Waters 2015; White et al. 2011). In fact, children are active in providing essential tasks, both emotionally and practically, toward the health and maintenance of their families (Alipio 2015). The intentionality or emotions behind an act of care within the context of migrating parents vary between anger, guilt, gratitude, and reciprocation, yet the care work by children, in particular, must be considered and envisioned as labor that is essential to maintaining the operations of a transnational family, thus combatting the adultism that is commonplace in migration studies (J. L. Waters 2015). My aim is to complicate the emotional geographies of children in transnational families—disentangling love and the actual acts of care work. Through *sukli (reciprocation of care work)*, Filipino children demonstrate a culturally localized understanding of transnational emotional exchanges between their adult migrant family members, moving away from a Euro-American perspective in analyzing the emotional geography of children dealing with migration (Alipio, Lu, and Yeoh 2015). Lastly, just as migration is a key social process that changes the emotional life of children (Boccagni and Baldassar 2015), the complex web of emotions and labor of Filipino children in transnational families within the context of the current neoliberal milieu tethers the very intimate emotional geographies in their childhood to larger political economic forces. Emotions are not just an intrapsychic process but are tied to larger political processes (Baldassar 2015; Lutz and Abu-Lughod 1990).

Learning How to be a Transnational Family through Practice

Althea contrasts her relationship with her mother with her relationship with Anna, her primary caretaker since infancy and also Anna's sister:

> I mean, I'm not that close with my mom, even the times when she came in here. Umm . . . not like Mommy Anna. I tell her everything. Because Mommy Anna is here and my mom is not here so *mas open ako sa kanya. Tapos 'yung 'pag 'yung mom mo nasa malayo, hindi mo siya . . . 'yung parang feeling mo wala. Natural lang na oo mama ko siya. Pero hindi katulad ni Mommy Anna na 'pag andyan siya tuwang-tuwa ako kasi andyan siya eh.*
>
> . . . so I'm more open with her. Then, when your mom is far, you don't . . . you feel like nothing. Of course, she is my mom. But not like Mommy Anna that when she's around, I'm so glad that she's there.

Mommy Anna's regular interaction with Althea gave their relationship ample time to grow into familiarity. In contrast, the emotional distance she feels from her mother is because of the intermittent interactions they have had in her life span. Rhacel Salazar Parreñas finds similar themes about the intimacy between migrant mothers whose returns are limited, arguing "the infrequency of mothers' visits to the Philippines without doubt aggravates negative impressions of transnational families" (Parreñas 2005a, 127). Althea's comment supports Parreñas's finding that intimacy fostered between parents and children needs time and that the demanding and overseas nature of her mother's work does not allow for a close relationship to develop between mother and daughter. When asked, Olivia agrees: "Cause you have been a migrant for almost twenty years . . . more than that. It's so hard. Way back then I don't know how to communicate with her." Olivia reveals vulnerability about her motherhood, or rather her inexperience and difficulty with performing duties ascribed to "good" mothers (Robinson and Milkie 1998).

Although migrant mothers are redefining motherhood in terms of how they can participate in their families from afar, gendered expectations about "good" motherhood remain static within Filipino culture. These narrow definitions about maternal instinct and intimacy, both culturally specific and internalized by family members left behind (like Althea), trigger both migrants and their families to morally judge migrant mothers. But they miss the complexities of learning how to mother from afar. First, motherhood is learned, not natural or instinctive, thereby making it impossible to get it right the first time around. Second, motherhood is a practice: Many women, migrant or not, can learn to correct their mistakes and forge ahead with different ideas and behaviors. Olivia admitted that her mothering is always changing.

> Because [our relationship] is so distant. It looks like, you know, what I do is very strict. When I heard something that she did bad—wrong, what I do is [get] very, very angry at her. And then, the more she will not open up. But then, suddenly, it's like it's, you know, it's three years ago, when I started realizing that "Hey! I am not there. I am not the one who raised her." And so, why will I like, you know, every time she did something wrong, uhm, what I do is [get] very angry, so I adjusted myself, and like, you know, try to like, you know, find a different approach to her, and then now she is starting to open up, but still, there is the fear when she did something wrong.

At least to me, in our third talk-story together, Olivia admitted that she was wrong to treat Althea with a heavy hand and that absence has been a crucial part of her migrant motherhood. Her insight about who raised her daughter (not her) then informed the way she wanted to adjust her parenting from afar.

Because I went back to Manila to spend time with Althea while building a relationship with Olivia, accompanying her to the parks where she took her charge on weekends, my longitudinal approach gave me both sides of their story. If I were only to represent Althea's perspective, this dyad's family narrative would likely be characterized by the brooding resentment of a daughter toward her migrant mother. However, understanding their story as always simultaneously unfolding and interpreted from abroad and the Philippines, the account of emotional strain emerges quite differently, as one thread in their transnational family narrative and history. It does not take precedence over all of Althea's and Olivia's interactions; rather, it is an aspect of their family's transnational story that reflects their past and will perhaps shape their future. The intense strain they feel at times in their relationship does not constitute their whole narrative as transnational mother and daughter. In fact, emotional tension is a dimension of learning how to deal with the strain of being apart and trying to foster a transnational relationship.

Exploring the reasons why resentment becomes a mainstay in their relationship in our second talk-story, Althea reflected, "*Hindi ko alam. Siguro may mali din ako. Pino-protektahan lang niya ako.* I don't know. Maybe I've done things wrong. She is just trying to protect me." Here Althea acknowledged that the strain in her relationship from her mother comes from a place of care and that she herself has a part in creating and maintaining the distance between them. But she returned to the topic of her mother's parenting, countering her mother's story of *sacrifice* with her own:

Tapos 'lagi niyang sinasabi na binigay ko na lahat para sa'yo, pero wala naman akong pagkukulang. Pagkukulang lang niya 'yung ganyang hindi niya ma-gets na 'pag nagagalit siya sobra-sobra. Sabi ko siguro sapat naman siguro 'yung ano 'yung sinusunod ko siya o hindi naman ako siguro nagpapa-rebelde. Kasi kung nagrebelde ako, nabuntis na ako or layas ako, nagda-drugs na ako, wala ako lahat niyan. Hindi niya nakikita 'yun, 'yung mga sacrifice ko.

Then, she always says that I gave up everything for you and she didn't do anything wrong. But the wrong thing that she doesn't understand—the times when she gets so mad at me. I think that maybe it's good enough that I do what she says or I don't rebel against her, because if I rebelled against her, I'd be pregnant or I would've ran away, I'd be on drugs, but I'm none of that. She doesn't see that, the sacrifice that I make.

Althea highlighted the decisions she has made to reject negative paths that her mother would disapprove of. In her narrative of daughterhood she emphasizes that she is holding up her end of the "immigrant bargain" (R. C. Smith 2006) by not acting out or rebelling against her mother. The type of care that she can give her mother, the type of care that makes the most sense for her, is to try to stay out of trouble. This is Althea's practice of daughterhood growing in the moments as she learns the minimum boundary that she has and can do to show her mother that she is indeed working toward the maintenance of their unspoken agreements. This sacrifice falls outside the Western idea of love and hate in the emotional framework of mothers and daughters, as Angie Y. Chung astutely argues in her study on Asian American children of immigrants' "sacrificial" love for their parents (Chung 2016). Althea's emotional dissonance is clear when she states that her mother never sees the sacrifices she is making in the Philippines. However, she still shows that the reason for rejecting drugs or early pregnancy is in honor of her mother's sacrifice of migration.

Educational imperatives become a driving force for children left behind to animate their part in multidirectional care. Althea described her long path to graduating from college: She was not interested in college but continued because of her mother's wishes. She admitted to a pattern of stops and starts in her education. Asked about Althea's inconsistent educational career, Olivia replied, talking to a figurative Althea, "'I did not send you to school to follow my footsteps. I'm not going to support you forever. What if something happens to me? Where are you—where do you turn? Maybe you take some classes while I'm still earning, while I'm still supporting you . . . take some more classes. Aim high.' Then she insists, that she wants to go and try, I say, okay. Maybe she will learn something out of it." In this comment,

Olivia's frustration with Althea's lack of commitment is salient. On the one hand, by arguing that she will not support Althea forever and imagining her disappointment in Althea, Olivia demonstrates that there is a limit to her patience when it comes to her daughter's education. On the other hand, she pledges to support Althea if she "learns something out of it." Scholars argue that migrant parents interpret educational attainment as an acquisition of cultural and linguistic capital for future economic stabilization (Alipio, Lu, and Yeoh 2015; Katz 2008), yet children left behind are often burdened with the onerous challenge of completing a degree that may or may not result in a "better future." Still, this very negotiation is quite laborious, requiring much care work on both sides of the transnational family.

In negotiating her relationship with her daughter, Olivia is defining her care work with her daughter through what some scholars call "co-presence"—families continue the work of communication, albeit with negative emotions (Baldassar 2007). Although feelings of frustration and hurt are present, families continue to communicate to check if one another are "really okay." The need for what Loretta Baldassar calls "co-presence" often prevails over hurt feelings in the communication strategies of transnational families. Like Althea and Olivia's story, much of the communication between mother and daughter often ensured co-presence and no more than that. During times of strain in the transnational relationships of families, members feel a need to inform one another at the very minimum that they are doing okay. A range of feelings accompanies the work of letting one another know that "everything is okay" and yet transnational family members continue to make the effort to maintain contact. Both Althea and Olivia felt deeply divided in their relationship, and yet both of them sought to understand why and continued to provide care for one another by managing their emotions (Hochschild 2003).

Ironically, neither mother nor daughter feels that the other sees or adequately understands her sacrifices. In their own ways, Althea and Olivia define obedience and migration, respectively, as sacrifices and therefore equivalent to providing acts of care. This supports earlier scholarship that shows givers and receivers define care in their own terms and therefore those definitions vary wildly.[6] Through her painful experience of transnational daughterhood, Althea still continues to accomplish tasks as a form of care to her migrant mother in consistent ways.

> 'Yung may nangyari nung nag-aaral ako . . . para lang maging proud siya sa'kin, kailangan ko ng tapusin. Kailangan ko i-graduate 'to. Eh hindi ko naman alam

na may isa pa akong bagsak, so ayun. Parang sinusunod ko lahat ng kagustu-
han, sabihin niya sa akin, utos niya sa akin. Pinahawan 'yung sablay ko para
lang matuwa siya sa akin.

When that thing happened when I was in school . . . just so that she's proud
of me I needed to finish. I needed to graduate. But I didn't know that there
was one class that I failed, so there. It's like I did everything that she wanted
me to do, what she told me to do, her bidding. So I cleared my failing grade
just so that she could be happy with me.

The betrayal each feels stems from the fact that they are defining these
acts as care regardless of their emotional dissonance: They do not agree on
what constitutes sacrifice as care. The distance between Althea and Olivia
heightens the problem that neither of them could see the types of work they
do for one another, much less appreciate the time and energy that goes into
ensuring responsibilities are met. In the multidirectional care model Althea's
actions toward completing a semester is a form of care work. The obligation
of education is fulfilled to satisfy her mother's sacrifice of migration and even
if she feels conflicted about finishing college, she commits to finishing her
courses and tries to resolve the penalties in her classes. Like Althea mentioned
before, she does not have to do any of the things her mother has set out for
her to do. After all, her mother is thousands of miles away, and given that
they are not on good terms, there is really no reason or constraint that keeps
her from doing what she wants. In fact, Althea does not feel fulfilled or pas-
sionate about college; it is more of a burden than anything else. And yet, her
commitment to finishing her degree is unwavering because she understands
that her degree will grant her mother a type of relief. Her graduation will be
a marker of pride for her mother who has spent most of their family's lived
memory abroad. It will mean that that whole time apart resulted in some
relief for a migrant mother and her daughter left behind could feel that her
mother was proud.

Each is isolated, worsening the unstable relationship they already have.
With trust and communication already weak, showing any vulnerability is
less and less an option. Although Althea and Olivia describe only fragmented
intimacy, they continue to attend to one another's emotional and financial
needs. With this experience, the care that Althea provides for her mother is
not drawing from an idealized form of love. It is not even benevolent; it is
merely transactional. Althea discussed her completion of school as finishing a task that could actually release her from her obligations to her mother.
Complete with eye rolling and head shaking, Althea's body language and

words pointed to the fact that graduating was a measure of reciprocation that she took no pride or enjoyment in. It was all for her mother and graduating would quickly release her from the ties to her mother. Moreover, finishing school is a type of labor that is key to keeping the sacrifices between transnational mother and daughter. Olivia leaves to give Althea a better life, works abroad so Althea can go to a better school, and stays abroad to support Althea's lifestyle. None of these acts may have been acts that Olivia felt good about or proud of, yet she considers them to be care work. For Althea, the actions that she takes of finishing her college education, or keeping her mother in the loop, are a part of those agreements. Although Althea may feel that finishing her degree is arduous and arbitrary, it is still work on her end of the bargain. She is motivated by the powerful emotion of guilt (Baldassar 2015) in her relationship and therefore does not draw from feelings of love to honor her mother; therefore, the work of graduation, with or without an idealized form of love, is still a form of care work.

I asked Olivia about Althea's finishing college and what she thought about her daughter's education. She remembered a time when she found out Althea did not pay her tuition with the money she sent. Olivia considered cutting off financial support to her daughter because she felt so betrayed about Althea's deception.

Noong na-find out ko na hindi nagbayad ng tuition fee, galit na galit ako! Ultimatum, sabi ko, that's it! Basta bibigyan ko lang siya ng enough for living purposes. Tapos, sabi naman ng teacher, sabi niya, wala daw contact ang mama niya, sabi na nasa abroad ang nanay niya—'Yung guardian naman niya, hindi ma-contact. So that means, wala talagang paraan na ma-contact ang kanyang pamilya. Siya lang daw ang pinapadalhan daw ng nanay niya ng pambayad. 'Yun ang pambayad din natin sa iba, so, it's not her fault. So that time, prinocess ko rin sa isip ko, tama nga. Kasalanan natin, kasalanan mo. Kaya tuloy, naging ano 'yung bata, dahil, parang wala parang hindi namin kini-care.

When I found out that she did not pay her tuition fee, I was so mad! I gave her an ultimatum, that's it! I'll only give her enough for living purposes. But the teacher said that they couldn't contact her mother, because her mother is abroad. And they can't contact her guardian either. So that means the school couldn't contact anyone. She was the only person that her mother sends money to, to pay for school. That payment went to other things too, so it's not her fault. So that time I processed it in my mind, she's right. It's both our faults, my fault. That's why the child got confused, because it was like no one was caring for her.

After Olivia fervently expresses that she was ready to give an ultimatum to Althea, enraged by the information about a missed tuition payment, the following sentiment was a statement about still caring for Althea's basic needs. This stark juxtaposition of withdrawal and concession to her daughter's livelihood is the kind of paradox of emotional dissonance that is the affective background to continuing basic family operations transnationally. In this story, Olivia talks about how she would continue to provide for her child's sustenance even in the midst of Althea's deception and her feelings of anger. In her comment, Olivia unpacks how Althea's choice to skip her tuition payment was actually caught up in a series of miscommunications between her, the school, Althea, and her guardian. Olivia felt right in her emotional response of anger to the fact that she did not know where her hard-earned money went. But still, she rationalizes the situation by describing the lack of care in Althea's life. In her use of the word "care," Olivia is not using an idealized notion of love and warmth; rather, she is pointing to the fact that Althea did not have guidance and proper follow-up with the school staff. Here we see that although Olivia's anger marks this event, her comment teaches us that, first, she is still willing to provide financial support to her daughter despite the missed payment, and second, that the care she identifies as necessary is not about love, but about completing the tasks of keeping Althea in school. Olivia is sharpening her practice of transnational motherhood by understanding that both she and her daughter were at fault in the tuition confusion, a pause that she would not have considered during the earlier phases of Althea's unwise decisions. As both Althea and Olivia mature in age and in their transnational relationship, they are expanding their definitions of care and how they interpret the bumps in the road for their family.

Sukli, the Uneven Exchange of Transnational Care Work

Children in transnational families act on care work even if they do not express that work through an idealized notion of love, warmth, or tenderness. The Filipino word *sukli*, repeated in the narratives of Filipino children in transnational families, captures the uneven and invisible ways that they assert care work for their migrant parents. *Sukli* can be translated in two ways: In the concrete, it means the monetary currency or change you are given after you've paid for something; in the abstract, it is deeply linked to the Filipino cultural value of *utang ng loob,* which can be loosely translated as reciprocation in the context of family obligation. *Sukli* describes children's acts of service toward their migrant parents and family's well-being, challenging the idea that they are passive recipients of care in the transnational family. It is true that children are contributing to their families in currencies and economies incommensurate to the capital their migrant family members send home; yet children's labor impacts their families greatly. Maya reflected on one of the times that her mother Rose was upset at her because of a bad grade on her report card.

> Pagkatapos ko tinext 'yung report card, hinintay ko ang tawag niya. Tapos, nung nag-usap kami parang 'yung ano, parang pinapahalagahan ko, parang iingatan ko bawat kung anong sinasabi niya talaga. Parang nandun 'yung goal ko na talagang gusto kong pakinggan kahit mahirap sundin, kahit saway na yun, para lang masuklian ko siya.

> After I texted her my report card, I waited for her call. Then, when we talked it's like, like I try to value, like take care and listen to everything she tries to say. It's like that's my goal, really try to listen to her even if it's hard to do it her way, even if she's telling me what to do, just so I can give something back to her in return.

The eldest of four children, Maya is responsible for communication with her mother, who is in New York City, as well as the upkeep of the house and, of course, the success of her educational career. In this moment of disappointment, Maya decided to text an image of her report card to Rose in the evening and await her phone call the following morning, given that Manila and New York City are exactly twelve hours apart in time difference. Maya understood that her mother would be unhappy, but listening and then trying her best to follow her mother's advice (and being fine with the fact that she might not be able to achieve her mother's wishes) was the way that she could honor Rose's sacrifice. Although families left behind are not able to fully reciprocate their migrant counterparts' contribution, and particularly not in the ways that migrants have imagined, Maya signals how families left behind understand what they can offer their migrant family members.

One way to understand the work of transnational care under emotional strain between separated family members is in the Tagalog word *sukli*, which Maya uses (as do many of the families I interviewed in the Philippines and migrant women in New York City). The abstract way children left behind are using this local cultural concept alludes to the unevenness in the exchange of care work within their families. I develop this concept because of the curious insistence of families in the Philippines on making sense of their care exchanges in this way. It was their way of saying that the money and the care work they do in the Philippines *for* their migrant family does not always feel equivalent. In an effort to develop emotional grammar (Mckay 2007) during times of intense, emotional situations, the notion of *sukli* can pinpoint labor in the care work, whether it is money or a text message, even if the expectations are different for migrant mothers and nonmigrant family members. As a migrant mother, Rose was terribly disappointed in Maya's bad grade, but still, Maya's commitment to communicating to her mother (and even her transparency) is a practice in care work to sustain trust and confidence in her relationship with her mother. And although Maya cannot return her mother's sacrifice with good grades, she states that listening to her mother is one way she can give back to her mother, albeit unevenly.

Members of transnational families—young people and their adult parents—define care through a broad range of acts: receiving and budgeting financial support through remittances from parents, maintaining transnational communication (Francisco 2013; Hoang and Yeoh 2014; Madianou 2011), graduating from college, obtaining necessities from parents (Hondagneu-Sotelo and Avila 1997), taking care of weekly household chores (Dreby 2010). However, when the conception of care is narrowly defined by monetary support, then care in the transnational family is reduced to the migrant, an adult or a child, who has moved elsewhere to seek financial stability for the family. Yet, from the perspective of a child in a transnational family care work envelops a wide spectrum of acts. From this lens, we can visualize the different actors and forms of care work transnationally, and in this study in particular, by focusing on children and youth as care workers in their own families and how they understand their experiences as active agents in the migration process. In fact, throughout this book, I demonstrate that financial remittance is not the sole currency of care in the transnational family. As scholars urge migration research on the transnational family to consider a lens of "care circulation" to better understand the mobility of labor within families (Baldassar and Merla 2013), *sukli* is a local emotional concept that allows us to explore this incommensurable exchange.

Migrant mothers can only do so much to regulate the behavior of their children in the Philippines. JJ, the 19-year-old son of Rose and brother of Maya, admits that he's not the strongest student and, at times, has a tendency to be lazy in attending early morning classes since he has to commute two hours to his college in the morning. This becomes a source of disagreement between him and his migrant mother and even his father living with him in Manila. Rose worries that JJ won't finish and that he will rebel against her wishes. They have had many serious talks over Skype about his schooling, but Rose thinks these conversations are only partly effective in convincing him to stick with his college schedule. In one of our talk-stories, I raised this issue with JJ and he said:

> *Iniisip ko talaga 'yung sinabi sa'kin ni Mama tapos pagbabayad niya tuition na hindi naman basta basta nilalabas 'yon. Minsan naiisip ko din na Manila pa 'yon, nakakatamad talaga 'di ba? Kasi kunwari ang aga ng klase, ang layo pa nun, parang nakakatamad pumasok. Iniisip ko din, nakakatakot kay Mama! Pero parang naiisip ko din 'yung ano kaya 'yun ang sukli niya sa aming tuition. So doon ako napapa-motivate pumasok.*

I really think about what Mama says, also when she pays for my tuition, that money doesn't just come out of nowhere. Even if sometimes I think about school is all the way in Manila, it makes you feel lazy, you know? For example, your class is early in the morning, and it's so far, it's like you don't feel like going. I also think about and I feel scared of Mama! But when I think about it too, that's why that's the least I can give back to her in return for my tuition. That's how I try to motivate myself to go to school.

In this context JJ talks about *sukli* as his way of returning his mother's diligent payment of tuition. Under pressure, JJ could easily disregard Rose's many conversations with him and be truant to his college classes. But making an effort to get to school is his keeping his end of the deal. *Sukli* is the right word here because the monetary amount of tuition is not actually equal financially or socially to JJ's effort to get up in the mornings and attend class. He is offering what he can in exchange for his mother's work abroad. Returning to the literal translation of *sukli*, what one gets in return for paying a full amount for an item is not the same amount of money given in the first place. Rose has paid through her migration, leaving her family, and working as a domestic in New York City, all of which results in the thousands of dollars she paid in college tuition. For JJ, his *sukli* is attending his classes and finishing college. These efforts and contributions to their relationship are not equal in any way yet they are attending to the labor that goes into maintaining their family. Both Rose and JJ have an unspoken agreement about the value of the actions (college tuition, going to school) they contribute to their relationship and although their contributions are not equal in currency, the differing expectations they have of one another are precisely what produces heated debates between mother and son. Rose believes that going to college is a simple task but at times it is quite difficult for JJ and therefore he interprets his reticent commitment to school as a form of care for his mother. In this way, JJ gives Rose what she paid, acknowledging that it is not equal in weight but may be equal in value.

Similarly, Zach, Vickie's son who has struggled with the same issues as JJ, says:

> *Sa'kin, because I'm still studying, ang sabi lang naman ni mama, magtapos. 'Yon lang ang hinihiling niya. Kahit na minsan, minsan talaga mahirap eh, tapos 'di kami nagkakasundo tungkol sa effort ko at ang kanyang ginugusto. Pero pinipilit ko pa rin, parang 'yon ang sukli ko sa kanyang sakripisyo.*

> For me, because I'm still studying, what Mama says is just to finish. That's all she's asking of me. Even though sometimes, sometimes it's really hard, then we don't see eye to eye on the effort I put in versus her expectations of me. Still, I force myself to do it in return for her sacrifice.

Zach explicitly addresses one of the issues that cause emotional strain and misunderstanding between him and his mother Vickie, living in New York City. He describes finishing his education almost as a chore; his only motivation is his mother's expectation for him to finish. However, in his use of *sukli*, Zach acknowledges his mother's experience abroad and weighs in against his everyday choice to either continue with his education or drop out. For him, this decision is not an easy one: Sometimes he thinks that going to school might not be in his best interest and sometimes his motivation wanes. In his eyes his effort is huge, taking up much of his will power. And yet he still understands that that effort is only part of what his mother offers to him as she is working abroad.

In our last *kuwentuhan* (talk-story) session, Maya and JJ talk about the conversations they have had with their mother about her wish for them to complete their education.

MAYA: *Hindi siya 'yung nanay na, na, "Kailangan suklian yan, tuition." Si Mama, hindi.*

JJ: *Si Mama sinasabi, "Ayusin mo man o hindi yung pag-aaral, sa akin lang gusto ko na magandang buhay para sa'yo. Para sa'yo din 'yan. Hindi 'yan para sa'kin."*

MAYA: *Ginagawa niya ang lahat para sa amin. Kaya nasa sa'min 'yun kung ano man ang maibibigay namin sa kanya.*

MAYA: She's not the kind of mother that's like, "You have to pay me back for the tuition that I paid." Not Mama.

JJ: Mama tells us, "Whether you do well or not in your studies, for me I just want you to have a better life. It's for you too. Not just for me."

MAYA: She does all of this for us. So it is up to us to do what we can in return.

Expectations of migrant counterparts toward their families left behind are a major source of strain and tension within transnational families. As Maya and JJ detail above, understanding what their mother's expectations are and what they are capable of supplying in the situation constitutes the mechanics of *sukli*. Grades are extremely important to children in the Philippines and mothers abroad, but the idea that children are doing their best to uphold their end of the immigrant bargain is often enough. In these terms, the labor in caring is defined by both providers and receivers of care in the transnational family.

Angered at Stubborn Gendered Norms

Girls and women in families left behind have stepped up into the roles of the migrant women in their families, causing resentment between daughters and mothers, in particular, but also between migrants and the women kin with whom they leave their children (Parreñas 2005a; Dreby 2010). The amount of work women kin and daughters take up in families left behind is a point of contention for transnational relationships, as are control or power in the household more generally. The emotional strain is compounded by the narrow gendered definitions of who is supposed to do care work in families left behind by migrant women. The patriarchal logics of the family are one of the reasons why children left behind harbor resentment and anger toward their families' situation of separation and migration. For daughters in particular, the strain they feel in their new family conditions does not always result in anger or resentment toward their mothers; instead, they express frustration at the inadequate reorganization of domestic work in their families. When Joan left, her oldest daughter Melann took over cooking, cleaning, and looking after the education of her older and younger brothers. But Melann expressed frustration about the lack of help that she received from her father, not about the migration of her mother:

> *Sa akin ngayon, mas galit ako sa tatay ko. Kasi he's supposed to be the one doing that. He's supposed to be the one providing for us, and yet wala siyang ginagawa dun. 'Di ba? Kasi ngayon parang wala si mama dapat siya, pinaparamdaman niya naman na kahit wala si mama, nandun siya. Pero siya never tumutulong sa gawaing bahay. Wala. Wala. Wala lang, parang wala na nga kaming nanay, wala pa kaming tatay.*

> For me now, I'm more angry at my father. Because he's supposed to be the one doing that. He's supposed to be the one providing for us, and yet he's not

doing that. Right? Because now that Mama is gone it's supposed to be him, he tries to make us feel that even if Mama isn't here, he's here. But he never helps with chores around the house. Nothing. Nothing. It's nothing, it's like we don't have a mother and we don't have a father.

Departing from the narratives of daughters resentful toward or estranged from migrant mothers, Melann offers a different perspective to analyze the emotional strain in transnational families. Her comment describes frustration with the gendered arrangement that is put in place when a mother leaves her family. She does not direct exasperation toward her mother; rather, she is angry that her father is not adjusting to the new conditions of their family. In spite of her angry feelings toward her father, Melann does not fail to meet the particular needs of her family. It is clear that the strain-inducing factor in Melann's situation is the contradiction in the ascribed gendered duties of her father's and mother's "social roles" as breadwinner and house maker. Although she feels abandoned by her father in terms of the care work left behind in their family, she has continued to do the work necessary to help raise her younger brother.

In fact, daughters left behind find their new roles meaningful despite the heavy burden of stepping into their mothers' roles in their families. In our *kuwentuhan*, Christopher, Melann's younger brother, and Melann talk about the heavy strain of missing their mother but also the unexpected product of that emotional strain.

CHRISTOPHER: *The thing is iba talaga kapag nanay ang nandiyan. Pero may positive din.*

MELANN: *Yung positive naman, mas naging mas close kaming dalawa. Kasi nga wala siyang nanay, ako yung nanay niya. Parang ganun.*

CHRISTOPHER: *Actually araw-araw sa gabi kakain kayo sabay-sabay. Negative 'yun eh ngayon 'pag gutom ka, may ulam diyan, kumain ka.*

MELANN: *Eh 'di kumain ka. 'Pag gutom ka kumain ka, may pagkain naman. (laughs)*

CHRISTOPHER: *Tapos habang kumakain, naubusan ka ng kanin, kasalanan mo 'yun, hindi ka kumain agad. (laughs)*

MELANN: *Ano? Bumili ka sa labas, magluto ka, may dunong ka naman.*

CHRISTOPHER: *Oo nga, magaling ka namang titser. Ako ay lalaking marunong magluto or kumain 'pag gutom. Wow!*

MELANN: *Wowin mo mukha mo! (laughs)*

CHRISTOPHER: *Pero sa totoo lang, nakaka-miss din yung sabay-sabay kumain.*

MELANN: . . . *at saka magsisimba.*

CHRISTOPHER: The thing is, it's really different when your mother's around. But there's positives too.

MELANN: The positive is that we got closer, us two. Because our mother isn't here, I'm his mother. Like that.

CHRISTOPHER: Actually every day at night we used to eat together. What's negative now is that if you're hungry and there's food, you just eat.

MELANN: You should just eat. If you're hungry, I mean, there is food. (laughs)

CHRISTOPHER: And when you're eating, and you run out of rice, it's your fault because you didn't eat right away. (laughs)

MELANN: What? Then buy some rice, or cook some, you've got a brain.

CHRISTOPHER: I know, you're a good teacher. I'm a man that knows how to cook or feed myself if I'm hungry. Wow!

MELANN: Wow your face! (laughs)

CHRISTOPHER: But in all honesty, you miss the times you eat together.

MELANN: . . . and going to church together.

I highlight this exchange between Melann and Christopher because it captures so precisely how children left behind talk about the things they miss about their mothers. It also shows how they are actively negotiating the gendered expectations of caring for each other. When Melann jokes that Christopher should eat when he's hungry instead of waiting around to be served by his older sister, she demonstrates that the responsibility for the domestic work her mother left behind must be shared. Christopher's acceptance that it is his fault for waiting too long to eat if the rice runs out signals that he understands that the new arrangement of his family depends on his own participation in caring for himself. Lastly, Christopher and Melann have repeatedly conversed about the gendered responsibilities that Melann assumed after their mother's departure and that new aspect of their family has become a uniting factor between these two siblings. Both of them have agreed that although their father is inactive in domestic duties, Christopher was not going to follow in his footsteps. Therefore, when Christopher is joking around about being a man who knows how to cook and clean, Melann gives it right back to him by saying that his skills are not something that should be glorified or wowed at. Here we are seeing that the gendered responsibilities in the transnational family that cause stress and strain on daughters are often being diffused by their initiatives to challenge the gendered notions of domestic work they are ascribed.

Separation places a heavy emotional burden on children. In this snippet conversation, Melann and Christopher are going in and out of the feelings of deep sadness, but they also are always talking about their survival strategies. They often talk of the pain and confusion they feel about why their mother is away; however, their reflections about their pain are also buttressed by the different ways they are building intimacy with one another. Emotional strain is a marker of tough moments in their lives, but it also serves as a launching pad to create and negotiate the gendered labor and emotional relations in their family.

Learning How to Struggle Through the Pain

Strain between Melann and her mother Joan also comes from miscommunication and fragmented reporting about the daily goings on and situations, what Loretta Baldassar has called "withholding of truths" (Baldassar 2007). Unlike Althea and Olivia, Melann and Joan have a frequent communication pattern, calling on Skype or chatting on Facebook every couple of days. But if care can be produced through a multidirectional care model, so can strain. One way this happens is when multiple people are reporting to a migrant mother about the happenings in her family. Even if lines of communication are open and multiple care providers are contributing to a multivalent caring arrangement, lines can still get crisscrossed and misunderstandings can arise:

> Tsaka ano, nung minsan nga parang may nagbalita sa kanya na 'yung boyfriend ko doon natutulog sa'min. Actually, minsan natutulog siya doon, lalo kasi may sakit siya, may hika. 'Pag sinumpong siya, hindi ko siya pauuwiin mag-isa. Oo, talagang . . . talagang . . . at saka hello? Anong mangyayari? 'Yung kwarto namin . . . (Melann laughs) ako dito, yung papa ko dito sa kabilang kama, yung kapatid ko sa itaas, so anong mangyayari sa'min? Kahit magkatabi kami matulog dahil dalawa yung kasama namin sa kwarto di ba? Ayun, pero 'yun, tapos pero parang upset . . . na-upset siya sa'kin. Disappointed daw siya, ganyan-ganyan. Sabi ko ano ba 'yan? Sabi ko, nakakainis naman hindi lang kita nakakausap, ganyan na 'yung ano, sabi ko. Sabi ko, wala kaming ginagawang masama. Andami kasing pumapapel sa amin eh.

There was this one time, that she had heard or someone told her that my boyfriend sleeps over at our house. Actually, he did sleep over a couple of times, especially when he's sick, he has asthma. When he has an asthma attack, I won't let him go home by himself. Yes, really . . . I mean really . . . and hello? Our room (Melann laughs), it's me here, my papa beside me on the bed right next to me, my brother is right upstairs, so what are we really gonna do? Even if my boyfriend and I sleep next to each other, there are people in the same room as us, right? There, even then she was so upset . . . so upset with me. She told me she was disappointed in me, like that. I said, what? I said, that is so unfair that I just wasn't able to talk to you about this issue, you're already judging me, I said to her. I said, we didn't do anything wrong. There's so many people involved with our family, that's why.

Melann's story is a demonstration of how one piece of news can be twisted into different stories that produce a huge misunderstanding between mother and daughter. Melann grits her teeth through the pain of feeling like she has lost her mother's trust. Because of the extended and multidirectional character of care in Joan and Melann's family, Tita Tina (Joan's sister and Melann's aunt) was the one who reported this overnight incident to Joan in New York City. Coming from someone other than Melann, Joan took the news as a blow to what she thought was an open and truthful relationship with her daughter. Although Joan felt like trust was broken, they continued to talk and clarify the issue. At this point, even if the two do not trust one another or are hurt by the things they are hearing about each other, we see that they still forge ahead with their communication as a type of care work.

Melann was able to explain the intentions behind her boyfriend sleeping over. I interpret the silences behind her word *talagang* (really) as moments where she could not understand why her mother would not give her the benefit of the doubt in this situation. Melann is a responsible daughter, and in her terms, she would have never taken advantage of her mother's absence to make bad decisions. However, because of the distance between the two, Melann has to do the work of communicating through these awkward growing moments to defend herself and also to clarify the issues that cause her mother worry and stress.

Joan says that communication as a type of care work is key to learning how to deal with periods of emotional strain in her family:

Ang ano ko lang is open sila sa akin. Kahit anong galit nila, ano sakit sa puso nila, talagang sasabihin sa'kin. At sinasabi nila. Sabi ko nga sa kanila, kahit na masama o mali, o ano, sabihin nila sa'kin. Pag-uusapan namin. Doon lang naman nagkakaroon ng kasunduan 'yun e. 'Wag lang maputol ang komunikasyon.

For me, I just want them to be open with me. Whatever anger they have, whatever heartache they have. Just tell me. And they do tell me. I told them, even if it's bad or wrong or whatever, they just let me know. We'll talk about it. That's how we can understand each other. Just don't cut off communication with me.

For Joan, even under the stress of hurt, anger, or pain, she insists that co-presence (like in Althea and Olivia's case) is not enough. Rather, it is the work of being honest and talking through the emotional struggles of the family that can trump emotional dissonance. Both she and Melann are demonstrating that communication as a type of care work could be a uniting process. Even if Joan is disappointed and Melann is insulted and even if they do not necessarily *want* to talk to one another, the act of keeping up with each other and then pushing through the feelings of betrayal can be considered care work. Moreover, both Joan and Melann are learning how to deal with situations that are unwanted but that they still need to attend to from afar. This moment of strain in their relationship lasted months and definitely informs their current relationship, but the struggle was only temporary. The pain and betrayal they felt is a part of their story but it is not all of it.

Conclusion

Moving away from characterizing emotional strain within families as dysfunctional or aberrant, I highlight these moments of hardship and difficulty as a part of the rubric of the emotions of transnational families: Even when transnational family members are angry or disappointed or resentful of one another, they continue to do work in keeping their transnational families operational. Sometimes the work of caring under these emotional circumstances is unhealthy, resulting in mental and physical damage. Other times, the amount of work that is necessary to smooth over rough patches is unequal. Children left behind often do the bare minimum to keep up their end of expectations while migrant mothers are working their fingers to the bone to keep up tuition payments. Or sometimes children left behind expend an extraordinary amount of effort to live up to the expectations of their mothers without getting the recognition they feel they deserve. The often invisible work that keeps families functional under difficult emotional conditions is not always characterized by love or nurturance. Yet on both sides of the transnational spectrum, all members of the family are engaged in labor that attempts to value and revalue the actions and sacrifices of their family members far away. When families in the Philippines make meaning of their acts of care as *sukli* toward the work of migrant members, they are acknowledging the different expectations, abilities, and forms in which care circulates within their families even under emotional reticence. This book is an exercise in re-visioning care work in exactly this way. And under the conditions of emotional reservation (to put it tamely), transnational families illustrate that the labor in caring is never left unattended.

The descriptions and quotes I provide describe time periods of strain that are anywhere from days, months, and years. Strain, although an important and illuminating aspect of family lives, does not characterize the complex and often changing narratives and experiences of families who are separated. The linear way in which I am able to narrate the story of strain in this academic text only allows me to encapsulate each story with a beginning and end. Yet the families in this study are not so simple. Their relationships are contentious, and often the source of pain and guilt remains even as they enact care work. Mothers, children, husbands, grandparents, all have entrusted me to tell the good in their families' histories. I am aware of the filters they have told their stories through and the ways they have told me about their "drama." Therefore, I interpret their talk-stories with what Ruthellen Josselson calls a "hermeneutic of suspicion" (Josselson 2004). And yet, I have also tried to contextualize these moments of strain within the whole narrative from different vantage points, looking at their lives with a "hermeneutic of faith" (Josselson 2004) that gives way to the vacillation in family peace and war. The glimpses into transnational family life seek only to recognize the labor that goes into the transnational family even through times where the emotional fabric of the family is thin. The stories and quotes detangle the myth that all care work in the transnational family has to be characterized with resounding love. Rather, through times of strain or entire relationships that are built on strain, transnational families are working to keep their families together. Strained relationships can be characterized through these temporary moments and as the emotional information that becomes the underpinning of whole relationships. Focusing on the fluidity of these relationships allows us to see that transnational families have a tremendous capacity for adapting and adjusting.

At times the resentment and strain felt by transnational family members, specifically daughters or women kin left behind, is not only anger toward the individual who has migrated. Resentment often stems from the social process under which transnational families are absorbing the heavy weight of the shifts in gendered work in the family. The narrow ideas of patriarchal culture, maintained through institutions like the family, and the gendered processes of Philippine migration result in conflicting ideas of ascribed social roles for men and women. The ascribed gendered work in family care has long been coming undone. But it is unraveling without a parallel process that dismantles the very cultural logics that keep gendered family care intact. The strain that daughters like Melann feel is a frustration with fathers who are unable to assert a new role as care providers in their transnational family context.

Further, strain necessarily emerges from the complex network of care providers in a transnational family. Using a multidirectional care model, I interpret care in the transnational family as a dynamic arrangement with numerous providers of care in different locations. Often emotional dissonance within a transnational family is placed within a linear timeline between two diametrically opposed members of a family. However, in my research, strained relations or emotions result from a more complex arrangement of care. With all hands and hearts involved in maintaining a transnational family, feelings are bound to be hurt and misunderstood. Simply put, there are many people invested in keeping a family together, albeit physically apart; thus, the stakes in doing emotion work (correctly) from all of the points of a transnational care network is much higher.

At times care circulation is reciprocal, and at other times, when it is not realized it can produce guilt and disappointment within family networks (Baldassar 2015; Vermot 2015). While these negative emotions can weigh down relationships, they are effective resources for family members to reinterpret different types of care work. Although care work circulated may not necessarily equate on an economic scale (money is not valued in the same way as a Skype call in a globalizing Asia), children in a transnational arrangement still invest work into sustaining caregiving under the emotional circumstances of "guilt trips" or resentment (Baldassar 2015). A multidirectional care lens calls attention to the need to broadly define the exchange—multiple in direction, forms, and actors—in care work that occurs in transnational family arrangements. More importantly, this framework illuminates the way in which children left behind are defining their contributions to their transnational families.

For transnational families, and in particular for children left behind, the risk in analyzing their emotional processes without taking into account the larger social forces of globalization will likely contribute to a discourse of deficit for young people in transnational families. Studies have shown that the popular cultural frame of children left behind as brooding and resentful subjects abandoned by migrant parents is inaccurate; in fact, children have a range of positive emotions to their experiences of migration and separation because they are actively engaged with maintaining family relations (Alipio

2015; Ní Laoire et al. 2010; Alipio, Lu, and Yeoh 2015). The emotionality assigned to young people in Filipino transnational families is a milieu of anger and disappointment that often shapes their roles in their families as passive and at times ungrateful recipients of care (Parreñas 2005a, 2005b, 2008). However, these ascribed emotions do not situate the affective background of young people in transnational families in the larger shifts in political economy that render their families in the condition of transnationality; rather, they are investigated from a Euro-American perspective of childhood that is often conceptualized in a private home and family characterized by co-presence and proximity. Emotional geographies of transnational families, both migrant and nonmigrant, are necessarily embedded in the social, political, and cultural ideologies that produce their family formations (Lutz and Abulughod 1990). The experience of childhood in the contemporary Filipino family, in particular, has been shaped by migration produced by sophisticated and aggressive neoliberal immigration policies (R. M. Rodriguez 2010; Guevarra 2009) that have prioritized family separation for almost a half century. As illustrated throughout this book, children left behind are agentic in interpreting their parents' migration and because of the persistent political economic conditions in the Philippines, they are leading families in creating new understandings of reciprocal and incommensurable care work.

To capture the relationship between global and intimate in the lives of transnational families, it is key to consider migration as a process rather than an event, making room for the narratives of children and young people in transnational families as continuous and in development, rather than static. As an adult analyzing children's lives, I challenge the idea that children left behind are stuck in one affective context for the entirety of their childhood. Conceptualizing the affective realities of children in transnational families as resentful in totality assumes that "good" care is correlated with spatial proximity between family members (Jameison 1998). When we assume that families can only have meaningful care if they live under the same roof, much less in the same nation-state, we excise the ability to analyze families' adaptability to rapid economic shifts that shape their family labor relations (Orellana et al. 2001). Further, I advance an argument about children's care work regardless of emotional dissonance as a reflection of the ongoing and historic trend of labor migration in sending countries like the Philippines. The half-century-long system of labor export has made migration part of Filipino culture, Filipino families, and, important to this study, Filipino young people's aspirations and life course planning (R. M. Rodriguez 2010; Guevarra 2009). Migration as a constant has and will continue to change how young Filipinos understand care work in their families, its geography, and how family members are supposed to adjust to those conditions. Lastly, the current emotionality assigned to children in transnational families left in homelands casts them aside as reactive to migration rather than seeing them as agents of resiliency and creativity responding to the changing meanings of "self" and "culture" (Mckay 2007). It does not allow them to evolve and mature their emotional grammar (Hoang and Yeoh 2012) to fit the (often difficult) conditions of their family; in actuality, children are responding to their family arrangements with an incredible capacity for resilience and creativity (Alipio, Lu, and Yeoh 2015; Hoang et al. 2015).

Conclusion

Producing Transnational Families and Possibilities Embedded

In 2004, Sharon traveled to New York City at age 52. She thought her duties as a mother were completed—having raised four children and having been a dutiful wife for thirty years to a successful Filipino businessman—and had turned her attention to caring for her ailing husband in their "third act." Although her husband was an American citizen, they established a home and made their lives in Manila. Her trip to New York City was supposed to be a short visit to take care of legal paperwork for her husband, who could no longer travel. But her husband suddenly fell gravely ill. Over Skype, Sharon, her children, and other family members in the Philippines collectively decided that she should stay in the United States to earn some extra money to cover the rapidly rising cost of her husband's medical care. After overstaying her tourist visa, Sharon could not go home to physically care for her sick husband or later to attend his funeral because she found a reliable and well-paying job as a nanny in New York City. The graduations and weddings of her adult children took place without her. In fact, Sharon is still in New York City working as a domestic worker to send money back to her children and grandchildren in Manila.

In my first interview with Sharon in early 2010, she told me what it's like to be away from her family:

> Communication—text, YM [Yahoo Messenger], Skype—makes me feel like I'm close to them. When they tell me what happens in their day-to-day life— it's like talking to Mom is taking care of Mom. For example, there was this time when Johnny got into an accident and they were taking care of him. They told me instead of hiding it. When they are honest and they share with

me, even if I'm worried, I feel like I'm there. Especially in those moments. Because it's not a one-way, not a one-way ticket, not just the moms who are taking care. They are doing their best to give comfort to their family members back home. But because back home, they understand the sacrifice, for them, for their father, they also include me. For me it's easier. Even if I cannot be with them, at least I can communicate. I was still the mother. Using these technologies, I was still the mother.

In her experience as a migrant mother away from home, Sharon considers her family's responsibility to one another as an answer to her sacrifice of being away from home. She recognizes that the care work in her transnational family comes from her abroad to her children back home, from her children to her in New York City, *and* among her family members in the Philippines. The frequent communication on different platforms keeps her abreast of daily life back home while giving her the opportunity to partake in important decisions in the lives of her family. These are simple processes that Sharon values in her, albeit compromised, role as a mother from afar. When she says, "I was still the mother," Sharon points to transnational processes that make meaning of the radical reconfiguration of her relationships with her family in the Philippines. Her story also showcases the ways in which (adult) children left behind are active in the redefinition of the transnational family. Migrants like Sharon interpret the Philippine-based family's gestures of inclusion from afar as opportunities to redefine the meaning of their new roles in the family while retaining a semblance of their premigration identities as mothers.

A few months after my conversation with Sharon in Queens, New York, I sat down with her son Max, living in Metro Manila, Philippines, with his brother and sister-in-law and their three children. Max is the eldest of Sharon's four children. When I interviewed him in October 2010, he was 36 years old, making enough as a freelance graphic designer to support himself and contribute a small sum to his brother's family. Their extended household also started receiving financial support from Sharon to buttress the monthly expenses after his father fell ill. Max became the primary caregiver for his father, as his three younger siblings had families of their own. Sharon and Max were in constant communication about the health of his ailing father and the status of his siblings. I asked him about his experience taking care of his sick father while his mother had to work abroad and he said:

I hoped some of her stress is relieved. I wouldn't really know kasi baka may kaunting guilt na dapat siya 'yun. Pero kung ako as a son, 'yun ang gusto ko na ma-free siya of that burden. And most of all na maramdaman niya na isa kami, we are one in that goal na maalagaan at mabigay yung best kay Dad.

Magkakasama kami doon, hindi lang kanya yun. 'Yung oras, 'yung malasakit, pati 'yung gastos, gusto ko maramdaman niya 'yun na magkakasama kami.

. . . I wouldn't really know because she may have felt guilty, like she should've been taking care of him. But as a son, I would like her to be free of that burden. And most of all that she feels that we are one, we are one in that the goal was to take care and give the best to Dad. We were all together in that endeavor, that's not only her responsibility. The time, the devotion, and the cost, I wanted her to feel that we were all together.

Max reflected on his desire to ensure that his whole family felt that they were one in caring for their sick family member, that they would all contribute to helping his father in his last days. He recognized that even if his mother was far away, her contribution to the costs of medical care was as valuable as the time and energy he put in at his father's bedside. Max's effort to make sure Sharon understood her contribution—that she was also playing a role during an intense family crisis—is what I am identifying as a form of care produced by nonmigrant family members to the migrant abroad. The care of their sick father divided up between Sharon's children is a form of care that answered the immediate need in Manila, but it also doubled up as a form of care to Sharon, reassuring her that even without her physical presence, her financial support helped the family deal with the hardship that confronted them. Max says, "we are one," to illuminate that everyone plays a role in keeping the family together, another articulation of multidirectional care. For Sharon and her children in the Philippines, care is shared and given value in the different forms and directions it takes—from migrant mother to the family left behind, from son to ailing father, between siblings—and then those care networks boomerang back to the migrant mother, reassuring her that her family is taking care of one another.

In New York City, Sharon continues to redefine care in her local networks. In the early part of 2011, a participant in this study and a distant acquaintance of Sharon, Melanie, faced homelessness when her apartment was suddenly evacuated. Sharon offered a small spare room in her flat to Melanie in a time of need. Although Sharon felt embarrassed that the room was an oversized closet in a basement apartment in Queens, Melanie was thankful and took the opportunity without hesitation. In my follow-up interview with Sharon, after I helped Melanie move into their newly shared apartment, I asked Sharon what inspires this sort of help between migrant Filipinas. She answered:

It's because we understand how hard for a woman not to have anyone in these situations. We are in the same boat. So we know the feeling. You try to help also. The feeling of being alone in a different country. Being in a place where it is new. The feeling that you are away from your immediate family. Working so hard as a housekeeper. Only making so little. *Malaking sakripisyo talaga 'yan, at isa sa kalooban 'yan ng migranteng Pilipino.* It's really a huge sacrifice, and we unite in spirit with every migrant Filipino in that.

Sharon's response activates three specific identities that allow her to relate and recognize the hardship and sacrifice that other migrant Filipinos go through. The intelligibility between Sharon and Melanie as migrants, mothers far from their families, and domestics in a global city is based on an imagined global community, linked to experiences and identities of being a migrant that are simultaneously transnational and local. The community of care for migrant Filipinos, as shown in Sharon's and Melanie's examples, draws from their similar experiences in the stretch between their lives in New York City and the Philippines, thus extending their ability to recognize and care for one another in their diasporic homes (Francisco, Abenoja, and Lim 2016).

I share Sharon's story because it animates the main interventions of this book. First, through the model of multidirectional care, I demonstrate that care in a transnational context is never a one-way formula. Care comes in different forms (i.e., financial support and remittances from migrants or emotional support from families left behind) and there is no one metric to recognize these labors as they assist in the functioning of the transnational family. Still, I consider all of the types of care work discussed in this book as social reproductive labor—work that reproduces family operations. Perhaps their importance and contribution to the stability of the family are incommensurable—remitting $500 to pay for medical bills is qualitatively different from clicking "like" on Facebook—yet they all contribute to the care of a transnational family. This book is an effort to explore and value the myriad types of care beyond financial support within transnational families.

Families in this book admitted that efforts to keep transnational families intact are mixed with moments when care work felt valued and times when the work felt underappreciated and ignored. Strain and exhaustion appeared over and over again in these family narratives as the burden of separation and distance proved to be a continuous obstacle in reaching common understanding in sharing family life. Yet they still attended to this labor of caring through the emotionally dissonant and conflict-free periods in a family history. The acts of caring do not belie the occasional feelings of betrayal, anger, or resentment of transnational family members; rather, they are consistent with the idea that transnational family members have a deep understanding of the context of their separation that requires a commitment to care work for the upkeep of familial operations.

The different actors and providers of care are the essential junctures that keep transnational families operating. When transnational family members articulate their intimate understanding of care work, they acknowledge the complex web of people attending to care work in both the proximity of the place left behind and the transnational relationships for migrant and non-migrant members of their biological and extended kin. Therefore, forms of care in transnational families are not only maintained by the practices of the migrants abroad. They are multiple. The care arrangements in homes and among families left behind is a form of care for their proximate members and also a form of care that is aimed at their migrant family members because often that work cannot be monetized and measured in currency. Rather, it is the implicit acknowledgment and meaning-making processes between transnational family members that give the work (of sons like Max) value.

Second, as Sharon and her family show, the use of communication technology illuminates that care work can be as simple as answering a text or calling on Skype within the model of multidirectional care in the transnational family. Both migrants and families left behind use a variety of communication technologies frequently to keep one another involved. While migrants send remittances from abroad, families in the Philippines send text messages, status updates, and video calls as a currency of care as well. Along with messages and support, the roles of care providers are often simultaneous and exchanged through this use of technologies such as Skype, Facebook, Yahoo Messenger, or short message services. Through these avenues, caregivers in the transnational family can vary in their roles as providers of content as a form of keeping family members from afar abreast of daily activities.

Lastly, the examination of transnational care through a multidirectional care model demonstrates that redefined forms of care and roles of care providers inform how migrants recognize one another and, more importantly, build networks to support one another abroad. Stitching together the circulation of care in migrant communities as part of the web of care reconfigured under transnational contexts, Filipino migrants create solidarity with one another as they draw from their experiences as domestic workers, migrants, and transnational family members and workers in the United States. Migrants, in essence, include a new circuit of care in their transnational formulation of care by fostering communities of care that operate as their families away from home.

At the beginning of the process of writing this book, I set out to examine how transnational families are rethinking and reorganizing care work. As I delved into my research, analysis, and writing, I found that a deeper examination of the meaning, forms, roles, and definitions of care is at the crux of proposing multidirectional care to demonstrate that care work in transnational families is manifold. These aspects of care work in the transnational family urge us to decenter care as a project of the lone migrant family member; rather, it values the care work that many people involved in transnational family arrangements contribute to sustaining familial relationships while separated. It urges us to think about families with an expanded view, to include biological kin and fictive kin, both at home and abroad. In illuminating the intricate circulation of care types, actors, and meanings, we see the inventiveness and endurance of migrants and their families under the dire conditions of migration.

And yet my central research aims included a consideration of the neoliberal conditions that produce transnational families. Therefore, I turn to another transnational dynamic: the acceleration of migration in an era of neoliberal globalization. As joblessness in the Philippines increases and low-wage work in the United States pulls a feminized stream of Filipinos into migration, separation from families and redefinition of care work compel us to see that people beyond migrants themselves are deeply affected by the necessity of migration for work. The very conditions that pull migrants and their families to be creative in keeping their families together are the same conditions that count on their separation for national profit of the Philippines.

Exporting Migrants, Enlisting Families

Although the multidirectional care model illuminates elaborate exchanges of care work, it is important to contextualize these impressive strategies of coping in the capitalist political economy that induce family separation through "migration-as-development" policies, namely, the Labor Export Policy in the Philippines. The invisible, institutional actor—the Philippine labor brokerage state—is reified in these discussions of reorganized care work in the Filipino transnational family. Valorizing multiple nodes and directions in the transnational care of families who are crafting strategies of survival could easily be justification for the continuation and even perpetuation of migration as a form of a family wage and livelihood in the Philippines and elsewhere around the world. However, the multidirectional care model is only possible because the Philippine neoliberal state relies on the upwards of $24 billion remittance industry as the cornerstone in the rubric of its national economy. The recruitment, regulation, deployment, and management of labor migration is not just offering up migrant workers to the global economy; it is equally reliant on the vast family networks of Filipino migrants and the innovative strategies of coping that families invent when they are under conditions of migration and separation.

The export of Philippine labor has been institutionalized in what scholars call a "labor brokerage state" (R. M. Rodriguez 2010; Guevarra 2009). The culture of migration has not only relied on a steady and continuous stream of migrants working abroad and sending money back to their families but also the participation and reconfiguration of care in the Filipino family. While the Philippine state harps on the traditionally Catholic filial obligation of Filipinos to produce generations of migrants within families, it draws both migrant and nonmigrant Filipino family members into the throes of transnationality to sustain their families. The state employs the whole family, albeit indirectly, to adjust and adapt to long-term separation and necessary migration; they are called to reorganize their lives to make meaning of migrant members' absence and work to overhaul their notions of family. If the state's rhetoric appeals to families left behind (and families *potentially* left behind) to validate labor migration, then an accurate reflection of the political economy of migration requires the contemporary family form—the transnational family—in the construct of the international division of social reproductive labor (Parreñas 2001b). Migrants are the prime citizen-subjects for labor export policies, but the family is the required hinge that keeps migrants moored to serial migration and a steadfast remittance industry.

It follows that if the global political economy of migration relies on both migrants and families to keep it going, then care work in this arrangement must also be examined through the contribution of *both* migrants *and* their families left behind. Families left behind activate many forms of resources and networks to fill the vacuum left by their migrant family members. They rely on their immediate biological family members to take up chores around the house and they turn to biological kin networks to reduce the strain of having one or more members abroad. A multidirectional care model applied to the Filipino transnational family allows for an expansive definition of the Filipino family left behind to include extended and fictive kin moving away from the centrality of the nuclear, heteronormative family as the operational form of Filipino families left behind. When we consider the expanded network as the operational organization of the transnational family, we can locate the multiple directions of care work coming from more people and places than just the immediate biological members of a migrant's family. Many Filipino families already operate on a multigenerational and extended network basis but these adjustments in transnational care work have been made in response to the continuous stream of migration from the Philippines and away from Filipino families. Families are drafted in a secondary way to support the nation's development strategy of exporting people, the very family members they give up to global markets. Given that the Labor Export Policy, the Philippines' entry to the neoliberal global economy, has held fast for almost a half century, it is clear that multidirectional care including extended kin in the Filipino transnational family has been engendered by the political economic climate of the nation and its culture of migration. This work reminds us to always link these strategies of multidirectional care to the larger social forces that produce them.

Technology is an integral dimension of the neoliberal condition and it has also become an essential part of the lives of migrant family members and families left behind living under the circumstances of neoliberal immigration policies. As the labor brokerage state seeks more and more women workers to ship across the globe as domestic workers, many Filipino migrants are unable to return to their country because of their precarious immigration statuses. Hence technology becomes the bedrock of their transnational relationships since most migrants in this study have undocumented status, which makes them unable to go home without penalty, or worse, without a viable option to return to the United States to earn a living. Most of the migrants in this study grit their teeth through years of hard work and separation to be able to put their children through school or pay for the healthcare of a sick family member. Oftentimes, they are unable to return because they are the primary breadwinners in their families and there are little to no options for work in the Philippines because of ongoing privatization, liberalization, and deregulation of the Philippine economy, stifling stable national industrial development (Padios 2017). Not to mention the debts migrants have incurred for their migration, fees for applying for visas to leave the Philippines, and increasing interest on those debts limiting migrants' options to return to their country and families without option for viable livelihood (Francisco and Rodriguez 2015). The significance of digital platforms like Facebook and Skype is the saving grace for many migrants because seeing their family members on a computer screen is all they have. Although participants laud the development of the plethora of web interfaces with which they can keep in touch with their families back home, the technology appeases a pain for migrants that would not be there if they were not pushed to migrate as a form of livelihood for their family or if immigration reform in the United States could provide possible avenues to legalization for undocumented people in the country. The increasing neoliberal turn in immigration policies to treat migrants as temporary workers—never permanent residents—leaves the technological prowess of migrants and their families as part of the complex system of neoliberal globalization.

The Labor Export Policy, a historical, aggressive, and sophisticated system of migrant export to markets globally, is a neoliberal immigration policy that has ultimately reorganized the formations and relationships of the Filipino family. The Philippine economy is over-reliant on a remittance industry that banks on the separation of family members to keep the nation's gross domestic product afloat. The Philippine labor brokerage state places migrants as the *bagong bayani* (modern-day heroes) of the Philippine economy while taking advantage of their family members who are often reorganizing their lives to account for their new transnational circumstances. Without a clear plan to create sustainable industries with the plentiful natural resources in the Philippines, the state's investment in the continued export of migrants seals a future of generational migration for families in the Philippines. Development must not consider people as mere remitters of capital but as human beings who long to raise their own children and care for aging parents with a viable avenue for livelihood in their own country. The worth of Filipino migrants is reduced to the money they send back to the Philippines while their ability to decide how they would like to raise their families or what type of work they would like to do is surrendered to the will of the global economy. Ensuing research must carry forward important studies like the sociologist Leisy Abrego's work on policies and enforcement that produce illegality as a condition of migrants that holds them and their families across borders. We must scrutinize the ways in which state-to-state relationships are supporting collaborative neoliberal immigration regimes (San Juan 2000) in both the First and Third Worlds that continue to separate families.

Normalizing Migration, Shifting Gender Ideologies

The contested performances and "doing" of gender is a thread that runs through the narratives of transnational families in this book that has produced conflicts and given way for new types of autonomy. Since a majority of participants identified as women, the ideals of femininity and "good" motherhood were often included in the internal and familial debates in the lives of migrants and their transnational families. Women have taken up an enormous amount of work in sustaining their families, expanding their notions of motherhood to include migration. As with Sharon's story, many Filipino women consider migration as a normalized notch in their definition of womanhood and motherhood as they seek to support their families by migrating abroad. Women's migration magnifies motherhood as it includes their staying abroad for long periods of time to pay for education and various family-related expenses. They are also expected to stay attentive to their families, keeping up with them through different forms of technology. In some ways, they are absorbing ascribed roles of fathers and mothers, as breadwinners and nurturers, albeit from afar. And although this practice in the expansion of motherhood may sound exhausting, it also provides women a sense of autonomy and power given that they are able to author these new dimensions on their own.

Away from the patriarchal constructs of the Philippines, or their own husbands, or even their own kin, migrant women are glad to be redefining their ideals of femininity to include their hard work abroad (Raymundo 2011). Feminists argue that women are doing this without challenging the patriarchal structures that design and determine their lives. Yet the articulation of pride and gratification in the narratives of migrant women in this study also suggests a different type of feminist sensibility—one that values the experiences and voices of migrant women under such constrained circumstances. This redefinition of femininity and "good" motherhood is mitigated by migrant women's ability to build solidarity with one another as migrants and workers in New York City. Their labor solidarity based on their transnational care arrangements may be an invitation to feminists to link ideas of gender equality to the racialized and class identities at work in the daily lives of migrant women (Aguilar 2000).

As the production of new femininities were articulated in this book, emergent and differing masculinities also surfaced. Through a multidirectional care lens, I included the network of kin left behind in interpreting how men in the place left behind were mediating gender normative roles and how they adjusted to them. Scholars have found that men often reject their domestic labor roles when wives or mothers migrate, largely because of entrenched cultural, social, and patriarchal logics that render men unable to perform their ascribed roles as breadwinners or providers. However, I find the personal and family backgrounds of men left behind crucial in understanding how and why men may or may not reject their new roles as homemakers. The role of the kin network left behind assisting fathers or sons left behind with the absence of their wives or mothers allows them to temper the difficult transition. Indeed, asking for help from kin actually affirms a different type of masculinity for fathers left behind, one that contributes to the well-being of the family. When their domestic work is valued or shared domestic labors are performed with kin, men left behind have a different source of value to draw from to redefine their self-esteem and masculinities. As the gendered processes call on women to migrate under neoliberal globalization in droves, challenging the ascribed gender roles for them, masculinities are also reorganizing under conditions of migration and separation (Fajardo 2011).

Past scholars argue that technology mediates gender in transnational families by reinforcing gender roles in the family (Parreñas 2008; Dreby 2010). However, in my work, I found that the frequency and visual register in these new forms of communication change the quality of interaction particularly in terms of gender. Husbands left behind open up lines of communication that were rarely used when their wives lived in the Philippines with them. The fact that their wives are away, often indefinitely, pushes some husbands to talk with their wives more as part of their daily routine. In the past, men would go to work and have limited time for conversation with their wives, but now the roles of breadwinner have changed. Frequent communication between husbands and wives and the ability to see their spouses' tired faces make room for a deeper understanding of the sacrifice migrant women make in migrating, living, and working away from their families. In this way, husbands in this study noted that they have come to a deeper understanding about the reversal of gender roles in their marriages. Additionally, husbands mentioned that camera technology also gives them the opportunity to ask their wives how to do a particular task or chore. These interactions sometimes slip into espionage and scrutinized observation, yet there is much to be learned about the different texture of contemporary technology and how it is shaping gender negotiations.

Kin networks and social recognition of fathers left behind can provide men with a different source to value their fatherhood and manhood. Technology eases tensions in the gender boundaries crossed by migration. Through the advancements in communication technology, specifically through the visual register on camera devices and social network platforms, frequency in contact between transnational family members allows for a deeper understanding of the sacrifices in migration, therefore modifying the perspective of husbands and fathers left behind on ascribed roles of domesticity. The families in this book demonstrate these possibilities and yet it is also probable that Filipino men will still reject their roles as homemakers, as patriarchal logics are deeply embedded in Filipino culture. However, I have provided evidence that if we study the transnational family through a multidirectional care model, we can count kin network support as care to men left behind and then we can also reflect on how masculinity can be defined in multiple ways within their new familial contexts sans their migrant women family members. When men can draw from different sources to value their manhood beyond the narrow hegemonic masculinity model, they can begin to realize their worth in terms of their contribution to their families.

This might not always be the case. Many men may fall back into their patriarchal beliefs after taking up domestic duties for some years. Others may reverse their ideas of male supremacy and usher in a new type of gender equality in raising their children. Gender ideologies do change over time but they are immutable without structural and cultural shifts. Statistically, more and more women who are mothers, grandmothers, sisters, and daughters will be undoubtedly pulled into the global economy as migrant workers, and inevitably men continually have to answer to the shifting gender ideologies that accompany increased, feminized migration. Hence, we need to keep paying attention to the ways that gender ideologies are shifting with the continuing political and economic investment in feminized migration within countries like the Philippines.

The Politics and Solidarity in Transnational Care Work

While migrants are adjusting to the different texture of their family lives under the conditions of long-term separation over long distances, their common understanding of the experience of transnational life as both rewarding and isolating is a useful resource to imagine and build political solidarity abroad. Migrants have found comfort in sharing struggles with others who understand the experience of being a migrant away from their family during times of great stress and moments of hardship. Points of solidarity between migrants can lead to the development of a network for support for one another in what I have discussed as "communities of care." Informed by the revision of family life transnationally, migrant women in this study invest in a community of care inasmuch as they relate to one another's experiences as a migrant, a transnational family member, and a worker. This formation of care work in the place abroad as an essential part of the sustenance of migrants is novel because it unhinges the ideas of care from the biological family into the homosocial, fictive kin networks in migrant communities. This dynamic has often been studied as separate from the framework of the transnational family; however, migrant women draw so clearly from their shared experiences of transnational care, the circulation between migrants is crucial to their ability to thrive abroad for as long as they do. As sociologists study migrant community building, I distinguish my theorizing on this particular formation by including it as a part of the formulation of the multidirectional care in transnational families.

Scholarship on immigrant social networks has theorized the functions and forms of networks that have assisted immigrants in their transition and settlement in their destinations (Ebaugh and Curry 2000; Hagan 1998; Portes 1995). The reasoning behind immigrants' investment in these social networks is largely attributed to functionalist and deterministic logics of assimilation and integration into destination countries. However, I instead highlight the similar structural positions migrant women occupy as the engine for participation in these networks and add a different dimension to these networks outside the already established purposes. Experiences of being a new migrant to the United States, maintaining a family from afar, and working as a precarious worker in a global city are nodes of intelligibility from which migrant women begin to recognize one another. These shared experiences become the basis for the network they build and participate in for both practical purposes and emotional support. These networks circulate a form of care that is informed by migrant women's experiences in their transnational families and redefine migrant camaraderie as a variation of "family" abroad.

Filipina migrants are also astutely refashioning their ideas of womanhood (Constable 2014) and membership in a family in establishing "chosen families" (Weston 1997) in the place abroad. In valuing homosocial practices and collectivities, they form a different type of family under the often isolating and difficult conditions of migration. The fictive families they choose in their communities of care work go beyond providing pragmatic and personal support to the individuals in that network. They are also sites of belonging where migrants can be seen in their various beings and becomings as brave migrants or flawed mothers or exploited workers. Queer theoretical frameworks on chosen families and queer kinship urge us to think of a community of care as a creative response from individuals contending with the displacing processes of neoliberal migration schemas, low-wage work, and racialized classism. It invites us to think of family outside the biological or heteronormative box. Most importantly, it puts the power of resilience in the hands of migrant women who are the ones doing the choosing: choosing to survive and choosing who can help them thrive.

These communities of care can also be fastened to feminist theoretical frameworks developed by women of color in the United States, specifically black feminist epistemologies, which situate the inventive forms of resistance initiated by women of color in the United States in a critique of systems of oppression. Black feminists have written about the alternative forms of women-centered networks and "othermothers" that have fortified and bolstered black communities in the United States since the days of slavery (Collins 2000).[1] As the gendered and racialized history of domestic work manifests in the lives of Filipino migrant women so is their ability to foster collectives that circulate vital care for one another in a world where they are being paid to give to their charges and are expected to give to their transnational families. When migrant women shared their stories of abuse and exploitation as domestic workers, conversations often led migrants to open up about their trials as well. The instability of their jobs and the often-substandard labor conditions they worked in are products of an American racial order in paid domestic work. This engenders a particular labor solidarity that not only speaks to the experiences of migrant women solely as transnational family members and as migrants but as precarious workers that are racialized as inferior and criminalized as deportable. The politics of a community of care is enmeshed in the racialized and classed history of domestic work in the United States but also always with their transnational family experience.

A deeper theorizing and analysis of communities of care demonstrates that Filipina migrant women activate this network on the basis of their shared identities: migrant, transnational family member, and worker. These Filipino, transnational, and migrant identities are produced through regimes of power relations that generate experiences of subjugation and powerlessness. Yet, migrants build networks to combat daily processes of isolation and hardship. These are the reasons why it is not enough to discuss communities of care simply as immigrant social networks that migrants use to trade and exchange resources. The processes of identifying (Hall 2003) with one another based on various diasporic social experiences combined with a critique of systems of power in the creation, maintenance, and operation of communities of care are important to highlight as the basis of these networks. The horizontal care within migrant communities is informed by the reorganization of care in migrants' transnational lives and their local everyday reality as workers in the diaspora. These are essential dimensions that often propel migrants to craft a politics of solidarity with each other and potentially with others across the Filipino labor diaspora (Francisco 2015b).

A Call to Action

In studying the transnational lives of migrants and their families left behind, I explored multiplicity in care work as it is reorganized in the context of migration and separation. The model of multidirectional care applied to the lives of Filipino transnational families describes the complex circulation of care work that maintains the different parts of the family by members of families in different sites. I insisted on understanding the Filipino transnational family in its expanded form, including biological kin in the Philippines and fictive kin in the United States. I argued that families' perspective on multiple directions of care must be contextualized within the historic and uninterrupted culture of Philippine migration and its labor brokerage state. The family's pivotal position as the anchor to migrant workers proves its invaluable role in the Philippine migration industry. Therefore, families are always already incorporated in the brokering of migrants as workers to the world. But now what?

The data in this study show that both migrants and families are impacted by the Philippine state's ideology of migration as a development strategy. This linkage is key in leveraging power in the hands of migrants and their families to be able to demand better options for livelihood and staying together. For example, in April 2015, Mary Jane Veloso, a Filipina migrant domestic worker, was arrested for drug charges and sentenced to death in Indonesia. Mary Jane, who had been trafficked as a drug mule across Indonesian borders, languished in jail for five years before she was put on death row (see Francisco forthcoming). On her arrival in Indonesia, she had no idea that the people who sent her to work as a domestic had stashed drugs in the lining of her baggage. Although Mary Jane was a victim of poverty in the Philippines and trafficking under an aggressive labor brokerage system, the Indonesian government's zero tolerance law sentenced her to death. In a global uproar that mirrored the case for clemency for a Filipino migrant woman on death row in Singapore named Flor Contemplacion twenty years earlier, thousands of Filipino migrant workers across the world mobilized and held actions to demand justice for Mary Jane. The international support from migrant workers used the very linkage this book proposes to pressure the Philippine government to exhaust all of its avenues to save Mary Jane's life. Many transnational activist networks led by the activist Philippine-based alliances Migrante International, GABRIELA, and BAYAN alongside their international chapters connected the dots between the Philippine Labor Export Policy and its effects on families left behind as a key logic as to why the Philippine state should intervene: Mary Jane's two sons would lose their mother who had been forced to migrate to support the basic needs of her children. Linking the relationship between the state and families reveals that macropolicies have profound impacts on and at times grave consequences for not only migrants but also their families. Today, a critical mass of Filipino scholars are doing the work of interrogating global capitalism and imperialism as it is producing precariousness in the lives of Filipinos in the Philippines and diaspora and it is imperative to continue linking up these critiques to social movements (Bonus 2000; Isaac 2006; Buenavista 2010; R. M. Rodriguez 2010; Guevarra 2009; Baldoz 2011; Cabusao 2011; Burns 2012; Velasco 2013; Kares 2014; Caronan 2015; Diaz 2016; Padios 2017; Tungohan 2017).

Migrant workers are at the center of an increasingly contentious global debate: desired as cheap labor but without the possibility of permanent residency. At the publication of this book, the anti-immigrant sentiment under the current US president Donald Trump will undoubtedly have increased. With the Trump administration's actions toward exclusionary immigration policies and deportations, migrants and their families' futures are even more uncertain. It is not enough that migrants are often discarded after their work and worth are squeezed from them; they will surely be criminalized as the rhetoric of illegality and nativism escalates in this country. However, migrant communities are rich with experiences of creative resistance and collective mobilization, remaking rights-claiming politics, activism, and democracy with their presence and community building (Coll 2010). With stories like those of Mary Jane Veloso (see Francisco forthcoming) and Fely Garcia (see chapter 4), migrants are drawing from their daily experiences of reorganizing and attending to complex webs of care to contribute to a critique of neoliberal policies like labor export in the Philippines and broken immigration systems such as the case of that of the United States. Once a domestic worker shares a negative work experience, others are then invited to share their similar (and perhaps worse) experiences; this process can encourage migrants to share their struggles but also engage in a collective process to identify strategies for coping and resisting. Communities of care can be a revolutionary idea of creating relationships that have agency and collective life at the center, instead of displacement and seclusion. Given that Filipino migrants live worldwide working under comparable precarious and unstable industries, the circuits of migration could also be the circuits in which transnational action and mobilization travels (Viola, Francisco, and Amorao 2014). Although experiences of exploitation vary greatly across geography, similar experiences of precariousness might be a point of solidarity for migrant communities toward coalition-building politics transnationally.

The stories in this book also underscore the importance of transnational families in inciting the political imagination and inspiring the collective action of migrants. Perhaps the grassroots political power of migrants can be harnessed in and through their different identification processes as migrants, family members abroad, and domestic workers, and even all at the same time. These social categories could be unifying within migrant communities and across communities of different races, ethnicities, classes, nativity (both migrant and nonmigrant), sexualities, and genders. Perhaps not everyone can relate to migrant narratives of displacement from home or family histories of generational migration but the relationships in this book, both stable and strained, humanize migrants and their families so that they are not the racialized "other" in the current façade of multiculturalism in the United States. The strengths and weaknesses in the practice of doing family make it possible for us to relate to one another in support of humanizing those whose lives are narrated as temporary, undocumented, and dispensable. The power of storytelling and the systematic development of migrant worker leaders can be tinder to light a fire of political intelligibility within migrant communities. But the flaws and contradictions of migrants make it difficult to create and sustain political organization with them. The role of gossip, interpersonal conflict, and the aspirations to middle-classness (both in New York City and in the Philippines) often blocks migrant workers from seeing one another as worthwhile allies in the pursuit of social justice. Still, their experiences as migrants, workers, and transnational family members can be generative points of solidarity and even something so basic and important as friendship.

With these stories, my call to action is for each of us to find our role and to join a local organization that echoes a global call to change our society to one that does not compel migrants to leave their families so they can put food on their table, one that does not undervalue and exploit migrants' important work in our homes and in raising our children, one that does not label migrants as criminal because of their immigration status. Rather, we need to be active in working, organizing, educating, and mobilizing our various strengths and skills to stand in solidarity with migrant workers' organizations and their campaigns for the recognition of their rights to stay with their families and be able to support them with a livable wage, or as workers who have a right to paid sick leave, or a break time, or a path to legalization.

The most salient and significant finding I discovered in writing this book is that the resilience of migrant workers in the United States and their transnational families in the Philippines is vast. The experiences of transnational families are perhaps better understood in what migrants described as *lakas ng loob* (strength of the spirit). I found that despite exploitative and dehumanizing conditions as domestic workers, migrants often found solace and strength in one another. Through the pain of missing one's family members, the strength that pushed families forward is their interdependence on one another. It is with their spirit that I hope we can all find the strength within our own spirits to find our roles in supporting the important political organizing work of migrants in the hostlands and their families in their homelands for a different world that may allow them to form their families with freedom, confidence, and love.

Methodological Appendix

To the women, men, and families of Kabalikat, the domestic workers who were not part of Kabalikat, and the community organizers who made this book possible:

After years of questions like What is "research"? When will you finish? How many more interviews do we need? How many more workshops? I hope I can explain the reasons why we did our research together, why we did it the way we did, and what kinds of things we can accomplish when research is done as a community effort.

I want you to know that we chose the particular methods we did, not just because they were fun to do, but because the way we collected your stories will help people understand your lives as part of a larger picture, a bigger system of politics and economics. The structures of power you already know about because you live it. I hope that writing down all these reasons, academic and political, will show that when we did our research together in all sorts of ways, we were essentially helping people understand that even when your lives are hard, there are ways of surviving and thriving. And at the end of the day, that was our project together. To remember how strong we can be for one another, despite the facts that your jobs are exhausting, your families miss you, rent is too high, winters are too cold, and New York City feels too lonely.

Writing down all these reasons is a practice in letting you know that our research interviews, or kuwentuhans, *karaoke afternoons, theater workshops, playwriting sessions, and* Diwang Pinay *are embedded in grassroots organizing logics, just as your migration and separation from your families are embedded in systematic neoliberal logics. But above all else, I want to write these reasons down because we've all already felt the transformation of research coming from the grassroots. Now I want to pause and tell you the thinking behind it.*

Every day I wake up and I wish I had your strength and bravery. Every day I wake up and I wish that everyone could see you as I see you: brave, heartbroken, hilarious, exhausted, and full of love. Your stories are all over this book. Rightfully, it's yours. But as soon as you shared it with me, with our community, it became all of ours in our own ways. Sana gumaan ng kahit konti ang inyong dala. *I hope that your heavy loads became a little lighter in the process. Thank you for sharing your lives with us. Thank you for working with us, nonmigrants, nondomestic workers, a way to be part of your struggle without appropriating it. Thank you because I learned so much. I hope other people can learn from you too.*

Sa inyong laging nagmamahal,
With love, always,
Valerie
Field notes, April 2011

I wrote this letter to the women of Kabalikat Domestic Workers Support Network two weeks after we staged a play entitled *Diwang Pinay: Kasaysayan sa Likod ng Kababaihang Migranteng Mangagawa* (Spirit of the Filipina: The Story Behind the Woman Migrant Worker). Culling stories from the individual and group interviews (*kuwentuhans*) (Francisco 2013) I conducted for this book, we wrote a play during a year-long series of theater workshops, playwriting sessions, and rehearsals. Fifteen days after the performance of this transformative play, I stared at a screen trying to write the first draft of this methods appendix for this book and all I could eke out was this letter to the participants: more than forty domestic workers of Kabalikat; more than thirty members of Gabriela New York, a progressive Filipino women's organization; and the staff of Philippine Forum, the Filipino Community Center in Queens that housed the Kabalikat program. After the intensive work on the play, pausing to write the logic of inquiry in my research felt like a passive exercise in justifying myself after the fact. But in reality, this research affected people, families, and communities, right when it started, as most research projects do. Likewise, the people in it shaped the methodology and outcomes of this project. Domestic workers, community organizers, community members, and students were always ready to contribute their own opinions and reasoning as to how we conducted research qualitatively and why we needed to turn interviews and focus groups into a play. This methodological appendix is an effort to track, explore, and insist that research processes are indeed shaped by the people in the study and in turn the research process shapes the participants anew as well. To this end, a subargument throughout this appendix is that with thoughtful and collaborative initiatives research processes can be useful for political organizing and grassroots mobilization.

In place of the stereotypical lone ethnographer, and in the spirit of collaboration and capacity building, many hands, minds, and hearts informed the design, implementation, and products of this research. Following indigenous and native scholars (L. T. Smith 1999; Tuck 2008) who argue that research is haunted by a long history of false ownership and colonial knowledge production, "we," the members of the research project, tried our hardest to distribute this research project's findings and products in a way that could benefit us all. Still, as a Filipina, an immigrant, and a woman of color scholar, I accept the privilege and burden of claiming this project as mine, understanding that this book may not represent the views of all of the members of the research. And yet, this book is not the sole product of this research. Thus, I will be using "I" when discussing particular intellectual choices about research design, plans, methodology and methods. With "we," I mark the moments, parts, and sections of the research when many of the various members of the community were involved. I also have the responsibility of speaking from my embodied privileges as an academic, a documented person (Fine and Torre 2006), and an "insider-outsider" among the participants of this study (Smith 1987; Haraway 1988; Collins 1986; Harding 2007). I was an insider with them sharing my cultural background as a Filipina and my experience of immigration as a formerly undocumented person. Yet I was an outsider as an academic, a 1.5-generation immigrant, and a green-card holder. I used my insider-outsider location to root my political commitments to the advancement of migrant worker power, to dedicate my time toward building relationships outside research purposes, and to critically analyze the institutions that produced transnational families. To this end, I weave together the intellectual and academic underpinnings for the methodology and, more importantly, the epistemological and political significance of the methods in which the research was carried out.

This project integrates multisited and transnational ethnography, institutional ethnography (IE), and participatory action research (PAR), methodological approaches that reflect the epistemological realities of those who live with and operate in the distinctive characteristics of the transnational

Filipino family in this historical and political moment. Collaborations and participatory methods include feminist, qualitative methods, and theater of the oppressed games as data collection strategies. The various methodological influences reflect the different needs of participants and the organization(s) that contributed to the production of the information in this book. Overall, we sought to study the mundane and the microsociological while insisting on linking experiences to the macromechanisms and macrologics that produced transnational families.

Traveling and Tracing Transnational Lives

Early in my research, domestic workers told me that if I really wanted to know about their experience of migration, I would have to go back to the Philippines to meet their families and to understand the effects of their absence on the ones they loved most. They urged me to return to our motherland to observe the political, economic, and social conditions that pushed them to leave in the first place. I would then have to match those social facts up with their current experience in New York City. "You have to get to whole picture, there and here, or else, *bitin* [loosely translated as not whole]," said Bernadette, a domestic worker who had lived in New York City for ten years. When I first walked into the homes of families in Manila, gifts from the migrants in hand, it was clear to me that migration changes everyone and everything that the process touches:

> *I knock and 9-year-old JJ answers; he is such a beautifully cheerful child. As soon as I step into Rose's family's home in Manila, I see only him and his bright and all-encompassing smile. His squinted eyes and mouth turned upward at the corners swallow me into a love that I was only lucky to receive because Ate Rose told them months in advance that I was on my way. Of course, when I enter JJ and Grace huddle their bodies together on the far wall under the photos of New York City buildings and trees covered in snow. Their eyes filled with wonder and their smiles teeming with welcome betray their body language. I stick my hand out to them and say, "It's nice to meet you." And immediately, as if touch bonded us as sisters or cousins or best friends they warm to me. As quickly as happiness enveloped me, I feel a pang of pain that Ate Rose had not been able to touch her kids in five years now. That the arms, my arms, that embrace her two youngest children were the same arms that held her in a tight hug before I left New York City.*

> *We are in the living room for five or so minutes and Kuya Mike (father of Pepe, Grace and Rose's co-parent) urges me to get started with the interviews as he's starting to grill the meats for dinner while dialing Rose's cell number in the United States. He assures me that he is seasoned in multitasking with all the kids he has. I ask if we can do the interview in the single room in the small but well-kept house. The living room is really the opposite side of the kitchen in a 20 x 10 foot room. The room where all five of them sleep on a bunk bed. It is clean. The floors are white and it looks like they swept and mopped before I came in. Because by the end of the night with the frequent ins and outs and the activities of undressing and unpacking going on in the room, it was littered with pillows out of place, wrappers thrown aside, and book bags and notebooks strewn all over the place. After interviewing JJ and Grace, Kuya Mike invites us to eat dinner. In the background, we hear JJ and Grace practicing the prayer before meals. When we come back to the food, Kuya Mike encourages the kids to recite it as he says it out loud too. Before we start to eat, Kuya Mike shows me his spread where I was pleasantly surprised to see all of my favorite foods. Pork barbecue, crab, and shrimp, and* pinakbet, *a vegetable stew. Ate Rose had mentioned to them that these were the things that I ate when we had gatherings in the United States. I was moved almost to tears because here is the food that Ate Rose cooked for me and at the other end of the world. Sitting next to her husband and kids, I'm breaking open the same crabs that I eat when I am in front of her.*
>
> Field notes, November 4, 2009

Traces of transnationality were present throughout my visit to Rose's family's house in Manila. As much as I was in Manila, whole parts of the home (i.e., refrigerator door of photos, wall of photos), my embrace, stories of Rose's children, our meal were, at once, in front of us, but also produced by transnational interaction. These families lived their lives squarely in Manila and in New York City and in-between, and my research had to take on this complex everyday spatiality. Everyday practices, processes, and relationships between people, institutions, and places are imperative to understanding the transnational life of immigrants (D. E. Smith 2006). Scholars agree with the domestic workers that, to understand migration, researchers must factor in the experiences and changes in the lives of nonmigrants, and so must conduct research in multiple sites of the transnational social field (Anzaldúa 1999; Levitt and Jaworsky 2007; Pessar 1999; Wimmer and Schiller 2002) or multisited ethnography (Burawoy 2003; Fitzgerald 2006; Marcus 1995).

Scholars and migrants alike understood that the experience of settlement in new places was tied to life at home, and that transnational life unfolded in between homelands and hostlands. If I wanted to study a transnational dynamic, I had to follow the transnational circuits that started in Manila, ran to New York City, and then back again (Levitt and Schiller 2004).

In the traditional ethnographic approach, a researcher plants herself in one place to do participant observation, write field notes, and interview members of a community or communities. It is impossible to study transnational life in this way. Therefore, through multisited ethnography, the unit of analysis for this book emerged: the transnational family. Shuttling back and forth between sites and family members allowed me to explore the dynamic in the local knowledges in the lives of both migrants and nonmigrants regarding the shifts in their social relations and even the larger changes in the political economic milieu that affected decisions to migrate or return home for good. I chose to conduct multisited research by traveling between New York City and Manila from 2009 to 2014, spending a total of eight months in Manila and five years in New York City. This decision to conduct multisited ethnography was also guided by my resolve in linking these seemingly disparate locations and lives to the capitalist world-system that produces a set of relations such as the transnational family.

A unique aspect of this multisited ethnography was my ability to integrate and study the transnational life and formations of care within constellations of families. In contrast to other studies of Filipino transnational family life (Asis, Huang, and Yeoh 2004; Parreñas 2005a; Wolf 1997) that do not connect samples of migrants with samples of their own families left behind, conducting multisited research with families gave me an opportunity to include family histories in my conceptualization of multidirectional care and caring under emotional dissonance. The erstwhile form of sampling might have constrained participants' answers to emphasize the negative consequences of migration and separation. Numerous visits to families left behind allowed me see growth spurts in children and the development of wrinkles in the faces of husbands, mothers, and fathers of migrants; then I was able to go back to New York City and see the tired hands of domestic workers as the hairs on their heads grayed. This methodology gave me a chance to see the ups and downs of a family throughout a short period of the family's history. I could see the circuits of multidirectional care, strained or not. Digital relationships also sustained these connections. I became Facebook, Instagram, and Skype friends with almost all of the family members I visited and interviewed. Online and in actual visits, I was able to observe and ask about the effects of separation and about the strategies transnational families use to remain connected.

I identified eleven constellations of families to follow in the years of fieldwork; these yielded twenty-five interviews with families in the Philippines. The fifty migrant women interviewed in New York City were gatekeepers in the snowball sampling and recruitment of their families. Migrants and family members left behind also talked within their families about my research and whether they were comfortable participating in it. This unique methodological choice gave families time to articulate grievances about long-term, long-distance separation and also how they were making their situations work. For me, staying inside the constellations of families gave me a comparable unit of analysis across families, as I could test the ideas of gendered shifts of labor or emotional strain across family constellations. I was also able to observe if what participants were sharing in interviews actually played out in their actions within their family structures. As I studied the transnational family as a unit of analysis, I could understand the family's care work in a continuum of interactions, including the choice of migration or the use of technology as a form of care. I could tease out forms of care that were otherwise considered as neglect or a compromised way of participating in a family.

Favoring family constellations helped family members define who "belonged" or "contributed" to the transnational family, including biological children; spouses; biological parents, grandparents, and siblings; biological kin networks; fictive kin; and friends. Past studies assumed that the Western idea of the nuclear family was the operative form of family in the Philippines; they found emotions of outrage and betrayal to be rife. In contrast, using an extended kin network frame gave room for families left behind to tell me about the broader range of resources that contribute to the success of the transnational family. Once we started talking about different providers of care contributing to the family, I could analyze the multiple directions of care within those extended networks.

Additionally, acknowledging biological kin and fictive kin as a crucial component of transnational families also allowed me to operationalize "communities of care" as a type of family produced under the conditions of migration and settlement in New York City. Multisited ethnography gave me an opportunity to observe transnational care work exchange and also see it in terms of the family structures that were being built between migrants in New York City. Studying in multiple sites allowed me to follow the transnational circuit as it played out in the lives of the migrants.

Multisited ethnography bolstered my analysis on place, a pivotal theoretical frame for this book (Fitzgerald 2006). In George E. Marcus's discussion of multisited ethnography, he argues that ethnography in the contemporary world should be situated in and of the world system, proposing that ethnography of the changes in culture under a globalizing world leads to an understanding of that system (Marcus 1995). The continuing role of *place* in this discussion highlights what Peggy Levitt and Nina Glick Schiller call "simultaneity" in transnationalism (Levitt and Schiller 2004). Many migrants' lives in a transnational context occur on many social fields, and changes in a migrant's hostland trigger changes in a migrant's homeland almost immediately.[1] A look at place allows us to attend to the nuances of changes in the different places in a migrant's transnational life (Guevarra 2006a). To track this, I had to pay attention to the changes that migration and separation produced not only *from* the places migrants called home and hostland, but also factoring in the political economic milieu in New York City and Manila essential to producing a transnational life. Places like New York City and Manila are themselves characters in the stories of transnationalism. Even if transnational life happens in the shuttling between home and hostland, homelands and hostlands have geographical and material form, and more importantly, imagined and experiential consequences. In New York City, I was attuned to the specificity and historicity of securitization in the years I spent doing my fieldwork. It was apparent to me that experiences of migrants in the global city of New York City did not revolve around incorporation or assimilation into the mainstream norm. Quite the opposite: The anti-immigrant sentiment and rise of raids and deportations in New York City made the idea of settling and assimilating to American society a fleeting thought. These particular political conditions shaped how migrants saw one another as refuge and resources, hence, how they invested in what I call a "community of care."

On the other transnational hand, Manila, the capital of the Philippines, was a place rapidly developing geographically in these years alongside the acceleration of feminized migration. Manila's neoliberal "development" through foreign direct investments and multinational corporations created a national economy that is ruled by privatization, deregulation, and liberalization (Tadiar 2004). With a dependence on migrant remittances and investment funding urban development, though Manila is increasingly modern it is built on a wobbly foundation. Most new employment is in the service, information economy (call centers) (Padios 2018) and tourism sector, and therefore migration as a form of livelihood becomes a mainstay in the lives of Filipinos. These observations conducted during my time in Manila informed my understanding of migration as "forced" instead of a rational choice for career or social mobility. Migration was often a coerced decision because of the lack of viable livelihood in the fleeting subcontractual jobs in the Philippines.

Through multisited ethnography, I was able to study the world system that produced these global cities and the transnational life of Filipinos. The transnational family was and is undoubtedly a product of neoliberal globalization and economic restructuring both in the Philippines and in the United States. Choosing to conduct multisited ethnography to understand transnational life in these places allowed me to analyze these structural problems of neoliberalism that connects the lives of Filipinos in the Philippines and abroad. At the same time it also showed me the creativity and imaginative solutions migrants and their families come up with on the contour lines of a globalizing world (Katz 2004). Multisited ethnography is an effort to follow the people or the "cultural formation in a world system" and to follow the political economy of migration, "an ethnography of the system" (Marcus 1995, 99). As my travels from the Philippines to the United States helped me realize the systems in place that produced transnational life for migrants and their families, I also developed a sharper critique of the role of labor migration as a type of national development in globalization given its unsustainability for families and the nation. Therefore, multisited ethnography was not solely a mere reflection of the transnational character of migrants and their families but it was also a political choice to study and critique the capitalist world-system under which those transnational lives are produced.

Migrants and Transnational Families, Experts at Living in Globalization

It is easy to consider transnational families at the will of political economic policies, thrown around with the wind. However, throughout my five years in the field, between New York City and Manila, the participants in this study demonstrated astute analysis of the very macromechanisms forcing their migration, rendering them "illegal" and keeping them separated. In New York City, a majority of the migrants I encountered were women; around 95% of my sample identified as women and participated in semi-structured individual interviews and *kuwentuhans*. The self-identified men in the study were often husbands of migrant women who also participated in the research. Eighty-five percent of both men and women participants left biological children in the Philippines upon their migration; a majority of those families left behind remain in the Philippines. Only one out of the eleven families included in the study was successful in gaining legal status and filing a petition for their children from the Philippines to come to live in New York City with them. If the participants did not have biological children, they left behind biological parents, siblings, nieces and nephews, and extended kin. Every single person in the sample had some tie to the Philippines; they were all financially supporting family members there. The median age of the migrant sample is 42 years old, with the youngest participant 28 and the oldest 67. The range of time in the United States in the sample, at the time of the interviews, was anywhere between two years and twenty-five years. Participants who reported their years away from home in the decades were often serial migrants who had lived and worked in multiple, different countries before landing in New York City. Ninety-five of the participants in the study can be categorized as undocumented with no foreseeable avenue of legalization under current immigration law. The string of people many migrants needed to support underscores their inability to legalize as migrants in the United States. Many migrants' decisions to overstay their tourist visas or fall out of status was guided by the fact that there was no option for them to support their families in the Philippines and there was no possibility of filing for documentation in the United States. These broken immigration policies were the rock and hard place many migrants were stuck between and they were keen in observing that these circumstances left them vulnerable.

In Manila, my interviews and *kuwentuhans* with families left behind included twenty-five members that were migrants' parents, husbands, children, siblings, aunts, nieces and nephews, and best friends. Fourteen were male and sixteen were female. The youngest participant in my first round of qualitative fieldwork in the Philippines was 10 years old and the oldest was 35 years old at the beginning of the study. Within the eleven families I focused on, ten families had generations of migrants from grandparents, parents, and siblings with labor migration histories, while other family members outside their New York City counterpart were also abroad. Scholars of childhood studies have argued that adultist research instruments cannot be merely replicated with children as it misses their competencies, thus affirming their ignorance and incapacity to understand their own lives (Morrow 2008; Huijsman 2011). Additionally, scholars of childhood and migration have argued that age greatly influences how children left behind or child migrants understand and interpret their transnational and migratory experiences (Hoang and Yeoh 2015; Ní Laoire et al. 2010). Therefore, based on the ages of the children in transnational families I varied my qualitative techniques with children from ages 7 to 12 to include photo elicitation and for younger adults from ages

13 to 25 to include *kuwentuhans* about social media interactions and social media interactions themselves. A majority of the adult children, ages 25–35, were contemplating migration in return for their migrant parents' sacrifice, and therefore I incorporated some of the questions from the migrant interview guide around the pressures to migrate and adjust to absences of family members to their premigration experiences (see appendixes A and B). With the income of their migrant family members, many of these families had stabilized their household economic status. Debts were slowly being paid off. Purchase of land and building and renovation of homes were taking place. They were able to send children to private elementary schools, high schools, and colleges. Families were also able to afford healthcare for aging or sickly family members. Although the quality of life in the basic necessities improved for families left behind, many of the families were not becoming upwardly mobile or transcending class lines in the Philippines. Many of the families were only making ends meet with the remittance income they were taking in each month. These were the details of forced migration under conditions of globalization that make transnational families experts on the consequences of neoliberalism. The pendulum of stabilization in families with migrants echoed the instability of global capitalism.

The marginalized categories that migrants and their families embody are assigned and produced through institutions of governance and migration under neoliberal globalization; though their transnational lives are often detached from these institutions, they live out the consequences of a migrant labor export policy. Using IE (D. E. Smith 2005; D. E. Smith et al. 2006), which examines such institutions and their machinations, I brought into focus the institutional conditions that produce the Filipino labor diaspora (Guevarra 2009; R. M. Rodriguez 2010). Their lives illuminate the underbelly of labor brokerage. Specifically, I used IE to track two sets of relations that migrants are enmeshed in. I address the work processes of migrant workers, specifically domestic workers in New York City, as the "fundamental grounding of social life" (DeVault 2006, 294), or "*social relations* people are drawn into through their work (with the term 'social relations' taken in its Marxist sense to mean not relationships but connections among work processes)" (DeVault 2006, 294). Second, the labor brokerage state of the Philippines is an institution that produces what IE terms "ruling relations," "an expansive, historically specific apparatus of management and control that arose with the development of corporate capitalism and supports its orientation" (DeVault 2006, 295). These institutions facilitate, mobilize, and regulate migrant labor through the specific bureaucracies of migration management.[2]

With an IE framework, I was able to tease out how migrant workers became intelligible to one another through their experiences as domestic workers in New York City, migrants to the United States, and transnational family members. The research process itself expanded migrants' understanding of the very institutions that produced their transnational lives, and at the same time people also used this process to gain networks and resources to survive their conditions. When migrants shared these experiences in *kuwentuhans*, they found meaningful connections with one another, leading to friendships and leads to new employment or housing in the case of some migrants who were looking for that type of help. However, through the theater workshops and theater performance, research participants found more political solidarities as they shared their collective experiences with the broader Filipino American community. The social relations that drew people together with shared understanding of being a migrant, domestic, and transnational family member were articulated through the collective production of this play, which exposed the good and bad commonalities in their work processes as migrant workers. Additionally, although not as exhaustively covered in this book, almost all migrants (in interviews, *kuwentuhans*, community workshops, and the play production) critiqued and analyzed the ever-growing culture of migration in the Philippines. Through IE,[3] migrants were experts in the mechanisms and consequences of the institutional and bureaucratic apparatus of migration as labor export.

Notably, I count transnational mothering and care work by nonmigrant families in homes left behind as crucial parts of understanding neoliberal globalization. In the popular narratives of the Philippines' migrants as "modern heroes," the scope of "good" motherhood now embraces the obligation for mothers to leave their families. Dutiful mothers sacrifice anything and everything for their families; therefore, migration is a necessary option to keep families afloat and futures promising. Still, when women enter the industry of paid domestic work or other low-wage industries targeting migrant workers, they are still bound to yet another invisibilized set of work processes in the gendered organization of transnational caring in their families. Further, the material and physical work of gendered care work done by families left behind in the Philippines also becomes a requirement, if not an obligation in a transnational family context. These work processes, ushered in by the reconfiguration of social reproductive labor through migration and long-term separation, are never the focus of the Philippine labor brokerage state or receiving families and governments in destination countries. I use IE to introduce the care work processes left behind as valuable, difficult, and fulfilling, and to understand multidirectional care as a type of expertise in adjusting care work under the conditions of globalization.

Participatory Action Research Inspirations

PAR methodology prioritizes the participation of subjects of research as critical to the planning, implementation, and analysis of a research project that would often exclude the voices, bodies, and opinions of the "researched." Informed by their indigenous knowledge of their own social conditions and the institutions they live in and through daily, people participate in creating integral parts of the research process such as objectives, design, recruitment, data collection, and timeline. But more importantly, PAR methodology also insists that research is an engaged practice that activates dialogue across and within communities. Principles of PAR insist that all communities should have access and a "right to research" the pressing issues that are important and urgent to their community (Appadurai 2006; Udvarhelyi 2011). During my participation as an organizer with the Kabalikat Domestic Workers Support Network during the campaign to repatriate Fely Garcia in 2007 (see chapter 4) and through my ethnographic field notes, I noted that domestic workers helping this stranger found unity in three major dynamics: a critique of the Philippine state's negligence with migrants' welfare, concern for Tita Fely's family left behind, and a worry that this fate could be shared by any of them. To explore these themes, I interviewed Rita, Joan, and Andrea, leaders in Kabalikat, and with the needs of the organization in mind, we began to develop a research plan inspired by PAR principles, a method of research that the Filipino community organizers were familiar with from their organizing connections in the ongoing national liberation movement in the Philippines (IBON Foundation 2004) and by various political education activities inspired by theater of the oppressed methods (Boal 2000). We also planned to develop a program to keep up the political energy and organizing momentum parallel to the collection of data.

Kabalikat leaders identified three sets of issues they wanted to learn more about: domestic workers' migration stories, the role of the government and the culture of migration in the Philippines, and the current case of why people came together for Tita Fely (see Appendix D). In emphasizing that family was the main reason for migration, the Kabalikat coordinators also noted the need to understand the roles and operations of the transnational family under forced migration as motivation for domestic workers to leave, work abroad, and possibly organize together. We decided that outside research, this process had

Photo Appendix 1. Domestic workers learning interview skills and participating in theater of the oppressed activities. Photo courtesy of Valerie Francisco-Menchavez.

to engage migrants in building their skills in political organizing and education through a theater program. Through multiple discussions, revisions, and approval of the membership, we decided to incorporate the aforementioned issues in a semi-structured interview guide with open-ended questions for all of the interviews with domestic workers in this project (see appendix A). We conducted most of the interviews, *kuwentuhans,* and later the play *Diwang Pinay* in Tagalog, or Filipino, the national language of the Philippines.

I began to conduct individual semi-structured, confidential interviews with the core members of Kabalikat and this experience gave participants the time and space to share their stories, deepening our understanding of individual experiences of migration, domestic work, and participation in a transnational family. Many of the participants would divulge their trajectories bit by bit to each other and to me, but as core members began to learn skills in group interviewing, they started to hold *kuwentuhans* and connect their individual interviews. This allowed them to understand their discrete experiences as part of a larger story. Outside interviews and *kuwentuhans,* various data collected through the theater program included information such as maps, journals, play scripts, short topical open-ended surveys, songs and dances, and web observations (i.e., screen captures, emails, videos), which I return to in greater detail below. I conducted twenty-six interviews with Kabalikat members before the theater workshops and *kuwentuhans* began. But before we started the community theater program, many of the Kabalikat members advised me to return to the Philippines and interview their children to get all sides of the migration story. As discussed above in my decision to conduct multisited ethnography, the exploratory study and trips to the Philippines were actually influenced by the participation of the migrants in the study.

Through the participatory research design of this study, the migrants included in this book led the direction into deepening the meaning of family as a common motivation for migration and separation (Foner and Dreby 2011; Massey et al. 1993; D. E. Smith 2006). Understandably so, family also became one of the most sensitive topics for migrants in the various forms of data-gathering avenues we undertook. Migrant family members, especially mothers, would talk about the most painful and intimate parts of their family lives with me in individual interviews and in group-based data-collecting activities only if and when they felt safe and ready. Therefore, the methods of the research also had to foster a sort of community of commonality wherein migrants could disclose their struggles and fears about being separated from their families in a network they were invested in. The years we spent building relationships with each other were and are key to these conversations. Indeed, that migrant mothers, aunts, sisters, and grandmothers embraced me was crucial to my ability to complete this study. Participants in New York City would phone home, Skype, or communicate through Facebook months before I would take a trip to Manila, telling their families to expect me.

When I arrived in families' homes in Manila on my first trip in the summer of 2009, I was greeted with familiarity as migrants from New York City had already sent pictures of me and told stories about my work and the research we were doing together before I even set foot in the Philippines. I was also greeted with feasts of my favorite Filipino foods—*alimasag* (crab), *hipon* (shrimp), and *kangkong* (greens). Humbled by the effort spent on a spread for my visit, I would present each family with gifts from the United States and small parcels (*padala*) from their family members in New York City. I was frequently surprised about how much families in Manila knew about my favorite foods, current events in New York City, weather changes there, and upcoming activities at the center. But it was most clear to me in these moments of transnational life that experiences of migration necessarily had to incorporate the stories of migrants and the people they left behind. Without this suggestion from the migrant workers, I could have easily focused in just on their lives in New York City. And even though it was a costly move and made my analysis much more complex, this story of changing families would have never been enough without the interviews of families in Manila.

In Manila, I asked family members about their experiences of their migrant members' departure, the changes in their lives since the separation, the ways in which they incorporate missing members into their family activities, their networks of support in the absence of their family members, and their opinions on the politics of migration (see appendix B). With children and young adults left behind, I used photos from family photo albums to ask them about life before and after the migration of their mothers. We also looked at social media network profiles along with blogs and discussed the content and interactions with migrant mothers on these technologies to explore current transnational relationships. Varying the methods with children were intently chosen to use children's dexterity in technological use in their experience of migration and transnationalism, highlighting a "child's standpoint" (Mayall 2002). The development of the methods for Manila-based family members reflected the topics in the New York City interview guide to retain some comparability between interviews.

In December 2009, we began to hold theater workshops in New York City following the logic of PAR projects that take up action to distribute research findings toward an array of political ends, such as legislative change or public awareness of an issue. Our "action" was a year-long theater program and play production, transforming interviews and *kuwentuhans* into a stage play. Kabalikat's objectives in putting on the program and the play were to build leadership and organizing skills in their organization so that the migrants involved could grow in their capacity to be worker leaders in political organizing (Francisco 2014). At the outset of the research plan we constructed together, we planned that the interviews could train members in skills such as contact building, interview skills, and critical analysis skills. With ten to thirty people regularly participating in *kuwentuhans* and other theater of the oppressed exercises, we discovered themes during what Stuart Hall calls "processes of identification" (1996, 2)—as cultural identities became politicized—between members of the organization and began to build a political analysis and critique of their experiences of forced migration, precarious work, and immigration issues in the United States. Theater workshops (theater exercises, writing, and acting) included not only Kabalikat women, but also other Filipino domestic workers and Filipino American community members. Theater of the oppressed games brought out a different quality of conversation where identification was not automatic, but based on play—a more carefree and light exchange between migrants. After twelve- to sixteen-hour workdays, migrants would attend meetings and be refreshed by laughter and moving their bodies in theatrical games to start bringing their cultural sensibilities of performance and "drama" (Manalansan 2003). From this community program, I was able to recruit twenty-four more domestic workers who were not Kabalikat members to participate in the study. The non-Kabalikat domestic workers' stories were mostly collected through individual interviews, but there were many times that these members would also participate in the workshops where I recorded *kuwentuhans*.

For ten months, we conducted monthly *kuwentuhans* during the theater workshops. We increased the frequency to weekly (every Sunday) for the last four months of play production. These *kuwentuhans* are similar to interview sessions, or focus groups with two or more people, with questions fielded by all participants, not just the researcher. Doing so gave research participants, workshop participants, and me, the researcher, an opportunity to see, hear, talk, act, and discuss the commonalities in individual stories.[4] And commonalities abounded. Still holding on to shared experiences and shared dislocations, we added an education portion to each monthly theater workshop. Workshop schedules consisted of components such as games from the theater of the oppressed methodology and an educational component that was analytical and built the skills of participants to contribute to political organizing and creating the theatrical production. In the half hour to an hour *kuwentuhan* segments with anywhere from five to fifteen people, I would introduce recurring themes from the individual interviews for discussion in the group, topics like separation, motherhood and children, sexuality and desire, husbands and infidelity, community, solidarity and diasporic family, and state and transnational migrant governance. These themes are dislocations and experiences of dispossession; however, during *kuwentuhans* the spirits of those in the room were uplifted as people saw that others had gone through similar struggles. Whether we were talking about Tita Fely and the Philippine consulate's negligent handling of her case or about missing the milestones in children's or family members' lives, participants discovered or discussed how their own experiences were experiences of others too. Among them, I observed how the themes in individual interviews actually shaped the lives of the migrants as a whole. Practically speaking, we heard and listened to multiple voices. Moreover, *kuwentuhans* were also an epistemological method that echoed the patterns of talk and gossip in migrant worker social life in what Esther I. Madriz calls "collective testimony" (Madriz 1998): Filipino migrant women are often in groups of two or more in conversation about almost anything—work, where to get good and cheap thermals, sexuality, and desire. *Kuwentuhans* arguably allow people from marginalized communities to be more open and honest about their experiences of oppression as common experiences emerged during the discussions. Because stories of migration are often tearful and agonizing stories of trauma, members of Kabalikat and I were engaged in building a community of support and healing. Whether it was group yoga sessions at the Filipino community center, attending church together, or holding karaoke afternoons, the work of critical healing in our community happened through solidifying collective living. In specific circumstances, I used my resources as a community organizer and professional to tap into various city agencies for legal, health, and social services.

Through 2010, in the spirit of participatory research and the theater of the oppressed, migrants validated the recurring themes in the individual interviews I conducted through their collective production of *Diwang Pinay*. In their group decision-making discussions of which story lines to take up in each scenes or which voices to include in the dialogue of the play, migrants' authorship of the cultural production was the initial analysis or open coding of the stories in this book for me. The migrants' troubled static notions of their experiences as migrants and workers challenged the ideas, for example, that mothering from afar was neglectful or working as a domestic was a dirty job. In *kuwentuhans* and discussion about and writing the script of the play, the domestic workers infused these experiences with complexity, retelling them as stories of pleasure and pain, freedom and constraint, and trials and victories. The educational component for this project was a segment devoted to leadership development and building the capacity of migrants to organize fellow domestic workers. PAR projects often reserve time for analytic sessions to invest in conscientization (Freire 2000)—the development of critical consciousness—through the research process but also to ensure that participants are involved in the design, implementation, direction, and skills of doing research (Fields et al. 2008; Minkler et al. 2003). This educational component is an important intervention to turn away from the tokenization of migrant workers as mere informants in the research process toward a more transformative, participatory process that contributes to building grassroots migrant power in various local campaigns in New York City (Cooke and Kothari 2001; Torre et al. 2012).

The development of a transformative participatory research process in New York City included more than just migrants; it invited and required the participation of Filipinos in the Filipino American community. Younger Filipino immigrants and Filipino Americans from ages 19 to 35, most of them women, college-educated, and professional, were crucial in facilitating theater workshops, organizing logistics and production details, transcribing interviews, and providing technological support. Filipino American women from GABRIELA New York and the staff of the Bayanihan Filipino Community Center-Philippine Forum took the more time-intensive responsibilities: revising scripts; looking for a theater; choreographing the dances; and designing the lights, creating art (see appendix C), and props. This crew of nondomestic workers numbered between thirty and forty people. The staff for the production was cross-cultural (Filipino and Filipino American) and intergenerational (age cohort and immigration cohort); we all varied in terms of education, legal documentation, work stability, income, housing, and language. Although PAR researchers have established that not all participation in PAR projects is egalitarian (Fields et al. 2008; Fine and Torre 2006), we made sure that all collaborators were included in the discussion about the balance in the parts they brought into the project. Elsewhere I have written about "deep participation" (Francisco 2010) in PAR projects, in which we invited everyone to participate with acute attention to our embodied identities, to make room for those who are often silenced, and to participate with intention so as to not silence our privilege. We followed a similar ethic during the research process.

When we staged the play *Diwang Pinay* at City University of New York, Hunter College, in March 2011, the writing of the script, production, direction, cast, dancers, art production, songs, choreography, and set design were all collaborative, volunteer efforts of a majority women staff that consisted of Kabalikat members, domestic workers, and Filipino immigrant and Filipino American community members (see appendix C). Although the play script is not included in this book, the analysis brought out by the *kuwentuhans*, performance-elicited narratives, and discussions reflecting the theater of the oppressed methods informed how I picked out the themes in the collective story, or as Rita said, *iisang istorya*, of Filipino migrants in New York City that is in this book and the structure of our play. For example, following Augusto Boal's "image theatre" (2000), the use of participants' bodies to sculpt a portrait or an image of their last memory of the Philippines (usually at an airport) elicited narratives about personal memories but also drew out discussion from all participants about their common narrative. Performance-elicited narrative coupled with participatory politics in research allowed me to study the circulation of affect, first experienced by individuals and then in a community of migrants.

Throughout the five years of data collection and analysis in both New York City and Manila, I employed a rigorous, triangulation strategy that is often used in mixed-method studies aiming to test for the validity of research findings, through cycles of individual interviews, field notes, observation, theater workshops, *kuwentuhans*, field notes, and observations (see appendix E). I ensured themes reflected across data sets, relying on grounded theory for themes to emerge for analysis (Charmaz 2014). Although we adjusted methods due to the participatory nature of the methodology, we did not

Photo Appendix 2. Migrant women and Filipina Americans in a scene about different cleaning tasks of a domestic worker. Photo courtesy of Julie Jamora.

alter this data collection and analysis cycle. The systematic character of my collection and analysis drove a scientific logic of inquiry between inductive and deductive reasoning. Additionally, through this cycle I maintained a hermeneutic of faith and a hermeneutic of suspicion (Josselson 2004) in the concepts that would surface and disappear. I wrote ethnographic field notes (Emerson, Fretz, and Shaw 1995) in all phases and sites about my experiences in the field interviewing and observing. These memos were greatly useful in my data analysis, which at times overlapped with data collection especially during the participatory discussions during theater workshops. But the field notes were most helpful as I started to piece together the academic gaps and where this book could make methodological advances. Further, field notes were crucial in forming new ideas about the massive amounts of data I collected so that when I conducted focused coding on the interview and *kuwentuhan* transcripts using qualitative analysis software, Atlas.ti, I was able to look back on the most common themes. More open coding occurred in between extensive field note-taking and analysis workshops with domestic workers during theater workshops.

The inspiration of participatory action methodology in this book demonstrates that the methods, conducting, and analysis of research processes possess transformative qualities that can create action and unity within a

Photo Appendix 3. Curtain call for the play *Diwang Pinay* featuring domestic workers who wrote and starred in the production. Photo courtesy of Julie Jamora.

community. For the Filipino Americans in this study who were not aware of the struggles of undocumented migrants in their community, hearing stories and helping shape the theatrical production became their own process of conscientization. For migrants who participated in the theater program and performance, the ability to articulate their struggle and the opportunity to be heard by people in their community were also powerful. They were able to see one another as political allies and partners in campaigns and as possible contributors to a community of care that extends outside shared experiences of dislocation. Many of those second-generation and migrant participants continue to organize and support the causes of Filipino migrant workers. As the participants of this research shaped the design, methods, and dissemination, they too were affected, impacted, and changed.

Conclusion

Filipinos are the second largest Asian American immigrant group in the United States, with three million recorded and roughly one million uncounted and undocumented (Chua 2009). Outside California, the northeast region of the United States is home to a large concentration of Filipinos. The 2011–2015 census estimated more than 75,000 Filipinos living in Metro

New York City. The Filipino foreign-born residents population increased 22% from 2000 (Asian American Federation 2011). Constituting 7% of New York City's Asian American immigrants, Filipinos, both documented and otherwise, are generally college-educated; are fluent in English; and take up occupations primarily as nurses, domestic workers, and teachers. Fifty-eight percent of Filipinos in New York City are women. They are becoming a formidable transient and settled community in New York City, much like Filipinos in other global cities. It behooves scholars to research the various sectors of burgeoning immigrant communities. Not all Filipinos are nurses. Not all Filipinos are upwardly mobile, model minority types. Some of them are undocumented immigrants. Some of them are low-wage workers. It is a sociologist's call to create generalizations about the social world we live in, but we must retain the nuance in our studies to reflect the various realities of the communities we research. More importantly, in this move to hetero-genize the knowledge we produce, it is of utmost importance that we begin with our methods.

This research design allowed for three distinct findings to emerge in this book. First, multisited ethnography focuses on transnational lives within constellations of families in two sites to expand the definition of family members and the forms of care work. This study adds to the emerging literature on the nonmigrant counterparts of those moving around all over the world. Second, in prioritizing the voices of migrants and their families left behind to study institutions of migration, care work, and family, I show the every-day life consequences of the neoliberal immigration policies in a capitalist world-system. Third, employing participatory methods debunks the idea that the process and products of research are reserved for experts. Research, often an invasive project, still interrupted the lives of Filipino migrants and their families, but in an informed way. Participatory methods allowed for this research (and the importance and right to research) to be translatable to audiences outside the academy through the theatrical production. Dia-lectically, it also changed the views, political participation, and community engagement of people who participated in the project, including me.

Throughout the longitudinal research process and the writing of this book, I have seen the power of sharing stories, collective action, and political par-ticipation change the lives of the people while forging new understandings. The charge of writing about power and resistance is a difficult one. Often, the process was one that unearthed chasms of pain and grief for community members involved. But once those feelings were allowed to be felt and then acknowledged by the participants through a process of listening, producing a play, conducting political education, organizing and leading local campaigns, or building a community of care, there was a way to build a foundation in place of the gulfs of dislocation and dispossession. We were able to imagine a new vision of how our stories could be told. We could choose to be the authors of our own narratives. Heeding the challenge of feminists of color to reframe the lives of women from a place of power rather than a place of powerlessness, this process taught me that only through engaging in collaborative and collective struggle will the story be shifted and retold.

Appendix A
NYC Interview Guide

Family—*Pamilya*

Ikuwento niyo po sa'kin 'yung buhay ninyo sa Pilipinas. Pwede po kayo ma-gumpisa noong bata pa kayo.

Tell me about your life in the Philippines. You can start from childhood.

Meron po kayong mga kamag-anak na nag-abroad?

Do you have relatives who migrated or went abroad?

Paano po kayo nag-desisyon na mag-abroad? Ano ang mga dahilan para sa inyong pag-a-abroad?

How did you make your decision to migrate? What are the reasons for your migration?

Paano ninyo po sinabi sa anak at pamilya ninyo? Okay naman sila?

How did you tell your children and family? Were they okay with your decision?

Ano po yung pinakamahirap na bagay sa pag-a-abroad ninyo?

What is the hardest part of migrating?

Sa ngayon paano kayo nagiging aktib sa buhay ng anak ninyo?

How do you keep up with your kids?

Paano kayo nakikisali sa inyong pamilya sa pamamagitan ng technology?

How do you participate in your family through technology?

Anong klaseng technology ang ginagamit ninyo para makipag-ugnay sa inyong pamilya?

What kind of technology do you use to keep in contact with your family?

May naitutulong ba ang technology? O nagiging sagabal ba ang technology?

Does the technology help the distance? Or does it make it worse?

Kung pwede, gusto ninyo ba na mag-abraoad ang mga anak o kapamilya ninyo?

If they could, would you want your kids or family members to migrate to work?

Migration—*Pag-a-abroad*

Ikuwento ninyo po sa'kin ang karanasan ninyo tungkol sa inyong pagaabroad.

Tell me about your migration story.

Pagdating ninyo, ikuwento po ninyo ang naranasan ninyong masaya at karanasan ng mabigat.

When you arrived, tell me about a happy and a difficult experience you had here.

Ikuwento ninyo po ang karanasan ninyo sa pagtatrabaho bilang isang domestic dito.

Tell me about your experience working as a domestic worker here.

Sa mga pamilya sa Pilipinas, ang kulturang pag-a-abraod ay common, bakit kaya?

In families in the Philippines, a culture of migration is common. Why is that?

Bakit po ang karamihan ng migrante ay babae at hindi lalake?

Why do you think more women leave the Philippines than men?

Consciousness—*Pagmumulat*

Ano ang importansya in Tita Fely at Putli para sa Kabalikat?

Why were Tita Fely and Tita Putli such important markers in Kabalikat?

Bakit hindi tumutulong ang consulado sa mga isyung ganyan?

Why do you think the consulate doesn't help?

Sa tingin ninyo, ano ang tingin ng consulado at gobyerno sa inyong mga domestic worker?

How do the consulate and the government see domestic workers?

Ano ang kakaiba sa samahan ng Kabalikat?
What is special about Kabalikat as an organization?
Ano 'yung mga bagay na pagkakaisa sa mga myembro sa Kabalikat?
What brings members of Kabalikat together?

The State—*Gobyerno*

Ano ang papel ng gobyerno sa pag-a-abroad ng Pilipino?
What is the government's role in migration?
Ano ang papel nila bago kayong umalis sa Pilipinas?
What was their participation or influence or role before you left?
Ano ang papel nila sa buhay ninyo 'pag nandito na kayo?
What was their participation or influence or role after you got here?

Appendix B
Manila Interview Guide

Family—*Pamilya*

Ikuwento ninyo sa akin yung buhay ninyo nung nandito si [pangalan ng ka-pamilya].

Tell me about life when [insert family member's name] was here.

- *Ano 'yung niyong paborito gawin?*
- What was your favorite thing to do?
- *Ano 'yung pinakamasaya na panahaon?*
- What was a fun memory?
- *Ano 'yung pinakamalunkot na panahon labas sa nung nag-abroad siya?*
- What was a sad memory outside of her migrating abroad?
- *Meron ba kayong magandang pakiki-samahan sa kanila?*
- Did you have a good relationship with her or him?

Migration—*Pag-a-abroad*

Ikuwento ninyo paano sinabi ni [pangalan ng kapamilya] na siya'y magta-trabaho sa abroad?

Tell me how [insert name of family member] told you they were leaving.

- *Ano ang dahilan niya kung bakit siya nag-abroad?*
- What were the reasons they left?

- *Ano'ng naisip mo?*
- What did you think about that?
- *Ano'ng naramdaman mo?*
- How did you feel?
- *Meron ka bang naisip na hindi mo nasabi?*
- Is there something you wanted to say but couldn't?

Nung umalis na siya, ano yung naranasan mo?

When they left, what was your experience like?

- *Ano ang mga bagay na naiba nung umalis siya? Pwedeng positibo o negatibo?*
- What changed when they left? Positive or negative?
- *Sino nag-asikaso sa inyo? 'Pag pasok o 'pag nagkasakit kayo?*
- Who takes care of you? For school or when you get sick?
- *Yung dating inaasikaso ng nanay mo, sino na gumagawa nung bagay na 'yon ngayon?*
- Your mom's duties in the past, who does them now?
- *Kailan yung panahon na namimiss mo yung Nanay mo?*
- When do you miss your mom most?
- *Kung may problema ka, sino ang sinasabihian mo? Tinatawagan mo ba siya? Kung hindi siya sino?*
- When you have issues, whom do you talk to? Call your mom? If not her, who?

Sa palagay mo, bakit siya nag-abroad?

In your opinion, why did she leave?

- *Nauunawan mo ba ang kanyang dahilan?*
- Do you understand why they left?
- *Meron ka bang ibang kilala (pamilya o kaibigan) na ganito rin ang sitwasyon nila?*
- Do you know other people (family or friends) whose situation is like yours?

The State—*Gobyerno*

Ano ang papel ng gobyerno sa pag-a-abroad ng Pilipino?

What is the government's role in creating conditions for migration for Filipinos?

Ano ang papel nila bago umalis sa Pilipinas ang inyong kamaganak?

What is their participation or influence or role before your family member leaves to work abroad?

Ano ang papel ng gobyerno sa buhay ninyo pagkatapos nagabroad ang inyong kamag-anak?

What is their participation or influence or role after your family member migrates?

Appendix C

Flyer for Diwang Pinay

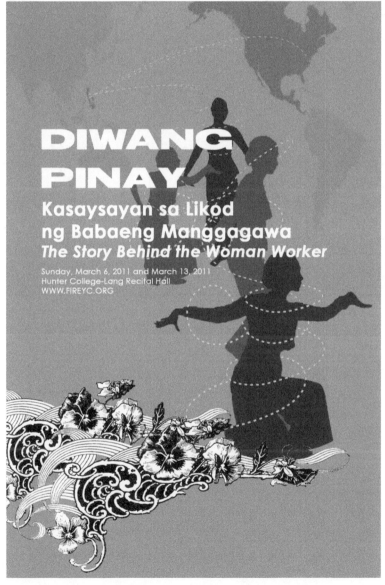

Photo Appendix C. Front of flyer for the stage production of *Diwang Pinay*. Art courtesy of Arlene Rodrigo.

DIWANG PINAY

Kasaysayan sa Likod ng Babaeng Manggagawa

The Story Behind the Working Women

Hunter College-Recital Hall
695 Park Avenue
New York, NY 10065

Location: 4th floor of the North Building at Hunter College
Access: 69th St entrance between Park and Lexington Ave

Subway: 4/6 to 68th St Hunter College, F to 63rd St and Lexington Ave

ALL AGES WELCOME!

March 6th 2PM Matinee Performance $10
March 6th, 7PM Evening Performance $20
March 13th, 2PM and 7PM Performance $20

Hosted By:

KABALIKAT
A FILIPINO SA FILIPINO FAMILY
PHILIPPINE FORUM
FILIPINO COMMUNITY CENTER
BAYANIHAN

Filipinos for Rights and Empowerment
for more information, visit us at www.ffreryc.org

Since February 2010, a group of Filipino women across generations, both age and migration, have gathered weekly to create an original staged play about migration, family and resilience. Diwang Pinay follows the story of Maria, a domestic worker in the NYC area who left the Philippines to support her family by migrating only to face challenges in a new city and figure out a way to survive. See the world through her eyes as a migrant and mother.

The process of creating this original work has bestowed a multigenerational group of Filipinas, immigrant and American-born, a unique experience to write, produce and direct stories about the lives of Filipino domestic workers living and working in New York City. This production is a collaboration between Kabalikat Domestic Worker Support Network, a program of the Philippine Forum and Filipinas for Rights and Empowerment (FiRE)-Gabriela USA.

Photo Appendix C. Back of flyer for the stage production of *Diwang Pinay*. Art courtesy of Arlene Rodrigo.

Appendix D

Research Questions and Methods Grid

Questions	Method
TRANSNATIONAL FAMILY	
• How do migrant women workers conceptualize and actualize participation in their families (i.e., mothering) from a transnational location? • What are the activities, technologies, and practices of migrant women to maintain family life from abroad? • How does migration problematize our notions of motherhood, gender, and family?	Field notes/participant observation Interviews Social media interactions and discussions *Kuwentuhans* Participatory analysis Theater workshops
FAMILIES LEFT BEHIND	
• How do families and kin left behind participate in the production of transnational families? • What types of care and emotion work do they do for the migrant family members? • How is technology changing the transnationality of family?	Field notes/participant observation Interviews Photo-elicited discussions Social media interactions and discussions *Kuwentuhans*

COMMUNITY RELATIONS

- What types of identifications emerged from migrant women's subjectivities as migrants, women, family members, and workers?
- In other words, how does the production of transnational families shape political mobilization?

Field notes/participant observation
Interviews
Kuwentuhans

STATE and the FAMILY

- How is the ideal Philippine family represented by the state through migration?
- In what ways does the Philippine government define ideal familial roles of motherhood, fatherhood, filial piety for children, extended family, etc.?
- How do migrant women integrate and negotiate these messages?

Interviews
Kuwentuhans

Appendix E

Research Methods Triangulation Cycle

Participant Observation and Field Notes

- Observe activities, gatherings, and events
- Identify important themes and concepts from observations
- Conduct participatory dialogue with research participants about findings
- Incorporate theoretical and research scholarship in the emerging data

Individual Interviews

- Semi-structured interviews based on topics culled from field notes
- Ensure participation in construction or revisions interview guide
- Take notes during interviews about new concepts, topics

Ethnographic Field Notes

- Write field notes on each interview interaction, specifically on recurring themes and new concepts
- Identify important themes and concepts from interviews
- Select recurring theme to introduce to *kuwentuhans* at theater workshop
- Incorporate theoretical and research scholarship in the emerging data

***Kuwentuhans* and/or Theater Workshops**

- Discuss a theme from individual interviews for *kuwentuhans*
- Conduct theater of the oppressed games
- Conduct educational segments

Notes

Introduction

1. The international labor force, with the prime neoliberal subject as the migrant worker, has become essential for neoliberal and capitalist accumulation. Under neoliberalism, the state and the family have been two highly contentious sites for social reproduction. As the neoliberal state (Harvey 2007) continues to retreat from welfare responsibilities and social services while surrendering to the whims of precarious labor markets (job losses, insecure contingent work), social reproduction has been reallocated to the family. To this end, the transnational family form is a product of the Philippines' neoliberalizing state and economy; the institutionalized export system and global migration as a "development strategy" has become the lynchpin of Philippine modernization. Accompanied by the neoliberal rhetoric of migration as independence and mobility, circulated as Filipinos choosing to pick themselves up from their bootstraps to find a better future for their families, the Philippine state is intentional in producing a racialized and gendered global labor force.

The institutionalization of labor export and migration that began in the early 1970s under the dictator Ferdinand Marcos has become part of the foundation of the Philippine national economy. Subsequent administrations have since developed and advanced a system of migration management and regulation for profit, in what Robyn Rodriguez calls a "labor brokerage state" (R. M. Rodriguez 2010). The remittance industry that brings in more than $25 billion annually has been the saving grace of the Philippines to pay back loans from structural adjustment programs incurred through the International Monetary Fund and the World Bank (Chipongian 2016). Remittance is integrated in the rubric of the national "development" in the metro areas of the Philippines and as a positive indicator for the United Nations' Millennium Development Goals.

2. Marxist feminists have long argued that the separation of public, waged, productive labor from private, unpaid social reproductive labor has devalued women's work

and roles in biologically, culturally, and materially reproducing social life (Laslett and Brenner 1989; Seccombe 1974; D. D. E. Smith 1989; Gordon 1992; Gimenez 1990; Luxton 2006).

3. The Philippine labor brokerage state has systematized migration for national economic stability in the wake of the neoliberal reforms that have privatized much of the country's social services and produced joblessness. The export of migrant labor, contractual and otherwise, and its lucrative remittance industry has proven to be a reliable neoliberal strategy to keep the Philippines an active player in the global economy. Following Karl Marx and Fredrick Engels's analysis of the state and the family (Marx and Engels 1942), I argue that state-sponsored migration is key to reconfiguring the contemporary Filipino family.

4. Scholarship on transnational families has analyzed the role of kinship networks as support systems to the dispersed family (R. C. Smith 2006; Dreby 2010); however, they are assumed to be in addition to the original nuclear family instead of a foundational component of the transnational family form.

5. Displacing the assumption of family as nuclear allows different family forms to emerge as they participate in various forms of circulation of care (Baldassar and Merla 2013). In the past, the nuclear form was the assumed operative form of the family. Yet the nuclear form limits the theorizing of care work since fictive or extended kin—their contributions and roles in care work and their definition of care—are rendered invisible as they are not considered part of the nuclear form. Expanding who is considered to be "in" the family allows for the possibility of studying a wider and more intricate network of care work in a family that is called to adjust their everyday practices and operations of caring for one another.

6. The transnational family and the reversal in gender roles and domestic labor within families who have migrant members has been well studied (Isaksen, Devi, and Hochschild 2008; Yeates 2009; Glenn 1992; Bridget Anderson 2000). Beginning in the late 1960s, the increased rate of feminization of migration—women migrating for labor or marriage, instead of men—began to change the ways families had to operate; the change ushered in a family unit that had to function against the odds of time and space (Guerrero 2000; Castles and Miller 2003; Zlotnik 2003). From Mexico, Central America, and Latin America, women began to migrate to "El Norte" in search of jobs, marking the beginning of families that lived and functioned across borders (Stephen 2007; Schmalzbauer 2004; Anzaldúa 1999). By the 1970s, most women who migrated for domestic work came from Southeast Asia, especially the Philippines, Sri Lanka, and Indonesia (Frantz 2008; Parreñas 2001b). Similarly, the increased migration of women from Eastern Europe to Western Europe to work in private households coalesced in the 1980s (Mather 2006; Bridget Anderson 2000). The movement of women for work through this upsurge in women's migration was often predicated on economic need and family survival. The feminization of migration as a characteristic of neoliberal globalization drew attention to the consequences of women's absence in the family.

7. Scholars agree that the migration of women, especially from the Global South to the Global North, to work in the care industry contributes to the decimation of

the "commons" that families build over time through their everyday interactions, especially for families who are transnational (Isaksen, Devi, and Hochschild 2008).

8. Scholars in the sociology of the family have argued that care is never a one-way street from active provider to passive receiver; rather, some have posited that care is relational and reciprocal (Milligan and Wiles 2010; Fisher and Tronto 1990).

9. Scholars argue that today's transnationalism is a set of "processes by which immigrants build social fields that link together their country of origin and their country of settlement," wherein migrants' relationship to the home country is not in contradiction to their settlement in the host country (Schiller, Basch, and Blanc-Szanton 1992, 6).

10. In what Peggy Levitt and Nina Glick Schiller call "dynamics of simultaneity," the place-based production of transnational families "takes us beyond the direct experience of migration into domains of interaction where individuals who do not move themselves maintain social relations across borders" (Levitt and Schiller 2004, 7). Technology also presents an avenue to express and withhold these dynamics of simultaneous care work.

11. Although one person's absence is hard and palpable, families left behind are also acutely aware of the situation they are left with; often there are many other members of the family still around and those relationships still require attention. For example, when family members or kin left behind take care of one another they see it as both a response to their migrant family member's sacrifice and a form of care for one another in the place left behind. When families left behind work to keep their lives together and they are successful in maintaining their lives, or even better, gain some advance in their quality of life, this is a form of care work for one another left behind and for their migrant family members. Therefore, a care circulation framework alongside a theory of simultaneity is necessary to adequately analyze the dynamics of care in transnational families.

12. In contribution to immigration and migration studies, I situate this analysis of communities of care toward what scholars have established in terms of social networks as essential to immigrant community formation and individual success in the United States (Bashi 2007; Kasinitz, Mollenkopf, and Waters 2004). Although the kinds of networks that emerge in communities of care have been studied in social science literature (Ebaugh and Curry 2000; Hagan 1998; Levitt 1998; Grasmuck and Pessar 1991; M. C. Waters 2001), I offer a different theoretical lens to discuss the basis and quality of social relations in these networks. Existing research on immigrant social networks argues that migrant assimilation is critical to understanding how immigrants build and contribute to their social networks and how migrants either thrive or fail in their new homes (Portes and Rumbaut 2006). Following Robert C. Smith's argument that transnational practices do not preclude assimilation (R. C. Smith 2006), I illustrate that the redefinition of the family as a community of care relies on transnational life as a resource.

13. Black feminist thought and queer theoretical frameworks move us toward looking at the role of neoliberalism and global migration in constructing sexual

identities, communities, and politics (Luibhéid and Cantu 2005; Manalansan 2003). These "social theories reflect women's efforts to come to terms with lived experiences within intersecting oppressions of race, class, gender, sexuality, ethnicity, nation and religion" (Collins 2002, 9).

14. Network theory in immigrant communities often only focuses on assimilative components of immigrant life (Hagan 1998; Elrick and Lewandowska 2008). But I contend that the political economy of migration ties migrants to transnational practices that don't often lead to a concern to assimilate, at least not immediately.

15. Migrant, worker, and mother are nodes of identification that migrant women use to recognize one another and recruit others into their communities of care. I highlight these identification processes (Hall 2003) because participants have described their recognition of one another as migrant, worker, and mother in such situated accounts. The migrants not only identify with one another—imprisoned by the label of "undocumented"—but they understand the emotional sacrifices they make living in between New York City and Manila. This in-betweenness is simultaneously imagined by transnational life and produced by situated and exclusionary pressures to assimilate. Still, migrants are adamant in seeing their fellow migrants do well in New York City while they maintain good relationships with their families at home. The assimilative purposes of immigrant social networks are often in relation to the upkeep of transnational life. This underscores transnational scholars' agreement that transnational practices and assimilation processes are not mutually exclusive; rather, they are nodes on a continuum (R. C. Smith 2006; Schiller, Basch, and Blanc-Szanton 1992).

16. In the 1960s, Carol Stack argued that families who live under conditions of structural retreat and lack often depend on intricate systems of biological and fictive kin for basic survival (Stack 1997). In opposition to the trope of culture of poverty, Stack argues that African American families creatively set up systems of resilience to deal with poverty, failing education systems, and joblessness. The concept of othermothers and kinship ties demonstrate that it is the *conditions* under which families live that reorganize social reproductive labor through women-centered networks. Embedded in the concept of othermothers is an analysis of the political and economic conditions that restrict and then inspire women of color to create forms of resilience. For migrants from the Global South living in the United States, the conditions of economic deprivation drive families to separate and then recuperate through reorganizing care.

17. Studies of Filipino migrants' communities in the diaspora have claimed that structural conditions produce displacement (Pido 1986; Parreñas 2001b; Espiritu 2003; Constable 1997; Ball and Piper 2002). They examine the conditions of the majority of Filipino migrants working in the care industry. Rhacel Salazar Parreñas, in her study of Filipino domestic workers in Rome and Los Angeles, investigates the diasporic "dislocations" of Filipina women in different "contexts of reception" (2001b, 8). Filipina women's common experiences as low-wage workers globally create tropes

of unity and solidarity among migrant women in diasporic locations. Although experiences of Filipina women are not the same everywhere, migrants find similarities in Filipina women's lives in the economic, political, and social contexts in Italy and the United States that thus gives rise to a coalitional ground between them. In her work, Parreñas almost speaks to the possibilities of networks for Filipino domestic workers, yet leaves the issue unattended.

In a study of Filipino domestic workers in Canada, Geraldine Pratt writes about the symbolic synonymy between migrants as a racialized and gendered population of laborers (Pratt 2004). She argues that domestic work is reified and inscribed onto Filipina women's bodies following a Canadian racial order and gendered disciplinary context, especially in public places and workspaces. Classed racism solidifies these inscriptions on Filipina women's bodies to produce powerlessness and vulnerability. Despite these discursive and political constraints, community organizing becomes a marker of Filipinas' reterritorialization of power, showing that political organizing is a strategy that Filipinas employ in reconstituting their identities (Tungohan 2017). Another study of Filipino migrants in Canada highlights the efforts of Filipina women to subvert and change policies that permit the exploitation of domestic workers in private homes (Stasiulis and Bakan 2005). Daiva K. Stasiulis and Abigail Bess Bakan argue that the similarities between authoritarian regimes that produce comparable conditions across the political, ideological, legal, and experiential dimensions of Filipina migrant women workers the world over can serve as a form of coalition building. These scholars deepen an analysis of Filipinas' capacity to form solidarity between one another. A key contribution in these studies is establishing the critique of political and economic systems in producing the precarious living and working conditions of migrant workers that can also hold the potential of migrant worker intersubjectivity and collectivities. However, lacking in this analysis is how Filipino migrants' transnational life figures into the reconstitution of their individual identities and community networks.

18. Black feminist thought theories and queer theories allow for macroexamination of the systems of power that have driven them to live in a migrant community balanced with a microsociological analysis of their everyday lives.

19. Yen Le Espiritu (2003), Robyn M. Rodriguez (2002), and Rhacel Salazar Parreñas (2001a) have argued that the creation of homes and community for Filipinos and Filipino Americans is inherently a political act, at times in imagining a transnational connection to the Philippine nation and also in critiquing the Philippine nation.

Chapter 1. Multidirectional Care in Transnational Families

1. The characteristics of family formation are transformed alongside social, political, and economic shifts in history (Hondagneu-Sotelo and Avila 1997; Dill 1988). Scholarship shows that the family form has absorbed changes under the conditions of globalization and migration by revising definitions, roles, and operations (Parreñas 2005a; Asis, Huang, and Yeoh 2004; Dreby 2010; Pingol 2001). As neoliberal

globalization puts new burdens on the family in the Global South, migration and separation are born out of decreased and privatized social services as well as increasing unemployment. Likewise, in the Global North, the privatization of public health care creates demand for low-wage workers to fill the gaps in the growing care crisis for aging populations and new families. Maruja Milagros B. Asis, Shirlena Huang, and Brenda S. A. Yeoh argue that the "transnational family—generally one where core members are distributed in two or more nation states, but continue to share strong bonds of collective welfare and unity—is a strategic response to the changing social, economic and political conditions of a globalizing world" (Asis, Huang, and Yeoh 2004, 199). In this study, the transnational family is exemplified specifically by long-term separation over great distances wherein migrant family members seek a livelihood abroad to support families left behind. In this arrangement, families strive to reorganize the operations of the family to maintain the functions of the family as well as ideals of family life.

2. Scholars in the sociology of immigration and transnationalism have introduced a variety of concepts to understand the reorganization of care and the transnational family under globalization (Hondagneu-Sotelo and Avila 1997; Parreñas 2005b ; Dreby 2010; Abrego 2014; Boehm 2012). Pierrette Hondagneu-Sotelo and Ernestine Avila's pivotal work about Latin American domestic workers in Los Angeles establishes that gender is organizing the changing social relations of family under migration and globalization. They argue that "transnational mothering radically rearranges mother-child interactions and requires a concomitant radical reshaping of the meanings and definitions of appropriate mothering" (Hondagneu-Sotelo and Avila 1997, 557). Migrant mothers often expand their definitions of motherhood by becoming the breadwinner while fulfilling intensive emotional and nurturing roles from afar. Joanna Dreby's powerful work with Mexican migrants in New Jersey and their families in Mexico explores how these separated family members still "do family" (Dreby 2010). She gives us a look at the work of maintaining a transnational family from different vantage points: migrant parents, caregivers, and children left behind. Migrant parents stay active in the lives of their families by providing financial support for basic needs and by maintaining regular communication through letters, pictures, phone calls, and cards (Hoang and Yeoh 2014). Still, the reorganization of the family—and what defines family—is ongoing; children and caregivers left behind are not merely passive recipients of money and goods. Dreby shows us that children leverage power over migrants' family members by "emotional withholding" (Dreby 2010, 142). Both migrants *and* families left behind reshape the meaning of family transnationally. In their compelling works on Mexican and Salvadoran transnational families, respectively, Deborah A. Boehm and Leisy Abrego insist that US policies create particularly difficult conditions for reunification and illegality that produces gendered experiences of care work for migrants and their families left behind.

Chapter 2. Skype Mothers and Facebook Children

1. *Nanay* is the Filipino word for mother.

2. During the holiday season of 2011, Coca-Cola in partnership with the Overseas Foreign Workers agency produced a short film entitled *Where Will Happiness Strike Next?* that followed three migrant workers who were sponsored and united with their families in the Philippines. The tearful and emotional short film showed how technology and transportation bridge the gap between transnational families, despite long-term separation and long distances.

Chapter 3. Communities of Care

1. Scholars examining social networks in migrant destinations often assess immigrant assimilation and acculturation—whether immigrants fare well and how they adapt. Alejandro Portes and Rubén G. Rumbaut argue that assimilation is often impeded by "contexts of reception," the local social hierarchies that greet immigrants upon their migration. Arguably, immigrants and second-generation immigrants rely on social networks to combat those challenges (Kasinitz, Mollenkopf, and Waters 2004).

Prior analyses of immigrant networks premigration and postmigration treat migration as an event rather than a process. However, Vilna Bashi, in her study of West Indian immigrant networks, proposes a hub-and-spoke model where a network expert (the hub) provides social capital needed for new immigrants to establish housing, work, and community in their new country. New migrants (the spokes) are often not obliged to return the favor to the hub, but are expected to pay it forward to new spokes in the social network. Bashi argues that in a transnational context, these hub-and-spoke networks traverse national boundaries, rolling out their social capital resources from the First World to the Third World and back again. According to Bashi, the immigrant social network is a dynamic and repetitive social process not a singular event. In their study of fictive kinship systems from Latin America, Yoruba, and Asian cultures, Helen Rose Ebaugh and Mary Curry focus on a cultural continuum in migration experiences (Ebaugh and Curry 2000). According to Ebaugh and Curry, certain forms of fictive kinship operate as social networks, and serve similar purposes of social and financial support as well as social control. Interestingly, these networks also serve to maintain cultural continuity and spiritual development for ethnic immigrants. Ebaugh and Curry's study thus provides an example of how the social network for immigrants is an ongoing process that grows and shrinks, stabilizes and destabilizes.

2. I rely on black feminist thought to analyze the emerging self-definitions of motherhood and womanhood of Filipino migrant women against the conditions of marginality they face as domestic workers and mothers or daughters who are separated from their families. In their communities of care in New York City, Filipina migrant women are re-

defining their experiences of oppression and isolation as a "standpoint" to create pockets of resilience. Patricia Hill Collins argues that "Black women's position in the political economy, particularly ghettoization in domestic work, comprised another contradictory location where economic and political subordination created the conditions for Black women's resistance" (Collins 2002, 11). Black women's experiences as slaves and later as domestic workers in white families presented an "outsider-within" perspective; black women were systematically excluded and subordinated into the dominant group's ideologies and lives yet they were integral to the daily lives of dominant white culture. Black feminist thought (Giddings 2009; Wallace 1990; Collins 2002) maintains that these conditions of oppression coupled with an outsider-within standpoint provided a unique backdrop for black women's solidarity with one another and thus a generative form of resilience and survival. Filipino migrant women's position in the current global political economy as exported migrant labor and disposable domestic workers in the urban economy of New York City's upper- and middle-class homes serves as the backdrop to their outsider-within standpoints. They are at once easily discarded migrant workers and requisite social reproductive labors for their employers and their families. Black feminist thought as a framework allows for the political economic subordination of Filipino migrant women to be integrated in the ways that they create new forms of resistance in their communities. Although the experiences of black women and Filipina migrants are distinct, the overlapping theoretical proposition of my black feminist epistemologies provides a useful frame in which to understand how Filipina migrants are constructing communities of care.

3. In her ground-breaking book *Families We Choose*, Kath Weston argues that GLBT people have been positioned outside the construct of the "family," even as a threat to the very idea of it (Weston 1997). Her study conducted during the mid-1980s described the family values debate that pointed to GLBT people as a threat to the family along with a confluence of shifting family concepts like open adoptions, blended families of divorced and remarried parents, and surrogate parenthood. Similarly, despite those challenges, GLBT people innovated and established "gay families" or "chosen families" from fictive kin, friends, and ex-lovers. In studying the family formations of queer individuals, she argues that we mustn't equate "chosen families" with a substitution or an alternative to a nuclear, heteronormative formation of family.

4. In an effort to highlight the agential capacities of migrants in this reformulation of immigrant social networks, I draw on queer theories' analysis of homosociality and sexuality in migration (Luibhéid and Cantu 2005; Luibhéid 2008; Manalansan 2005; Gopinath 2005), queer family formations among subjects with marginalized identities (Weston 1997; Eng 2010; Morgensen 2011), and black feminist analysis on motherhood and kin networks in African American and black communities (Stack 1997; Collins 1995; Giddings 2009; Wallace 1990). Concepts in queer theory and black feminist thought reach beyond mere categories of affinity and biology. These

theoretical frames urge us to interrogate the systems of power that influence marginalized peoples to form strong and reliable networks of care and resistance to combat experiences of oppression. These conceptual frameworks hinge on epistemology and thus provide a deeper frame to theorize the nuance in people's choices to build community as well as how they participate within that community. Further, these theories destabilize the heteronormative assumption that organizes much of the migration scholarship on families and immigrant social network. In this chapter, I follow queer migration scholars in exploring how "'the age of migration' is centrally implicated in the construction, regulation and reworking of sexual identities, communities, politics and cultures" (Luibhéid 2008, 169).

5. Although I build on Weston's idea of "chosen family," I heed the critiques of this concept in the scholarship on queer kinship as homonormative and keep in place the privileges of the heterosexual family (Duggan 2002). David L. Eng also argues that the model of pairing or marriage in the chosen family subscribes to a racialized intimacy that is often distributed unequally, underwriting white supremacy (Eng 2010). Addressing homonormativity in the queer kinship of migrant women in New York City, I lean on Judith Butler's definition of kinship as a "kind of doing" (Butler 2002, 34) in relation to the specificity of their relationship to the global political economy, the racialized domestic industry they work in, and one another.

Chapter 4. Caring Even if It Hurts

1. Scholars have established that belonging to a transnational family has its inherent challenges: lack of communication (Dreby 2010; Aranda 2003), loss of intimacy (Baldassar 2007, 2013; Parreñas 2005b; Pe-Pua et al. 1998), reproduction of gendered roles in domestic labor (Dreby 2010; Parreñas 2005a; D. E. Smith 2006; Wilding and Baldassar 2009; J. L. Waters 2002), and feelings of resentment and abandonment leading to emotional distance between transnational family members (Baldassar 2007; Parreñas 2001a, 2005a). "Emotional discourses of 'love and loyalty,' long-distance communicative practices and visits enacting mutual care, and embodied experiences of togetherness can dominate transnational kin relationships. Evidently, such relationships can also be marked by tensions and disagreement, or may even be absent" (Svasek 2008, 220). Although scholars acknowledge that transnational family relationships can be tense or produce emotional discord, few studies analyze the care work that happens even under these circumstances. The conflation of nurturance and love as the standard of transnational care work exaggerates the presence of any type of emotive dissonance as a form of strain or resentment in the transnational family. And although feelings of abandonment and resentment are very real for family members left behind and/or migrant members, many of them continue to attend to care work from afar.

The theme of resentment marks the experience of young people in Filipino transnational and immigrant families. Rhacel Salazar Parreñas finds that Filipino children left behind have high and unrealistic expectations of their migrant mothers, which often lead to feelings of abandonment and dissatisfaction (Parreñas 2005a). Adult children in transnational families took issue with their migrant mothers' absence, Parreñas argues, because they could not accept "their family as the right kind of family" (Parreñas 2005a, 136), wherein the exchange of material comforts and emotional intimacy was not sufficient. Migrant mothers often expand their definition of mothering work; however, their children may not recognize or identify their mothers' redefinitions.

In my work, I have found similar themes emerge; however, absent in Parreñas's theorizing is recognizing the acts of care that continue regardless of the emotional contradictions within the transnational family. For example, in her study, she cites many children who express their discontent with their mothers being away and, in the same breath, continue to honor their mothers' sacrifice with good grades or faithful communication. However, detangling the emotional discourse of love and loyalty from the acts of care of disagreeable children can be useful. This separation of the assumed emotionality of nurturance in caring allows us to acknowledge that children in transnational families are unhappy with the arrangement they're in, but we can also understand that their disappointment is not only in their mothers' absence but also in the political economy of the family separation.

2. Caring in the family has been studied and defined in a sentimentalized and essentialized nature attributed to women (Finch and Groves 1983; H. Graham 1983; Parsons and Bales 1955). The labor in caring within a family is often conflated with feelings of love, warmth, and nurturance. Jane Collier, Michelle Z. Rosaldo, and Sylvia Yanagisako join other feminists by arguing against "the Malinowskian view of The Family as a universal institution—which maps the function of 'nurturance' onto a collectivity of persons (presumably 'nuclear' relations) associated with specific spaces (the home) and specific affective bonds (love)" (Collier, Rosaldo, and Yanagisako 1997, 74) is not translatable across cultures (Thorne and Yalom 1982). This ideology of the family is linked with the oppression of women wherein the index of women's value is their efficacy as mothers (Collier, Rosaldo, and Yanagisako 1982). In this logic, an unloving mother or an uncaring daughter is a failed woman.

3. Family members engage in care work even in contradiction with intentions of nurturance. Scholars have found that care work, specifically done by women, draws from emotion management (Hochschild 2003). As mothers, daughters, and sisters attend to tasks of family care they are constantly employing emotion work when feeling frustrated about the assumed gendered division of domestic labor (Hochschild 2003). Women will often do tasks in domestic work that others can do for themselves and therefore completing these tasks is often accompanied by negative emotions about the tasks. In one study, 75% of women indicated feeling at odds with their care behaviors while the majority of men did not report emotive dissonance (Dressel and Clark 1990).

4. Other definitions of care work that separate emotionality from the labor of caring highlight that women are employing maternal thought and strategy in their acts and actions that are not always fueled by nurturance (Ruddick 1995; Seery 1996). In their study of family care, Paula L. Dressel and Ann Clark note that family members state

that "anything that one does for, or with, [family members] constitutes care" (Dressel and Clark 1990, 774). Although Dressel and Clark find that families believe in a romanticized ideal of care that then reifies care work as an arena of love and nurturing, they also explore the conduct of care work that at times belies family members' romantic ideals of care work. In their findings, families strive for nurturance but most of the time family members do the tasks of caring without love or warmth. They state that when "care is inherent in anything one does for or with a family member, the simplicity of that statement camouflages a variety of motives surrounding acts of care" (Dressel and Clark 1990, 777). For example, routine activities such as bathing and preparing meals are not tied to positive emotions; rather, they are acts of care that are part of one's daily duties. For the most part, these routine tasks are reified as loving gendered care work, often taken up by women and mothers.

5. In other studies of transnational families in other ethnic groups, scholars explore the role of emotive dissonance in transnational families, specifically how children use emotionality in shaping family operations (Dreby 2010; Orellana et al. 2001; Pe-Pua et al. 1998). Joanna Dreby argues that "children wield influence over migrant parents as the beneficiaries of their sacrifices" (Dreby 2010, 142). In other words, Mexican children left behind gain relative power in their families when they bargain with their parents through displays of emotional withholding. In my research, I find that children and family members left behind utilize emotional withholding as a form of negotiation with their migrant family members. But accepting these exchanges as a form of care work can help us understand that the institution of family is governed by a set of power relations that is not always narrated by love or loyalty. Still, these ebbs and flows in dysfunction make up a family structure. Transnational family members are using space and time differences as an actor mitigating their family operations, often counting on absence as leverage in the bargains they are making. Whether they need something or are trying to brush something under the rug, these exchanges in emotional withholding are all part of transnational family operations.

6. Family scholars and feminist writers have argued, however, that not all labor in the family is a labor of love (Lee and Mjelde-Mossey 2004; Montgomery, Gonyea, and Hooyman 1985; DeVault 1999). Scholars argue that definitions of nurturance must take the relationship between giver and receiver into consideration as well as who benefits from the care. "It is likely that family activities get defined as family care activities on the basis of interactional dynamics of both the giver and the receiver" (Dressel and Clark 1990, 771). The giver may not feel emotional attachment about the care being provided, but the receiver can feel fulfilled about the care given. Likewise, receivers of care may not always feel positive about the type of care work they receive, but that care work is still meaningful to caregivers. "The realization that acts of care may be self- rather than other-directed challenges a popular notion of who benefits from care" (Dressel and Clark 1990, 776). The giver of care does not necessarily have to have the intention of love and warmth to do the work of caring; the caregiver may have the objective of merely completing a task that satisfies a role of care provider.

Conclusion

1. Patricia Hill Collins argues that an "outsider-within" perspective produced an intersubjectivity between black women slaves that then led them to innovative strategies to cope with the cruelty of their circumstances (Collins 2000).

Methodological Appendix

1. In Pierrette Hondagneu-Sotelo and Ernestine Avila's pioneering article title, "I'm Here but I'm There," simultaneity becomes key in understanding the changes ushered in by migration, in that as much as the migrant's everyday life changes so does her family's (Hondagneu-Sotelo and Avila 1997).

2. For Filipino migrants, these two sets of relations are not as obvious as workplace studies that employ IE as methodology in community organizations (Mykhalovskiy and McCoy 2002) or nursing work in hospitals (Rankin and Campbell 2009).

3. IE has been instrumental to many research projects that are "studying up," examining institutions and structures of power like colonialism and race (Bannerji 1995), the welfare system (Weigt 2006), child protective services and social work (Brown 2006), and women's invisible care work (DeVault 1994). The corpus of work utilizing IE has sought to excavate various slivers that describe mothering work or care work; "whether it's done by a legal 'mother' or by another, or shared between two (or among more) adults, mothering work sustains household life. Social policy relies in various ways on the performance of such work, but typically accounts for it only in a language of 'values,' rather than recognizing it as work done in definite material conditions" (DeVault 2006, 297). In common, these scholars tackle systems of power from the vantage points and perspectives of women who have an intimate knowledge of these institutions. IE, after all, developed out of Dorothy Smith's theorizing on feminist sociology and method wherein women's experience took primacy in interpreting the mainstream tropes about women's work and lives. But instead of simply making women's stories available for people to interpret, it is the work of IE researchers to tease out how women, among other marginalized communities, understand, navigate, and negotiate processes of social organization, "exploring and describing the various social and institutional forces that shape, limit and otherwise organize people's actual and everyday/night worlds" (Mykhalovskiy and McCoy 2002, 19).

4. See also Robert C. Smith's work on "grounded group interviews" where "you can get informants with different perspectives to challenge each other, frame their understandings differently, or otherwise capture some of the dynamic quality of the social life observed" (R. C. Smith 2006, 357).

References

Abrego, Leisy. 2014. *Sacrificing Families: Navigating Laws, Labor, and Love across Borders*. Stanford University Press.

Agoncillo, Teodoro A., and Milagros Guerrero. 1974. *History of the Filipino People*. R. P. Garcia.

Aguila, Almond Pilar. 2011. "Living Long-Distance Relationships through Computer-Mediated Communication." *Social Science Diliman* 5 (1–2): 83–106.

Aguilar, Delia D. 2000. "Questionable Claims: Colonialism Redux, Feminist Style." *Race & Class* 41 (3): 1–12.

Alicea, Marixsa. 1997. "'A Chambered Nautilus': The Contradictory Nature of Puerto Rican Women's Role in the Social Construction of a Transnational Community." *Gender and Society* 11 (5): 597–626.

Alipio, Cheryll. 2015. "Filipino Children and the Affective Economy of Saving and Being Saved: Remittances and Debts in Transnational Migrant Families." In *Transnational Labour Migration, Remittances and the Changing Family in Asia*, edited by Lan Anh Hoang and Brenda S. A. Yeoh, 227–54. Palgrave Macmillan.

Alipio, Cheryll, Melody C. W. Lu, and Brenda S. A. Yeoh. 2015. "Asian Children and Transnational Migration." *Children's Geographies* 13 (3): 255–62.

Anderson, Benedict R. O'G. 1991. *Imagined Communities: Reflections on the Origin and Spread of Nationalism*. Verso.

Anderson, Bridget. 2000. *Doing the Dirty Work?: The Global Politics of Domestic Labour*. Palgrave Macmillan.

Ansell, Nicola. 2009. "Childhood and the Politics of Scale: Descaling Children's Geographies?" *Progress in Human Geography* 33 (2): 190–209.

Anzaldúa, Gloria. 1999. *Borderlands: The New Mestiza = La Frontera*. 2nd ed. Aunt Lute.

Appadurai, Arjun. 1990. "Difference and Disjuncture in the Global Cultural Economy." *Theory, Culture and Society* 7: 295–310.

Appadurai, Arjun. 2006. "The Right to Research." *Globalisation, Societies and Education* 4 (2): 167–77.

Aranda, Elizabeth M. 2003. "Global Care Work and Gendered Constraints: The Case of Puerto Rican Transmigrants." *Gender & Society* 17 (4): 609–26.

Asian American Federation. 2011. "New 2010 Census Data Show Increasing Diversity in New York City's Asian Community." Retrieved October 1, 2011. http://www.aafederation.org/press/pressrelease.asp?prid=126&y=2011.

Asis, Maruja M. B. 2006. "Living With Migration: Experiences of Left-behind Children in the Philippines." *Asian Population Studies* 2 (1): 45.

Asis, Maruja M. B., Shirlena Huang, and Brenda S. A. Yeoh. 2004. "When the Light of the Home Is Abroad: Unskilled Female Migration and the Filipino Family." *Singapore Journal of Tropical Geography* 25 (2): 198–215.

Bailey, Marlon. 2014. "Engendering Space: Ballroom Culture and the Spatial Practice of Possibility in Detroit." *Gender, Place & Culture* 21 (4): 489–507.

Baldassar, Loretta. 2007. "Transnational Families and the Provision of Moral and Emotional Support: The Relationship Between Truth and Distance." *Identities* 14 (4): 385–409.

Baldassar, Loretta. 2015. "Guilty Feelings and the Guilt Trip: Emotions and Motivation in Migration and Transnational Caregiving." *Emotion, Space and Society* 16: 81–89.

Baldassar, Loretta, Raelene Wilding, and Cora Baldock. 2007. "Long-Distance Care-Giving, Transnational Families and the Provision of Aged Care." In *Family Caregiving for Older Disabled People: Relational and Institutional Issues*, edited by I. Paoletti, 201–28. Nova Science.

Baldassar, Loretta, and Laura Merla, eds. 2013. *Transnational Families, Migration, and Care Work: Understanding Mobility and Absence in Family Life*. Routledge Research in Transnationalism, vol. 29. Routledge.

Baldoz, Rick. 2011. *The Third Asiatic Invasion: Migration and Empire in Filipino America, 1898–1946*. NYU Press.

Ball, Rochelle, and Nicola Piper. 2002. "Globalisation and Regulation of Citizenship-Filipino Migrant Workers in Japan." *Political Geography* 21 (8): 1013–34.

Bannerji, Himani. 1995. "Beyond the Ruling Category to What Actually Happens: Notes on James Mill's Historiography in The History of British India." In *Knowledge, Experience, and Ruling Relations: Studies in the Social Organization of Knowledge*, edited by M. L. Campbell and A. Manicom. University of Toronto Press.

Bashi, Vilna. 2007. *Survival of the Knitted: Immigrant Social Networks in a Stratified World*. Stanford University Press.

Baumeister, Roy F., Arlene M. Stillwell, and Todd F. Heatherton. 1994. "Guilt: An Interpersonal Approach." *Psychological Bulletin* 115 (2): 243.

Bernhard, Judith K., Patricia Landolt, and Luin Goldring. 2009. "Transnationalizing Families: Canadian Immigration Policy and the Spatial Fragmentation of Care-Giving among Latin American Newcomers." *International Migration* 47 (2): 3–31.

Boal, Augusto. 2000. *Theater of the Oppressed*. Pluto.

Boccagni, Paolo, and Loretta Baldassar. 2015. "Emotions on the Move: Mapping the Emergent Field of Emotion and Migration." *Emotion, Space and Society* 16: 73–80.

Boehm, Deborah A. 2012. *Intimate Migrations: Gender, Family, and Illegality among Transnational Mexicans.* NYU Press.

Bonizzoni, Paola, and Paolo Boccagni. 2014. "Care (and) Circulation Revisited: A Conceptual Map of Diversity in Transnational Parenting." In *Transnational Families, Migration and the Circulation of Care: Understanding Mobility and Absence in Family Life,* edited by Loretta Baldassar and Laura Merla, 78–93. Routledge Research in Transnationalism, vol. 29. Routledge.

Bonus, Rick. 2000. *Locating Filipino Americans: Ethnicity and the Cultural Politics of Space.* Temple University Press.

Brown, Debra J. 2006. "Working the System: Re-Thinking the Institutionally Organized Role of Mothers and the Reduction of 'Risk' in Child Protection Work." *Social Problems* 53 (3): 352–70.

Brown, Rachel H. 2016. "Re-examining the Transnational Nanny: Migrant Carework Beyond the Chain." *International Feminist Journal of Politics* 18 (2): 210–29.

Bryceson, Deborah Fahy, and Ulla Vuorela. 2002. *The Transnational Family: New European Frontiers and Global Networks.* Berg.

Buenavista, Tracy Lachica. 2010. "Issues Affecting US Filipino Student Access to Postsecondary Education: A Critical Race Theory Perspective." *Journal of Education for Students Placed at Risk* 15 (1–2): 114–26.

Burawoy, Michael. 2003. "Revisits: An Outline of a Theory of Reflexive Ethnography." *American Sociological Review* 68 (5): 645–79.

Burns, Lucy Mae San Pablo. 2012. *Puro Arte: Filipinos on the Stages of Empire.* NYU Press.

Butler, Judith. 2002. "Is Kinship Always Already Heterosexual?" *Differences: A Journal of Feminist Cultural Studies* 13 (1): 14–44.

Cabusao, Jeffrey Arellano. 2011. "Decolonizing Knowledges: Asian American Studies, Carlos Bulosan, and Insurgent Filipino Diasporic Imagination." *Kritika Kultura* 16: 122–44.

Carling, Jørgen, Cecilia Menjívar, and Leah Schmalzbauer. 2012. "Central Themes in the Study of Transnational Parenthood." *Journal of Ethnic and Migration Studies* 38 (2): 191–217.

Caronan, Faye. 2015. *Legitimizing Empire: Filipino American and US Puerto Rican Cultural Critique.* University of Illinois Press.

Castles, Stephen, and Mark J. Miller. 2003. *The Age of Migration: International Population Movements in the Modern World.* 3rd ed. Guilford.

Chang, Grace. 2000. *Disposable Domestics: Immigrant Women Workers in the Global Economy.* South End.

Charmaz, Kathy. 2014. *Constructing Grounded Theory.* Sage.

Chipongian, Lee C. 2016. "OFW Remittances Reach $25.8 B in 2015." Manilla Bulletin, February 16, 2017. http://2016.mb.com.ph/2016/02/19/ofw-remittances-reach-25-86-in-2015.

Chua, Peter. 2009. *Acting Kalagayan: The Social and Economic Profile of US Filipinos*. National Bulosan Center.

Chung, Angie Y. 2016. *Saving Face: The Emotional Costs of the Asian Immigrant Family Myth*. Rutgers University Press.

Coe, Cati. 2008. "The Structuring of Feeling in Ghanaian Transnational Families." *City & Society* 20 (2): 222–50.

Cohen, Cathy J. 1997. "Punks, Bulldaggers, and Welfare Queens: The Radical Potential of Queer Politics?" *GLQ: A Journal of Lesbian and Gay Studies* 3 (3): 437–65.

Coll, Kathleen. 2010. *Remaking Citizenship: Latina Immigrants and the New American Politics*. Stanford University Press.

Collier, Jane, Michelle Z. Rosaldo, and Sylvia Yanagisako. 1982. "Is There a Family? New Anthropological Views." In *Rethinking the Family: Some Feminist Questions*, edited by Barrie Thorne and Marilyn Yalom, 25–39. Longman.

Collins, Patricia Hill. 1986. "Learning from the Outsider Within: The Sociological Significance of Black Feminist Thought." *Social Problems* 33 (6): S14–S32.

Collins, Patricia Hill. 1995. "The Meaning of Motherhood in Black Culture." In *Women: Images and Realities*, edited by Amy Kesselman, Lily McNair, and Nancy Schniedewind. Mayfield.

Collins, Patricia Hill. 2002. *Black Feminist Thought: Knowledge, Consciousness, and the Politics of Empowerment*. Routledge.

Connell, R. W. 1998. "Masculinities and Globalization." *Men and Masculinities* 1 (1): 3–23.

Connell, R. W. 2005. *Masculinities*. Polity.

Constable, Nicole. 1997. *Maid to Order in Hong Kong: Stories of Filipina Workers*. Cornell University Press.

Constable, Nicole. 2014. *Born Out of Place: Migrant Mothers and the Politics of International Labor*. University of California Press.

Cooke, Bill, and Uma Kothari. 2001. *Participation: The New Tyranny?* Zed.

Curran, Sara R., Steven Shafer, Katharine M. Donato, and Filiz Garip. 2006. "Mapping Gender and Migration in Sociological Scholarship: Is It Segregation or Integration?" *International Migration Review* 40 (1): 199–223.

Deaux, Kay. 2009. *To Be an Immigrant*. Russell Sage Foundation.

DeVault, Marjorie L. 1994. *Feeding the Family: The Social Organization of Caring as Gendered Work*. University of Chicago Press.

DeVault, Marjorie L. 1999. "Comfort and Struggle: Emotion Work in Family Life." *Annals of the American Academy of Political and Social Science* 561 (January): 52–63.

DeVault, Marjorie L. 2006. "Introduction: What Is Institutional Ethnography?" *Social Problems* 53: 294–98.

Diaz, Robert. 2016. "Queer Unsettlements: Diasporic Filipinos in Canada's World Pride." *Journal of Asian American Studies* 19 (3): 327–50.

Dill, Bonnie Thornton. 1988. "Our Mother's Grief: Racial Ethnic Women and the Maintenance of Families." *Journal of Family History* 13 (1): 415–31.

Dobson, Madeleine E. 2009. "Unpacking Children in Migration Research." *Children's Geographies* 7 (3): 355–60.

Douglass, Mike. 2006. "Global Householding in the Asia Pacific." *International Development Planning Review* 28 (4): 421–26.

Dreby, Joanna. 2009. "Gender and Transnational Gossip." *Qualitative Sociology* 32 (1): 33–52.

Dreby, Joanna. 2010. *Divided by Borders: Mexican Migrants and Their Children*. University of California Press.

Dressel, Paula L., and Ann Clark. 1990. "A Critical Look at Family Care." *Journal of Marriage and Family* 52 (3): 769–82.

Duggan, Lisa. 2002. "The New Homonormativity: The Sexual Politics of Neoliberalism." In *Materializing Democracy: Toward a Revitalized Cultural Politics*, edited by Russ Castranovo and Dana Nelson, 175–94. Duke University Press.

Ebaugh, Helen Rose, and Mary Curry. 2000. "Fictive Kin as Social Capital in New Immigrant Communities." *Sociological Perspectives* 43 (2): 189–209.

Ehrenreich, Barbara, and Arlie Russell Hochschild. 2004. *Global Woman: Nannies, Maids, and Sex Workers in the New Economy*. Holt.

Elrick, Tim, and Emilia Lewandowska. 2008. "Matching and Making Labour Demand and Supply: Agents in Polish Migrant Networks of Domestic Elderly Care in Germany and Italy." *Journal of Ethnic and Migration Studies* 34 (5): 717–34.

Emerson, Robert M., Rachel I. Fretz, and Linda L. Shaw. 1995. *Writing Ethnographic Fieldnotes*. University of Chicago Press.

Eng, David L. 2010. *The Feeling of Kinship: Queer Liberalism and the Racialization of Intimacy*. Duke University Press.

Espiritu, Yen Le. 2003. *Home Bound: Filipino American Lives across Cultures, Communities, and Countries*. University of California Press.

Fajardo, Kale B. 2011. *Filipino Crosscurrents: Oceanographies of Seafaring, Masculinities, and Globalization*. University of Minnesota Press.

Ferguson, Roderick A. 2004. *Aberrations in Black: Toward a Queer of Color Critique*. University of Minnesota Press.

Fields, Jessica, Isela González, Kathleen Hentz, Margaret Rhee, and Catherine White. 2008. "Learning from and with Incarcerated Women: Emerging Lessons from a Participatory Action Study of Sexuality Education." *Sexuality Research and Social Policy* 5: 71–84.

Finch, Janet, and Dulcie Groves. 1983. *A Labour of Love: Women, Work and Caring*. Routledge.

Fine, Michelle. 1994. "Working the Hyphens: Reinventing Self and Other in Qualitative Research." In *Handbook of Qualitative Research*, edited by Norman Denzin and Yvonna Lincoln, 70–82. Sage.

Fine, Michelle, and María Elena Torre. 2006. "Intimate Details." *Action Research* 4 (3): 253–69.

Fisher, Berenice, and Joan Tronto. 1990. "Toward a Feminist Theory of Caring." In *Circles of Care: Work and Identity in Women's Lives*, edited by Emily Abel and Margaret Nelson, 35–62. SUNY Press.

Fitzgerald, David. 2006. "Towards a Theoretical Ethnography of Migration." *Qualitative Sociology* 29 (1): 1–24.

Foner, Nancy. 2005. *In a New Land: A Comparative View of Immigration*. NYU Press.

Foner, Nancy, and Joanna Dreby. 2011. "Relations Between the Generations in Immigrant Families." *Annual Review of Sociology* 37: 545–64.

Francisco, Valerie. 2010. "From Where I Sit." *International Review of Qualitative Research* 3 (3): 287–310.

Francisco, Valerie. 2013. "'Ang Ating Iisang Kuwento,' Our Collective Story: Migrant Filipino Workers and Participatory Action Research." *Action Research* 12 (1): 78–93.

Francisco, Valerie. 2014. "Using Participatory Action Research with Migrant Filipino Workers." In *Border Regime: Discourse, Practices, Institutions in Europe (or Grenzregime, Diskurse, Praktiken, Institutionen in Europa)*, edited by Lisa-Marie Heimeschoff, Sabine Hess, Stefanie Kron, Helen Schwenken, and Miriam Trzeciak, 269–81. Assoziation A.

Francisco, Valerie. 2015a. "The Transnational Family as a Resource for Political Mobilization." In *Migrant Domestic Workers and Family Life*, edited by Maria Kontos and Glenda Tibe Bonifacio, 231–53. Palgrave Macmillan.

Francisco, Valerie. 2015b. "Spatiality as Strategy: Transnational Migrant Worker Solidarity and the Filipino Labor Diaspora." In *Last Call for Solidarity: Opportunities and Limits of Transnational Solidarity of Trade Unions and Social Movements (or Last Call for Solidarity: Chancen und Grenzen transnationaler Solidarität von Gewerkschaften und sozialen Bewegungen)*, edited by Shuwen Bian, Sarah Bormann, Martina Hartung, and Jenny Junghelsüng, 157–69. VSA Von A Bis Z Press.

Francisco, Valerie. 2018. "Save Mary Jane Veloso: Solidarity and Global Migrant Activism in the Filipino Labor Diaspora." *Perspectives on Global Development and Technology* 17: 202–218

Francisco, Valerie, Geleen Abenoja, and Angelica Lim. 2016. "Filipina Lives: Transnationalism, Migrant Labor, and Experiences of Criminalization in the United States." In *The Immigrant Other: Lived Experiences in a Transnational World*, edited by Rich Furman, Greg Lamphear, and Douglas Epps. Columbia University Press.

Francisco, Valerie, and Robyn Rodriguez. 2016. "Coming to America: The Business of Trafficked Workers." In *Legislating a New America: The Immigration and Nationality Act Amendments of 1965 and Its Contribution to American Law and Society*, edited by Gabriel Chin and Rose Cuison-Villazor, 274–91. Cambridge University Press.

Frantz, Elizabeth. 2008. "Of Maids and Madams: Sri Lankan Domestic Workers and Their Employers in Jordan." *Critical Asian Studies* 40 (4): 609–38.

Freire, Paulo. 2000. *Pedagogy of the Oppressed*. Continuum International.

Fuchs, Christian. 2009a. "Information and Communication Technologies and Society: A Contribution to the Critique of the Political Economy of the Internet." *European Journal of Communication* 24 (1): 69–87.

Fuchs, Christian. 2009b. "Some Theoretical Foundations of Critical Media Studies: Karl Marx's Philosophy of Communication." *International Journal of Communication* 3 (34): 369–402.

Gerber, David A. 2001. "Forming a Transnational Narrative: New Perspectives on European Migrations to the United States." *The History Teacher* 35 (1): 61–77.

Giddings, Paula J. 2009. *When and Where I Enter*. HarperCollins.

Gimenez, Martha. 1990. "The Dialectics of Waged and Unwaged Work: Waged Work, Domestic Labor, and Household Survival in the United States." In *Work Without Wages: Comparative Studies of Domestic Labor and Self-Employment*, edited by Jane Lou Collins and Martha Gimenez, 25–45. SUNY Press.

Glenn, Evelyn Nakano. 1985. "Racial Ethnic Women's Labor: The Intersection of Race, Gender and Class Oppression." *Review of Radical Political Economics* 17 (3): 86–108.

Glenn, Evelyn Nakano. 1992. "From Servitude to Service Work: Historical Continuities in the Racial Division of Paid Reproductive Labor." *Signs* 18 (1): 1–43.

Goffman, Erving. 1978. *The Presentation of Self in Everyday Life*. Harmondsworth.

Gopinath, Gayatri. 2005. *Impossible Desires: Queer Diasporas and South Asian Public Cultures*. Duke University Press.

Gordon, Linda. 1992. "Why Nineteenth-Century Feminists Did Not Support 'Birth Control' and Twentieth-Century Feminists Do: Feminism, Reproduction and the Family." In *Rethinking the Family: Some Feminist Questions*, edited by Barrie Thome and Marilyn Yalom, 40–54. Northeastern University Press.

Graham, Elspeth, Lucy P. Jordan, Brenda S. A. Yeoh, Theodora Lam, and Maruja Asis. 2012. "Transnational Families and the Family Nexus: Perspectives of Indonesian and Filipino Children Left behind by Migrant Parent(s)." *Environment & Planning A* 44 (4): 793–815.

Graham, Hilary. 1983. "Caring: A Labour of Love." In *A Labour of Love: Women, Work and Caring*, edited by Janet Finch and Dulcie Groves, 13–30. Routledge and Kegan Paul.

Grasmuck, Sherri, and Patricia R. Pessar. 1991. *Between Two Islands: Dominican International Migration*. University of California Press.

Greenhouse, Steven. 2007. "Legislation Pushed to Require Minimum Wage for Domestic Workers." *The New York Times*, June 1, sec. New York Region. Retrieved August 23, 2017. https://nyti.ms/2vrbakW.

Guerrero, Sylvia. "Gender and Migration: Focus on Filipino Women in International Labor Migration." *Review of Women's Studies* 10 (1–2): 275–98.

Guevarra, Anna Romina. 2006a. "The Balikbayan Researcher." *Journal of Contemporary Ethnography* 35 (5): 526–51.

Guevarra, Anna Romina. 2006b. "Managing 'Vulnerabilities' and 'Empowering' Migrant Filipina Workers: The Philippines' Overseas Employment Program." *Social Identities: Journal for the Study of Race, Nation and Culture* 12 (5): 523–41.

Guevarra, Anna Romina. 2009. *Marketing Dreams, Manufacturing Heroes: The Transnational Labor Brokering of Filipino Workers*. Rutgers University Press.

Hagan, Jacqueline Maria. 1998. "Social Networks, Gender, and Immigrant Incorporation: Resources and Constraints." *American Sociological Review* 63 (1): 55–67.

Hall, Stuart. 1992. "Who Needs 'Identity'?" In *The Question of Cultural Identity*, edited by Stuart Hall and Paul du Gay, 1–17. Sage.

Hall, Stuart. 2003. "Cultural Identity and Diaspora." In *Theorizing Diaspora: A Reader*, edited by Jana Evans Braziel and Anita Mannur, 233–46. Wiley-Blackwell.

Haraway, Donna. 1988. "Situated Knowledges: The Science Question in Feminism and the Privilege of Partial Perspective." *Feminist Studies* 14 (3): 575–99.

Harding, Sandra. 2007. "Feminist Standpoints." In *Handbook of Feminist Research: Theory and Praxis*, edited by Sharlene Nagy Hesse-Biber, 45–70. Sage.

Harvey, David. 2007. *A Brief History of Neoliberalism*. Oxford University Press.

Hoang, Lan Anh, Theodora Lam, Brenda S. A. Yeoh, and Elspeth Graham. 2015. "Transnational Migration, Changing Care Arrangements and Left-behind Children's Responses in South-East Asia." *Children's Geographies* 13 (3): 263–77.

Hoang, Lan Anh, and Brenda S. A. Yeoh. 2011. "Breadwinning Wives and 'Left-Behind' Husbands: Men and Masculinities in the Vietnamese Transnational Family." *Gender & Society* 25 (6): 717–39.

Hoang, Lan Anh, and Brenda S. A. Yeoh. 2012. "Sustaining Families Across Transnational Spaces: Vietnamese Migrant Parents and Their Children Left Behind." *Asian Studies Review* 36: 307–25.

Hoang, Lan Anh, and Brenda S. A. Yeoh. 2015a. "Children's Agency and Its Contradictions in the Context of Transnational Labour Migration from Vietnam." *Global Networks* 15 (2): 180–97.

Hoang, Lan Anh, and Brenda S. A. Yeoh, eds. 2015b. *Transnational Labour Migration, Remittances and the Changing Family in Asia*. Springer.

Hochschild, Arlie Russell. 2003. *The Managed Heart: Commercialization of Human Feeling, With a New Afterword*. University of California Press.

Hochschild, Arlie Russell, and Barbara Ehrenreich. 2002. *Global Woman: Nannies, Maids and Sex Workers in the New Economy*. Metropolitan.

Hondagneu-Sotelo, Pierrette, and Ernestine Avila. 1997. "'I'm Here but I'm There': The Meanings of Latina Transnational Motherhood." *Gender & Society* 11 (5): 548–71.

Horst, Heather A. 2006. "The Blessings and Burdens of Communication: Cell Phones in Jamaican Transnational Social Fields." *Global Networks* 6 (2): 143–59.

Horst, Heather A., and Daniel Miller. 2006. *The Cell Phone: An Anthropology of Communication*. Berg.

Huijsmans, Roy. 2011. "Child Migration and Questions of Agency." *Development and Change* 42 (5): 1307–21.

IBON Foundation. 2004. *IBON Manual on Facilitating Participatory Research*. IBON Foundation, Inc.

Isaac, Allan Punzalan. 2006. *American Tropics: Articulating Filipino America*. University of Minnesota Press.

Isaksen, Lise Widding, Sambasivan Uma Devi, and Arlie Russell Hochschild. 2008. "Global Care Crisis." *American Behavioral Scientist* 52 (3): 405–25.

Jamieson, Lynn. 1998. *Intimacy: Personal Relationships in Modern Societies*. Polity.

Josselson, Ruthellen. 2004. "The Hermeneutics of Faith and the Hermeneutics of Suspicion." *Narrative Inquiry* 14 (1): 1–28.

Kares, Faith R. 2014. "Practicing 'Enlightened Capitalism': 'Fil-Am' Heroes, NGO Activism, and the Reconstitution of Class Difference in the Philippines." *Philippine Studies: Historical and Ethnographic Viewpoints* 62 (2): 175–204.

Kasinitz, Philip, John H. Mollenkopf, and Mary C. Waters. 2004. *Becoming New Yorkers: Ethnographies of the New Second Generation*. Russell Sage Foundation.

Katz, Cindi. 2004. *Growing Up Global: Economic Restructuring and Children's Everyday Lives*. University of Minnesota Press.

Katz, Cindi. 2008. "Cultural Geographies Lecture Childhood as Spectacle: Relays of Anxiety and the Reconfiguration of the Child." *Cultural Geographies* 15 (1): 5–17.

Kim, Hosu. 2016. *Birth Mothers and Transnational Adoption Practice in South Korea: Virtual Mothering*. Palgrave Macmillan.

Kleinman, Sherryl, and Martha A. Copp. 1993. *Emotions and Fieldwork*. Sage.

Kvale, Steinar. 1996. *InterViews: An Introduction to Qualitative Research Interviewing*. Sage.

Lan, Pei-Chia. 2006. *Global Cinderellas: Migrant Domestics and Newly Rich Employers in Taiwan*. Duke University Press.

Laslett, Barbara, and Johanna Brenner. 1989. "Gender and Social Reproduction: Historical Perspectives." *Annual Review of Sociology* 15 (1): 381–404.

Lee, Mo Yee, and LeeAnn Mjelde-Mossey. 2004. "Cultural Dissonance Among Generations: A Solution-Focused Approach with East Asian Elders and Their Families." *Journal of Marital and Family Therapy* 30 (4): 497–513.

Levitt, Peggy. 1998. "Social Remittances: Migration Driven Local-Level Forms of Cultural Diffusion." *International Migration Review* 32 (4): 926–48.

Levitt, Peggy. 2001. *The Transnational Villagers*. University of California Press.

Levitt, Peggy, and B. Nadya Jaworsky. 2007. "Transnational Migration Studies: Past Developments and Future Trends." *Annual Review of Sociology* 33: 129–56.

Levitt, Peggy, and Nina Glick Schiller. 2004. "Conceptualizing Simultaneity: A Transnational Social Field Perspective on Society." *International Migration Review* 38 (3): 1002–39.

Licoppe, Christian, and Zbigniew Smoreda. 2005. "Are Social Networks Technologically Embedded?: How Networks Are Changing Today with Changes in Communication Technology." *Social Networks* 27 (4): 317–35.

Luibhéid, Eithne. 2008. "Queer/Migration: An Unruly Body of Scholarship." *GLQ: A Journal of Lesbian and Gay Studies* 14 (2–3): 169–90.

Luibhéid, Eithne, and Lionel Cantu. 2005. *Queer Migrations: Sexuality, U.S. Citizenship, and Border Crossings*. University of Minnesota Press.

Lutz, Catherine A., and Lila Ed Abu-Lughod. 1990. *Language and the Politics of Emotion: Studies in Emotion and Social Interaction*. Cambridge University Press.

Luxton, Meg. 2006. "Feminist Political Economy in Canada and the Politics of Social Reproduction." In *Social Reproduction: Feminist Political Economy Challenges Neo-Liberalism*, 11–45. McGill-Queen's University Press.

Mabalon, Dawn Bohulano. 2013. *Little Manila Is in the Heart: The Making of the Filipina/o American Community in Stockton, California*. Duke University Press.

Madianou, Maria Mirca. 2012. "Migration and the Accentuated Ambivalence of Motherhood: The Role of ICTs in Filipino Transnational Families." *Global Networks* 12 (3): 277–95.

Madianou, Maria Mirca, and Daniel Miller. 2011. "Mobile Phone Parenting: Reconfiguring Relationships between Filipina Migrant Mothers and Their Left-behind Children." *New Media & Society* 13 (3): 457–70.

Madriz, Esther I. 1998. "Using Focus Groups With Lower Socioeconomic Status Latina Women." *Qualitative Inquiry* 4 (1): 114–28.

Mai, Nicola, and Russell King. 2009. "Love, Sexuality and Migration: Mapping the Issue(s)." *Mobilities* 4 (3): 295–307.

Manalansan, Martin F. 2003. *Global Divas: Filipino Gay Men in the Diaspora*. Duke University Press.

Manalansan, Martin F. 2005. "Migrancy, Modernity, Mobility: Quotidian Struggles and Queer Diasporic Intimacy." In *Queer Migrations: Sexuality, U.S. Citizenship, and Border Crossings*, edited by Eithne Luibhéid and Lionel Cantu Jr., 146–60. University of Minnesota Press.

Manalansan, Martin F. 2006. "Queer Intersections: Sexuality and Gender in Migration Studies." *International Migration Review* 40 (1): 224–49.

Manzerolle, Vincent R., and Atle Mikkola Kjøsen. 2012. "The Communication of Capital: Digital Media and the Logic of Acceleration." *tripleC—Cognition, Communication, Co-Operation* 10 (2): 214–29.

Marcus, George E. 1995. "Ethnography in/of the World System: The Emergence of Multi-Sited Ethnography." *Annual Review of Anthropology* 24: 95–117.

Marx, Karl, and Fredrick Engels. 1942. *The Origin of the Family, Private Property and the State*. Alick West.

Massey, Douglas. 1999. "Why Does Immigration Occur? A Theoretical Synthesis." In *Handbook of International Migration: The American Experience*, edited by Philip Kasinitz, Charles Hirschman, and Josh DeWind, 34–52. Russell Sage Foundation.

Massey, Douglas S., Joaquin Arango, Graeme Hugo, Ali Kouaouci, Adela Pellegrino, and J. Edward Taylor. 1993. "Theories of International Migration: A Review and Appraisal." *Population and Development Review* 19 (3): 431–66.

Mather, Celia. 2006. "Out of the Shadows?" *International Union Rights* 13 (1).

Mayall, Berry. 2002. *Towards a Sociology of Childhood: Thinking from Children's Lives*. Open University Press.

Mckay, Deirdre. 2007. "'Sending Dollars Shows Feeling': Emotions and Economies in Filipino Migration." *Mobilities* 2 (2): 175–94.

Milligan, Christine, and Janine Wiles. 2010. "Landscapes of Care." *Progress in Human Geography* 34 (6): 736–54.

Minkler, Meredith, Angela Glover Blackwell, Mildred Thompson, and Heather Tamir. 2003. "Community-Based Participatory Research: Implications for Public Health Funding." *American Journal of Public Health* 93 (8): 1210–13.

Montgomery, Rhonda J. V., Judith G. Gonyea, and Nancy R. Hooyman. 1985. "Caregiving and the Experience of Subjective and Objective Burden." *Family Relations*, 19–26.

Morgensen, Scott Lauria. 2011. *Spaces Between Us: Queer Settler Colonialism and Indigenous Decolonization*. University of Minnesota Press.

Morrow, Virginia. 2008. "Ethical Dilemmas in Research with Children and Young People about Their Social Environments." *Children's Geographies* 6 (1): 49–61.

Moynihan, Daniel P. 1965. *The Negro Family: The Case for National Action*. US Department of Labor.

Mykhalovskiy, Eric, and Liza McCoy. 2002. "Troubling Ruling Discourses of Health: Using Institutional Ethnography in Community-Based Research." *Critical Public Health* 12: 17–37.

New York Times. 2010. "Domestic Workers' Rights," June 6, sec. Opinion. Retrieved August 23, 2017. https://nyti.ms/2w0090N.

Ní Laoire, Catríona, Fina Carpena-Mendez, Naomi Tyrrell, and Allen White. 2010. "Introduction: Childhood and Migration—Mobilities, Homes and Belongings." *Childhood* 17 (2): 155–287.

Ninh, Erin Khuê Khuê. 2011. *Ingratitude: The Debt-Bound Daughter in Asian American Literature*. NYU Press.

Ong, Aihwa. 1999. *Flexible Citizenship: The Cultural Logics of Transnationality*. Duke University Press.

Orellana, Marjorie Faulstich, Barrie Thorne, Anna Chee, and Wan Shun Eva Lam. 2001. "Transnational Childhoods: The Participation of Children in Processes of Family Migration." *Social Problems* 48 (4): 572.

Padios, Jan M. 2018. *A Nation on the Line: Call Centrs as Postcolonial Predicaments in the Philippines*. Duke University Press.

———. 2017. "Mining the Mind: Emotional Extraction, Productivity, and Predictability in the Twenty-First Century." *Cultural Studies*: 1–27.

Park, Lisa Sun-Hee. 2005. *Consuming Citizenship: Children of Asian Immigrant Entrepreneurs*. Stanford University Press.

Park, Lisa Sun-Hee. 2017. "The Trouble With Love in Home Care Work: Affective Labor and the Possibilities of Queer Families." Paper presented at the Annual Association for Asian American Studies Conference, Portland, OR, April 12–15, 2017.

Parreñas, Rhacel Salazar. 2001a. "Mothering from a Distance: Emotions, Gender, and Intergenerational Relations in Filipino Transnational Families." *Feminist Studies* 27 (2): 361–90.

Parreñas, Rhacel Salazar. 2001b. *Servants of Globalization: Women, Migration, and Domestic Work*. Stanford University Press.

Parreñas, Rhacel Salazar. 2001c. "Transgressing the Nation-State: The Partial Citizenship and 'Imagined (Global) Community' of Migrant Filipina Domestic Workers." *Signs* 26 (4): 1129–54.

Parreñas, Rhacel Salazar. 2005a. *Children of Global Migration: Transnational Families and Gendered Woes*. Stanford University Press.

Parreñas, Rhacel Salazar. 2005b. "Long Distance Intimacy: Class, Gender and Intergenerational Relations between Mothers and Children in Filipino Transnational Families." *Global Networks* 5 (4): 317–36.

Parreñas, Rhacel Salazar. 2008. "Transnational Fathering: Gendered Conflicts, Distant Disciplining and Emotional Gaps." *Journal of Ethnic and Migration Studies* 34 (7): 1057–72.

Parsons, Talcott, and Robert F. Bales. 1955. *Family, Socialization and Interaction Process*. The Free Press.

Paul, Anju Mary. 2011. "Stepwise International Migration: A Multistage Migration Pattern for the Aspiring Migrant." *American Journal of Sociology* 116 (6): 1842–86.

Pea, Roy, Clifford Nass, Lyn Meheula, Marcus Rance, Aman Kumar, Holden Bamford, Matthew Nass, et al. 2012. "Media Use, Face-to-Face Communication, Media Multitasking, and Social Well-Being among 8- to 12-Year-Old Girls." *Developmental Psychology* 48 (2): 327–36.

Pe-Pua, Rogelia, Clyde Mitchell, Stephen Castles, and Robyn Iredale. 1998. "Astronaut Families and Parachute Children: Hong Kong Immigrants in Australia." In *The Last Half-Century of Chinese Overseas*, edited by Elizabeth Sinn, 279–97. Hong Kong University Press.

Pessar, Patricia. 1999. "Engendering Migration Studies." *American Behavioral Scientist* 42 (4): 577–600.

Pido, Antonio J. A. 1986. *The Pilipinos in America: Macro/Micro Dimensions of Immigration and Integration*. Center for Migration Studies.

Pingol, Alicia. 1999. "Absentee Wives and Househusbands: Power, Identity and Family Dynamics." *Review of Women's Studies* 9 (1–2): 16–45.

Pingol, Alicia. 2001. *Remaking Masculinities: Identity, Power, and Gender Dynamics in Families with Migrant Wives and Househusbands*. UP Center for Women's Studies.

Portes, Alejandro. 1995. "The Economic Sociology of Immigration: A Conceptual Overview." In *The Economic Sociology of Immigration: Essays on Networks, Ethnicity, and Entrepreneurship*, edited by Alejandro Portes, 1–41. Russell Sage Foundation.

Portes, Alejandro, and Rubén G. Rumbaut. 2006. *Immigrant America: A Portrait*. 3rd rev. ed. University of California Press.

Powell, Kimberly. 2010. "Making Sense of Place: Mapping as a Multisensory Research Method." *Qualitative Inquiry* 16 (7): 539–55.

Pratt, Geraldine. 2004. *Working Feminism*. Temple University Press.

Raffaetà, Roberta. 2015. "Hope Emplaced. What Happens to Hope after Arrival: The Case of Ecuadorian Families Living in Italy." *Emotion, Space and Society* 16: 116–22.

Rankin, Janet, and Marie Campbell. 2009. "Institutional Ethnography (IE), Nursing Work and Hospital Reform: IE's Cautionary Analysis." *Forum Qualitative Sozialforschung / Forum: Qualitative Social Research* 10 (2). Retrieved November 10, 2011. http://www.qualitative-research.net/index.php/fqs/article/view/1258/2720.

Raymundo, Sarah. 2011. "In the Womb of the Global Economy: *Anak* and the Construction of Transnational Imaginaries." *Positions: East Asia Cultures Critique* 19 (2): 551–79.

Reynolds, Tracey, and Elisabetta Zontini. 2006. *A Comparative Study of Care and Provision across Caribbean and Italian Transnational Families*. Families & Social Capital ESRC Research Group.

Riak-Akuei, Stephanie. 2005. "Remittances as Unforeseen Burdens: The Livelihoods and Social Obligations of Sudanese Refugees." *Global Migration Perspectives* 18. Global Commission on International Migration. Retrieved August 23, 2017. http://www.refworld.org/docid/42ce4d354.html.

Robinson, John P., and Melissa A. Milkie. 1998. "Back to the Basics: Trends in and Role Determinants of Women's Attitudes Toward Housework." *Journal of Marriage & Family* 60 (1): 205–18.

Rodriguez, Edgard R. 1996. "International Migrants' Remittances in the Philippines." *Canadian Journal of Economics* 29 (2): 427–32.

Rodriguez, Robyn M. 2002. "Migrant Heroes: Nationalism, Citizenship and the Politics of Filipino Migrant Labor." *Citizenship Studies* 6 (3): 341–56.

Rodriguez, Robyn M. 2010. *Migrants for Export: How the Philippine State Brokers Labor to the World*. University of Minnesota Press.

Ruddick, Sara. 1995. *Maternal Thinking: Toward a Politics of Peace; with a New Preface*. Beacon.

San Juan, E., Jr. 2000. *After Postcolonialism: Remapping Philippines-United States Confrontations*. Rowman & Littlefield.

San Pascual, Maria Rosel. 2014. "Living Through the Parameters of Technology: Filipino Mothers in Diaspora and Their Mediated Parenting Experiences." *Plaridel: A Philippine Journal of Communication, Media and Society* 11 (1): 1–28.

Sassen, Saskia. 1999. *Globalization and Its Discontents: Essays on the New Mobility of People and Money*. The New Press.

Schiller, Nina Glick, Linda Basch, and Cristina Blanc-Szanton. 1992. "Transnationalism: A New Analytic Framework for Understanding Migration." *Annals of the New York Academy of Sciences* 645 (1): 1–24.

Schmalzbauer, Leah. 2004. "Searching for Wages and Mothering from Afar: The Case of Honduran Transnational Families." *Journal of Marriage and Family* 66 (5): 1317–31.

Seccombe, Wally. 1974. *The Housewife and Her Labour under Capitalism*. Red.

Seery, Brenda L. 1996. "Four Types of Mothering Emotion Work: Distress Management, Ego Work, Relationship Management, and Pleasure/Enjoyment Work." PhD diss., Penn State University.

Semple, Kirk. 2011. "Few Domestic Workers Know About Law Protecting Them." *The New York Times*, April 14, sec. New York Region. Retrieved August 23, 2017. https://nyti.ms/2wosbWT.

Smith, Dorothy E. 1987. *The Everyday World as Problematic: A Feminist Sociology*. University of Toronto Press.

Smith, Dorothy E. 1989. "Feminist Reflections on Political Economy." *Studies in Political Economy* 30 (1): 37–59.

Smith, Dorothy E. 2005. *Institutional Ethnography: A Sociology for People*. Rowman Altamira.

Smith, Dorothy E. 2006. *Institutional Ethnography as Practice*. Rowman & Littlefield.

Smith, Linda Tuhiwai. 1999. *Decolonizing Methodologies: Research and Indigenous Peoples*. Zed.

Smith, Robert C. 2006. *Mexican New York: Transnational Lives of New Immigrants*. University of California Press.

Stack, Carol B. 1997. *All Our Kin: Strategies for Survival in a Black Community*. Basic.

Stack, Carol B., and Linda M. Burton. 1993. "Kinscripts." *Journal of Comparative Family Studies* 24 (2): 157–70.

Stasiulis, Daiva K., and Abigail Bess Bakan. 2005. *Negotiating Citizenship: Migrant Women in Canada and the Global System*. University of Toronto Press.

Stephen, Lynn. 2007. *Transborder Lives: Indigenous Oaxacans in Mexico, California, and Oregon*. 2nd ed. Duke University Press.

Svasek, Maruska. 2008. "Who Cares? Families and Feelings in Movement." *Journal of Intercultural Studies* 29 (3): 213–30.

Tadiar, Neferti Xina Maca. 2004. *Fantasy Production: Sexual Economies and Other Philippine Consequences for the New World Order*. Hong Kong University Press.

Thorne, Barrie, and Marilyn Yalom, eds. 1992. *Rethinking the Family: Some Feminist Questions*. Rev. ed. Northeastern University Press.

Tolentino, Rolando. 2010. *Gitnang Uring Fantasya at Materyal na Kahirapan sa Neoliberalismo: Politikal na Kritisismo ng Kulturang Popular*. University of Santo Tomas Publishing House.

Torre, Maria, and Michelle Fine. 2006. "Participatory Action Research (PAR) by Youth." In *Youth Activism: An International Encyclopedia*, 456–62. Greenwood.

Torre, Maria, Michelle Fine, Brett Stoudt, and Madeline Fox. 2012. "Critical Participatory Action Research as Public Science." In *APA Handbook of Research Methods in Psychology*, edited by Harris Cooper. American Psychological Association.

Tuck, Eve. 2008. "Re-Visioning Action: Participatory Action Research and Indigenous Theories of Change." *The Urban Review* 41 (September): 47–65.

Tungohan, Ethel. 2012. "Reconceptualizing Motherhood, Reconceptualizing Resistance: Migrant Domestic Workers, Transnational Hyper-Materialism and Activism." *International Feminist Journal of Politics* 15(1): 39–57.

———. 2017. "The Transformative and Radical Feminism of Grass-roots Migrant Women's Movement(s) in Canada." *Canadian Journal of Political Science* 50 (2): 479–94.

Udvarhelyi, Éva. 2011. "Reflections on a Politics of Research for the Right to the City." *International Review of Qualitative Research* 3 (4): 383–402.

Velasco, Gina. 2013. "Performing the Filipina 'Mail-Order Bride': Queer Neoliberalism, Affective Labor, and Homonationalism." *Women & Performance: a journal of feminist theory* 23 (3): 350–72.

Velayutham, Selvaraj, and Amanda Wise. 2005. "Moral Economies of a Translocal Village: Obligation and Shame among South Indian Transnational Migrants." *Global Networks* 5 (1): 27–47.

Vermot, Cécile. 2015. "Guilt: A Gendered Bond within the Transnational Family." *Emotion, Space and Society* 16: 138–46.

Vertovec, Steven. 2009. *Transnationalism*. Taylor and Francis.

Viola, Michael, Valerie Francisco, and Amanda Solomon Amorao. 2014. "Carlos Bulosan and a Collective Outline for Critical Filipina and Filipino Studies." *Kritika Kultura* 23: 662–83.

Waldinger, Roger, and David Fitzgerald. 2004. "Transnationalism in Question." *American Journal of Sociology* 109 (5): 1177–95.

Wall, Karin, and Claudio Bolzman. 2014. "Mapping the New Plurality of Transnational Families: A Life Course Perspective." In *Transnational Families, Migration and the Circulation of Care: Understanding Mobility and Absence in Family Life*, edited by Loretta Baldassar and Laura Merla, 61–78. Routledge.

Wallace, Michele. 1990. *Black Macho and the Myth of the Superwoman*. Verso.

Waters, Johanna L. 2002. "Flexible Families? 'Astronaut' Households and the Experiences of Lone Mothers in Vancouver, British Columbia." *Social & Cultural Geography* 3 (2): 117–34.

Waters, Johanna L. 2015. "Educational Imperatives and the Compulsion for Credentials: Family Migration and Children's Education in East Asia." *Children's Geographies* 13 (3): 280–93.

Waters, Mary C. 2001. *Black Identities: West Indian Immigrant Dreams and American Realities*. Harvard University Press.

Weigt, Jill. 2006. "Compromises to Carework: The Social Organization of Mothers' Experiences in the Low-Wage Labor Market after Welfare Reform." *Social Problems* 53 (3): 332–51.

Weston, Kath. 1997. *Families We Choose*. Rev. ed. Columbia University Press.

Weston, Kath. 2005. "Families in Queer States: The Rule of Law and the Politics of Recognition." *Radical History Review* 93: 122–41.

White, Allen, Caitríona Ní Laoire, Naomi Tyrrell, and Fina Carpena-Méndez. 2011. "Children's Roles in Transnational Migration." *Journal of Ethnic and Migration Studies* 37 (8): 1159–70.

Wilding, Raelene, and Loretta Baldassar. 2009. "Transnational Family-Work Balance: Experiences of Australian Migrants Caring for Ageing Parents and Young Children across Distance and Borders." *Journal of Family Studies* 15 (2): 177–87.

Wimmer, Andreas, and Nina Glick Schiller. 2002. "Methodological Nationalism and the Study of Migration." *European Journal of Sociology / Archives Européennes de Sociologie* 43 (2): 217–40.

Wise, Amanda, and Selvaraj Velayutham. 2006. "Towards a Typology of Transnational Affect." Sydney: Macquarie University, Centre for Research on Social Inclusion Working Paper 4.

Wolf, Diane L. 1997. "Family Secrets: Transnational Struggles among Children of Filipino Immigrants." *Sociological Perspectives* 40 (3): 457–82.

Wyman, Mark. 1993. *Round-Trip to America: The Immigrants Return to Europe, 1880–1930*. Cornell University Press.

Yeates, Nicola. 2009. *Globalizing Care Economies and Migrant Workers: Explorations in Global Care Chains*. Palgrave Macmillan.

Zlotnik, Hania. 2003. "The Global Dimensions of Female Migration." *Migration Information Source* 1.

Index

VALERIE FRANCISCO-MENCHAVEZ is an assistant professor of sociology at San Francisco State University.

The University of Illinois Press
is a founding member of the
Association of American University Presses.

University of Illinois Press
1325 South Oak Street
Champaign, IL 61820-6903
www.press.uillinois.edu